THE
HOUSE
ON THE
HILL

THE
HOUSE
ON THE
HILL

SUSAN DUNCAN

BANTAM
SYDNEY AUCKLAND TORONTO NEW YORK LONDON

A Bantam book
Published by Penguin Random House Australia Pty Ltd
Level 3, 100 Pacific Highway, North Sydney NSW 2060
www.penguin.com.au

Penguin
Random House
Australia

First published by Bantam in 2016
This edition published in 2017

Addresses for the Penguin Random House group of companies can be found at
global.penguinrandomhouse.com/offices.

National Library of Australia
Cataloguing-in-Publication entry

Duncan, Susan (Susan Elizabeth), author
The house on the hill/Susan Duncan

ISBN 978 0 14378 049 6 (paperback)

Duncan, Susan (Susan Elizabeth)
Women journalists – Australia – Biography
Mothers and daughters – Australia – Biography

Internal design and typesetting by Midland Typesetters, Australia
Printed in Australia by Griffin Press, an accredited ISO AS/NZS 14001:2004
Environmental Management System printer

Penguin Random House Australia uses papers that are natural, renewable and
recyclable products and made from wood grown in sustainable forests. The logging
and manufacturing processes are expected to conform to the environmental
regulations of the country of origin.

For Bob, who brings light to the darkest corners

PROLOGUE

Once I believed there could be no other place for me than a cream-coloured house on a high, rough hill overlooking the tawny-green waters of Lovett Bay. It was there, amongst spotted gums so thick and tall they blanked the sky, that I found love and peace, and a sustainable joy at a time of life when I was certain the best was behind me. His name was Bob. Not Robert. Just Bob. His mother, he told me, only called him Robert when he was in trouble.

But now there is a house on a high, quiet hill that overlooks the thin blue lines of distant mountains and the emerald slopes of the Manning Valley. It is shaped like a butterfly with wings that flare out from a lean, flat body and hovers alone in a sea of green grass, as though poised for flight. Although as a friend once remarked, 'If there's ever a gale strong enough to shift that house, we're all doomed.'

The house, sharp-edged, glassy with solid brick walls for substance, is reached by turning off bitumen onto a rough dirt road that crosses a small floodway and winds through cattle country. If there's been steady, heavy rain, the kind that puts smiles on farmers' faces and straightens their cricked backs for a day or two, there's a shallow run-off from the gullies that is easily forded in even a small car. But when storms gather high in the ranges and rain pelts down in sheets like corrugated iron, the trickle swells into a deep, churning torrent the colour of stewed tea, and you are stuck on one side or the other. Mostly, the floodwaters recede within a few hours. Only occasionally does it take a day or two before a depth indicator, pummelled by time into tipsiness, shows the water level is low enough for a four-wheel drive to make it safely across. So it's wise to check the weather forecasts regularly but not to trust them entirely. A sudden summer tempest can erupt out of nothing and nowhere, and then it becomes a matter of waiting out the deluge.

At certain times of the year, the road is ruched with flowering kangaroo grass. It turns soft pink in the evening light and bends and sways in even a lazy puff of air so it seems as if the land is rippling like sunstruck water. In mid-summer, blady grass has delicate, feathery blooms, which give a pale white sheen to the countryside at dawn, like a light dusting of snow. Just looking at it cools you down when the mercury is thrusting upwards of thirty-five degrees and the air is so dead still that even the welcome swallows give up their acrobatics and go off somewhere to wait out the heat.

Beyond the floodway, the road is rutted and rocky. In some areas, heavy rain has washed away the surface to form sharp little gullies that can ambush careless drivers and send cars skidding off course. I've been caught once or twice and now travel carefully and slowly. So slowly, a neighbour says, that when she sees me coming she rushes so she doesn't get stuck on my tail and made late for work.

The greatest threat, though, is a moment too long spent gazing at calves frolicking in a lush paddock or black ducks flying or, once, a wayward jabiru picking its way around the edge of a dam. Or swerving to miss witless plovers, or craning backwards to marvel at a pheasant on a fence post, her broad speckled wings spread wide to dry after a sudden downpour. Or noticing a hungry kookaburra scanning for dinner from a powerline. Or dodging water hens, blue-black with lipstick-red helmets, in a rush to find a deeper dam. Or gazing at flocks of flashy rosellas. Or peering skywards to see if the clouds are fat with the promise of rain or fluffy nothingness, showy but without substance. Or following the colourful arch of a rainbow, chasing the pot of gold like an excited child. Or feeling limbs go pleasurably loose when a coppery sunset brushes the hills with shiny light. Or a full moon dusts the crests with silver.

Out here, where the broad and deep Manning River runs like a pulsing vein from the north-eastern slopes of the Great Dividing Range to a magnificent double delta that ends in the Tasman Sea, there's none of the eyeball-skewering white glare of the outback. Light glows yellow and warm, softening harsh edges, easing the noon flatness. The land has the smell and texture of fecundity, too. Fresh-cut lucerne or rye. Eucalyptus. The stewy aroma of cattle. Very early in the morning, the unripe scent of dew. They follow you to town, those smells. On a hot day, when cow shit clings to the undercarriages of farm vehicles, the supermarket car park is as fragrant as a sale yard on market day. A nauseating stench to some, sweet perfume to others.

This property with the butterfly house is called Benbulla, and it climbs in three increasingly steep crests to a neck-straining point near the sky. The distance from the bitumen to the farm gate is two-point-four kilometres through open farmland and stringy ribbons of eucalypts that peel off to the sides in dark gullies or rise blue in the distance. A few isolated homes nestle on low-lying crests. Built from timber, brick or corrugated iron, they reflect changing times and fortunes, the gradual carving up of once impressive properties into smaller lots of one hundred acres or so.

Along the way there's an old dairy shed, tilted northwards as though it's been given a great shove, brought almost to its knees. A vine, perhaps a choko, holds it barely upright. Chokos were planted everywhere during the Great Depression, which is when the shed looks as though it was built. Four corner posts, peeled tree trunks, support a rusted corrugated roof. Panels missing here and there, lifted by the wind perhaps, or rotted to brown powder and now part of the earth. Rough-hewn timber for fence rails. It's a museum piece, a slice of rural history that stands within a sealed-off enclosure, as though someone cares deeply about the memories stored inside and wants to preserve them. Farmers, I discovered, can be a sentimental lot, although threats to livestock, pasture or livelihood are mostly dealt with swiftly and cleanly. Wild dogs. Weeds. Theft. They're all fair game.

After a while, we give the hills names: the Bottom Hill, the Home Hill and the Great Hill. From the peak of the Great Hill, a pair of wedge-tailed eagles often appear like great winged warriors, and way below, damp watercourses bind a gently rolling landscape of rivers, creeks, dams and culverts with velvety green seams. In the blurry distance, rounded, flattish and cone-shaped hills, like hard silicone breasts, surge in long swathes, shaded violet and blue. On a tempestuous day you can see weather coming, and it takes only a split second to judge whether the washing on the line will escape a drenching or not.

It is an odd feeling, finding myself back in the heart of farming country. Even though I was born a rural kid, my memories of those early days living in a migrant camp near the Albury–Wodonga border aren't always fond. At the age of five, after a day at school, I trudged home along lonely roads, dodging swooping magpies and breaking into a run if cattle, curious beasts, followed me for the length of a paddock. All summer I trod warily, a skittish child, watching for deadly snakes while my skin burned and peeled and freckles grew big as coins. In winter, when the sky was the colour of tin and the ground frosted white, my hands turned blue and my feet went numb with cold. Almost every day, my mother warned of the dangers of strangers in cars on those long stretches of desolate roads. 'If they offer you a lolly, run,' she said. But she never said where.

Even with the hazy gold patina that nostalgia applies to most recollections, while I knew no different, as a child I didn't love country life. Not a bit. Some deep and appealing imprint of a wide, brown land and open skies must have secretly lodged in my DNA, though, because there have been times when I've returned from extended stints living in foreign countries when just the smell of eucalyptus or the first drops of rain on dry earth stirred a slurry of emotion. Tears.

I wonder now whether we are drawn to the world of our youth as we age? If that is why, for no particular reason, one land-scape triggers relief and another anxiety. Or perhaps our needs are different from one decade to the next. Perhaps it is as simple as that.

1

THE GREAT SHIFT FROM SALTWATER BAYS to grassy paddocks, from boats to tractors, began innocently enough with a phone call at the tail end of 2007. A bloke called Michael Baker was on a make-or-break mission to save the family brickworks. If his tall red chimneys kept gushing black smoke into the blue skies around Wingham, he told Bob, one day there'd be a knock at his door and he'd be ordered to *clean up or close down*. Five generations turned to dust on the back of a stranger's signature. Even the thought must have felt like a sharp pain. 'We need a new kiln. Can you help us?' he asked.

Bob was 63 years old, a civil engineer who specialised in combustion. I was 55, a journalist turned author. We were both *technically* retired. No mortgages, no dependents, enough resources to see us comfortably through – provided we didn't go mad or fall for one of those scams aimed at people looking for an easy windfall. Old people, mostly. Desperate. In our separate ways, we'd always lived prudently, understanding cash was a tool that gave us choices but that nothing saved us in the end. In other words, we weren't giant risk-takers, although we were always willing to have a go if the odds weren't stacked against us.

'From what I understand,' Bob said, 'the brickworks are already operating leanly and finding the money for a new kiln will be tough. I might spend a year busting my gut on a design that will end up in the bottom drawer forever.'

There were other issues: the future of bricks in a new high-tech, quick-fix, temporary world was anybody's guess. Family members were bitterly divided about the long-term benefits when piled against the short-term investment. Wingham, a small town on the mid-north coast, was three and a half hours north of Pittwater if the traffic behaved – a significant drive. After a while, Bob returned Michael's call. The answer, with regret, was no.

—

With barely a tremor, we immersed ourselves in summer on Pittwater. There were great shifts, though, from those first uncertain days when I fell on to the isolated shores of Lovett Bay, wrecked by grief and searching for a place to belong. Not sure whether I'd made a catastrophic or brilliant decision to buy a tin shed, cut off from the city life I was used to, the throngs and bright lights and the illusion of being relevant in the bigger scheme of things. A purchase further complicated by the fact that it was separated from the bustle by a great body of water I came to call 'the moat', and accessible only by boat. As it turned out, it was the finest decision I'd ever made. Sometimes risks turn into gifts, if you're lucky. And I was.

In those early days, I threw myself into offshore living with an almost manic energy. The Woody Point Yacht Club twilight sailing races. Elvina Bay fire shed fundraiser dinners. Fishing from the shore at the foot of the front yard. A fire blazing in an old washing machine drum to cook the catch. Kayaking at dawn. Walking amongst wallabies, lyrebirds, brush turkeys, black cockatoos. Snakes. Listening. Seeing. Peeling off worn-out layers. Emerging renewed. Values redefined.

'I'll never leave Pittwater,' I used to insist. 'I love the wildness, the water and the huge throbbing heart of the community with a passion I can barely express.' Those who had long known the gypsy that lurked in my flibbertigibbet soul would raise a sceptical eyebrow so I would feel forced to add, 'When I finally leave here, it will be in a body bag.' I could not, on any level, imagine an existence outside our life on Pittwater.

We lived in a beautiful, bagged brick house built as a summer residence for the poet Dorothea Mackellar. Made grandiose by muscular columns that ran the full length of a ballroom-sized verandah, it was a pleasing, subtle balance of timber, stone, brick and panes of wavy glass, laid out in exquisite proportions. It had weathered time with grace and strength for nearly one hundred years, surviving bushfires, and in the words of the poet, *droughts and flooding rain*. Once remote and as mysterious as Mackellar, it still intrigues and remains an iconic presence on the western foreshores. Although when you eat and sleep, clean, cook, chase away spiders and, occasionally, a snake; mow the lawn, rake leaves and repair small fissures in stone retaining walls, it is those ordinary chores that define life, not the history or glamour or fame of the past.

Each day we woke to views of ancient escarpments, a waterfall that drizzled in drought, turned torrential during storms; sand flats that at low tide glowed golden in the evening light and at high tide pulsed with fish, stingrays, jellyfish, cormorants, a pair of majestic sea eagles and, once or twice, carpets of starfish like earthbound constellations.

It was a second marriage for both of us at a time when we were experienced enough to understand that passion might power a relationship at first, but it was how we handled the aftermath that mattered most. 'Are you happy?' It was a question I asked regularly in the insecure early days.

'Very. Are you?'

SUSAN DUNCAN

A different question came later when the sparkle had faded and we'd begun the inevitable slide into familiarity and routine: 'Any regrets?'

'Do you?'

'No!'

'So why do you ask?'

'You could have married a much younger woman with two healthy breasts and a libido with twenty years to run before conking out.'

A pause. Quite long. Finally: 'Sex is the tiniest component of a marriage. If it's all you've got, you're in trouble.'

'Component? Once an engineer, always an engineer, eh?' Attempting lightness, backing off. Tense shoulders relaxing. Managing a grin. But it's not easy, this growing old. Like youth, you have to be halfway through it before you get an unnerving glimmer of what it entails. Not that it matters. From the first bawling moment out of the womb, you're fully committed.

—

There were endless days of gently cutting through water that whispered sweetly under the hull all the way home. The musky smell and taste of salt. Rare nights, too, when phosphorescence exploded out of black depths, a blizzard of green light, sparkling and weird. And always at the end of any excursion, the character-building climb to the house, panting up a weathered sandstone pathway, which dipped on one side, as if being beckoned by the green waters of the bay. Fighting through cobwebs that sprang up in even a short absence. Breathless at the top. Occasionally, a late-night cognac on the verandah, slumped in our wicker chairs, soaking in the tranquillity.

When the season was wet enough with grass too moist and leaves too green to catch alight, Bob built a small fire in the heat-cracked stone fireplace on the lawn. We'd pull up chairs, fluff old cushions, whack them under our rumps and cook a chop or two. Sip our wine, stare into the flames and talk late into the night. Just the two of us. Although sometimes we wouldn't say much.

Seasons, measured by those unwavering offshore rituals — twilight racing and fire shed dinners — were a gentle, rocking calendar with the flurry of Christmas anchoring the end of one year and signposting the beginning of another. All this wrapped in the warmth and security of knowing we lived amongst good (mostly) people in a wonderful (mostly) community made up of fishermen, shipwrights, artists, architects, layabouts, writers, journalists, photographers, musicians, cooks, chefs, builders, electricians, city commuters and work-at-home freelancers. An eclectic, passionate, stimulating and generous-spirited lot. Mostly.

Rarely a day passed when we didn't sit over a cuppa and slice of cake amongst those heroic verandah columns, thanking whatever kind force had brought us to Pittwater and to each other. 'Life doesn't get much better than this,' we'd say, adding that it would be utter madness to even think about leaving for longer than a holiday. We repeated these thoughts so often it was like saying grace at breakfast, lunch and dinner.

———

The shift in passions was a subtle process. After almost ten faithful years of twilight sailing, I'd begun dreading rounding the markers with a sixty-strong fleet bearing down, sails cracking, skippers screaming 'buoy room!', when anyone could see the pressure we were under from the wind, the chop, the crowding. My heart raced. I felt fear instead of excitement.

Sometimes I found myself talking about the *old days* — as in *good old days* — at the noisy post-race dinners on the verandah. 'It never used to be about winning,' I'd grumble, heaping plates with spaghetti bolognese, passing the parmesan, pointing at the bread and salad. 'Sailors used to be kinder, looser, more gentlemanly.

Getting around the course without spilling your drink was victory enough.' Bob insisted the boats had always been competitive. The difference, he said, was felt in the numbers. Twenty boats, once. Now sixty. Occasionally eighty. Our quirky little yacht club (no clubhouse, anything that floated could enter, no cash left in the kitty at the end of the year) seemed to me to have lost sight of its core, larrikin values. But I was a lone voice. Essentially, times had changed and I'd simply failed to keep up.

One windy evening, when clouds scudded pink in the sky and fluffed back at us from the water, we tacked into position to round the Stokes Point marker. As we turned, a flashy timber bowsprit from a yacht on the port side was aimed straight at my gut and bearing down at frightening speed. I screamed. There was shouting. Sails cracking. Boats heeling. The wind roaring. Paralysed but with nowhere to go, eyes closed, I waited to be skewered – the first mortality in the Woody Point twilight races. Not the kind of notoriety that did you much good.

'There was no real danger,' Bob told me afterwards.

'Not from where I was sitting,' I replied angrily, still feeling the fear.

'Once you would have laughed it off.' Silence. 'Felt exhilarated by the experience,' he added, puzzled, as if searching for signs of the woman he once knew.

Soon after, I stopped sailing altogether. A year later we cut back the post-race dinners to occasional instead of regular events. Start of the season. End of the season. Perhaps one or two get-togethers in between if the crew were visitors or newcomers to the area. It was simpler – or do I mean less effort – to make a heap of sandwiches for Bob to take on board. Good sandwiches, though. Slow-cooked pork shoulder, rocket, red onion, chutney. Roast chicken, celery, shallots, lime rind, pistachios, mayonnaise. Cold roast lamb, cucumber, mint, yoghurt, tomato. Ham, tomato, gruyere, seeded mustard. All about the bread, of course. Huge crusty slabs of it, thickly sawn by a steady hand and slathered with butter. Some traditions cannot be bypassed. And good food is no more difficult to make than bad.

After I quit the boat and as one sailing season drifted into the next, I listened to Bob's enthusiastic retelling of the races when he arrived home. The bingle. The snapped traveller. The damaged knee. The storm. The lightning strike. The narrow escapes. The niggling interpretations of rarely invoked rules to justify ungentlemanliness. I felt not a pang of regret at missing the action, happy to stay home with our Jack Russell terrier, who'd rebelled against coming on board years ago. Smart Chippy. But Bob's face was alight, inspired by challenge. Even the occasional close call.

Much later, I realised withdrawing from an iconic offshore tradition signalled a mental and physical shift. I was aware I could no longer trust myself to think or act quickly enough in a crisis. What if I put someone else at risk because my knees seized at an inconvenient moment or my arms weren't strong enough to hold the main during a jib in strong winds? What then?

There were other signposts, obvious in hindsight but barely noticeable at the time. In bad weather, I began to ask Bob to taxi me to and fro to do the grocery shopping. On fine days, forced to hang off two or three boats deep at a jammed commuter dock, I hesitated, even baulked, at jumping from one vessel to the next to reach the pontoon, unsure of my balance and my ability to judge distance through the triple lenses of my glasses.

Once, wearing brand-new, state-of-the-art multifocals, I missed my footing on the gunnel completely. One leg sank deep in the narrow channel of water between two boats before I dragged myself back to safety, bruised, beaten and teary with shock. 'I'm tough,' I reminded myself that day. 'I'm tough,' I repeated when a kind offshorer asked if I was ok. 'I'll have a coffee at The Point. That'll get me back on track,' I added. Eventually, I continued on my way. *So close*, I thought, *to being crushed between the boats.* I shrugged it off, but not as easily as I used to.

At some point, too, we gradually reduced and then gave up our fishing expeditions and our shore-side campfires on early autumn evenings when the bay was filled with pearly luminosity, the sun dropping behind the escarpment. The light pewter then. Water slick with an oily sheen that made you want to reach out to stroke it. Instead, we watched the day fade and night creep in from our easy chairs on the verandah, where the electric stove was in easy reach. The dishwasher, too. Convenient, yes, but leaning on those handy little helpers came at a cost. They eroded intimacy with the earth, sea and sky. Set up a sterile, odourless, noiseless barrier between the bush, the teeming wildlife – the very bodies that heightened awareness, gave layers to living. But few of us recognise the narrowing that's taking place until old pleasures turn into memories. By then, we've slipped into new habits and there's no going back.

Somehow, in a sneaky sleight of hand, we had become residents of the twilight zone; a nebulous, grey area where we belonged neither to middle nor old age. Stuck in limbo, I called it. Too old to sign on for long-term projects. Not ready, though, to settle for daytime television and fluffy slippers. Although I am speaking for myself. Bob seemed to be mostly immune.

I was subject, on a daily basis, to insidious little reminders of what lay ahead: new body parts hurting for no apparent reason, weight redistributed in unwelcome areas, skin thin enough to bleed with the slightest bump. Making grunty noises getting up from a chair or sinking into it. Sliding feet along floors in a whispery shuffle – a habit that drove my father mad when I was a kid – instead of treading at least firmly if lithely was out of reach. Dreading the onset of winter. Dealing with the infuriating diffi- culty of opening jars and packets. Alarmed by a hideous new habit of counting: peels off a carrot, morsels for the dog bowl, logs in the wheelbarrow. Anything. Everything. Stopping at twelve or moving quickly through to fourteen. Thirteen disallowed for reasons I didn't want to explain even to myself. Wondering if these aberrations were just another checkpoint along the road or a portent of an unthinkable future. Days, even years, blurring so that a decade ago felt like yesterday and yesterday often felt like ancient history.

I'd also noticed the use of an alarming new hectoring tone in my voice. It erupted regularly during the evening television news. 'Nothing changes,' I'd harangue. 'Africa is still starving, warring or dying from one plague or another. Once it was the Red Brigade, Baader-Meinhof and Black Panthers. Now it's religious extremists. Every generation thinks it's going to save the world but the world remains stubbornly unsaved. And don't talk to me about social media or Twitter or whatever all that invasive, time-wasting rubbish is called. It's no better than the days of the Colosseum when the masses gave a thumbs up or thumbs down without knowing any of the facts. Politicians are still lying or, at best, spinning. We're trashing everything beautiful on the planet to run more hair dryers or build cheap, ugly shit that busts after one go. And the dollars aren't even going into our pockets. They're floating off into the atmosphere. Disappearing into whatever the hell a global economy means.' Stopping there sometimes, but more often building up a head of steam: 'And what about farmers being told they no longer have the right to choose how their land is used? What about them, when a drill gets sunk and all the underground water turns poisonous and there's nothing left to do but end the pain with a rope or a bottle of pills? What about those poor bastards, eh? And what are we going to cook if the land is dead and nothing grows? Tell me that. Is there no end to the eternal stupidity of the human race?' Almost shouting: 'And marketing is taking over the world. Making fools of us all. Does one generation never learn from the mistakes of another?' Bob would give me a patient look. The dog would slink off to a quieter spot. I'd have the grace to blush. But when you've lived long enough to witness endless and repeated cruelties and traumas, anger – born out of helplessness – flares more often than compassion.

Worst of all, I'd acquired a quite nasty little habit of rewriting history even as I judged the behaviour of others. As if I'd never drunk too much, skived off or made foolish choices. As if I'd never had a youth at all. Falling headlong into the same hoary, self-exonerating trap for which I impatiently condemned my mother. At heart, I understood it was borderline criminal to casually shed one skin, dismiss old truths – or at least hide from them – and blithely move on untainted by the past. Everyone for whom I cared deeply knew the facts and couldn't be fooled anyway. Turning into a self-congratulating bore creeps up on you, though. It's one of the many ignoble outcomes when you take a blameless seat in the audience instead of joining in the tournament.

But sometimes, on a dark, moonless night, when I was woken by a rustle or yowl or chirrup or thump that was unfamiliar enough to penetrate the fog of sleep, my mind without permission gnawed away at the past, which as everyone knows can never be undone. I broke the loop by counting the blessings of a privileged life. Rolled over and touched the warm, smooth skin of my husband's back. And was grounded again. But it was strange, this increasing focus on the irreversible. Unbidden snatches of memory I'd thought entombed rose to the surface, triggering one question, then another and another, and I'd lie unsettled and restless until the ghostly predawn light cast a grey sheen on the bay. Why rattle the cage, as my mother would say, adding for good measure: *why rock the boat?* What cannot be undone should be left unsaid forever. And in the cool sharpness of daylight, where even shadows struggled to keep hold of their mysteries, the past gave up its power and, for long periods, shrank away.

Like anyone who's lived long enough, I've known days when I foundered in loneliness and grief, times when I rebelled against every moral fibre to justify questionable desires. Some years, no matter how hard I struggled, good fortune seemed to belong to others. Once, no, twice, death hammered loudly at my door, turned back by the miracles of modern medicine. By some strange quirk of fate, luck – call it what you want – I have always kept a roof over my head, food on the table. Found, and somehow sustained, the love of a good man. Known more success than failure. So why the escalating urge to confront my mother with a secret I thought I would carry with me to the grave? My life had passed the point of no return. I'd survived. That was enough. Only it wasn't. I wanted – needed – to cancel out the gorilla that has walked beside me since childhood and pounded self-worth into barren dust. My mother held the key. She also had a right to know, didn't she, the reason I hovered on the threshold of fury when we were together? Even if, in the end, it destroyed the already splintery bond between us.

This is the perfect moment, I sometimes thought when the two of us were circling each other before one of our regular battles. Or when one of her darts hit a bullseye that threw me off balance for a while. But even as questions rose to my lips, I backed off. Swallowed them whole. Unable to scale the slippery cliff face between parent and child.

———

My mother, Esther Jean, on the cusp of her ninetieth decade, was the sharpest reminder that none of us were immune to the shifting realities of aging and the inevitable consequences of living. There was the year she furtively swiped the Christmas cracker knick-knacks – small but useful things such as honey spoons, plant tags, egg timers – stuffing them in her handbag and hightailing it back to her bedroom to hide them. We laughed, family and the customary waifs and strays who gathered each year at a long table on the lawn, but we wondered too whether this signalled a mind beginning to fall away.

'Ooh, Esther,' called curly-haired Lisa from Elvina Bay with a laugh in her voice, 'five honey spoons. You must love the stuff.'

My mother, who hears even the quietest whispers through brick walls, pretended deafness and kept going with the single-minded determination of a dog with a bone. Hunched over her Zimmer frame, her backside slipping closer than ever to the ground, but still heavy-boned and fleshy, she ploughed through the thick turf of the lawn. Lifting her head in frustration when wheels stalled at a lumpy spot. Jiggling sideways to escape the rut.

Lisa, blonde curls all over the place, bounded to her side: 'Need a bit of help, Esther, do you? And have I mentioned that you look gorgeous in that outfit?'

Esther grinned and wiggled her hips flirtatiously. Once she would have curtsied.

Later, when I confronted my mother with the sparkly bag full of Christmas goodies, she said innocently, 'Did *you* put them there?' As if it was the first time she'd set eyes on the stuff.

I sighed and smiled, mock serious. 'If you lose your marbles, you realise I'm going to have to club you,' I said. A joke, invoked regularly.

'You won't have to,' she snapped. 'I'll do it myself.' Eyes flashing, lips drawn in a hard line, chin thrust forward, she was the feisty Esther of old. Caught red-handed, she dug in harder. At her bedroom doorway, I paused. No matter how flaky the deed, there was often a subplot.

'What do you want all that stuff for anyway?' I asked.

'For the girls,' she said with a hint of petulance. 'I like to give them little gifts.' The 'girls' were the small collection of white-haired octo and nonagenarians whom she occasionally joined at a dining table in the retirement village.

'Ah,' I said, nodding. *A rational theft, then.* 'Did you enjoy the pork today?' I asked, closing the subject. 'Your recipe,' I added, in what was meant to be a compliment and offering of peace.

She raised an eyebrow. 'Well, don't blame me.'

And so, the status quo resumed.

2

THEY USED TO WARN BLINDLY BESOTTED YOUNG MEN on the verge of marriage: *look at the mother and you will see what the daughter will become.* When I was young I laughed at the suggestion. For a start, I was tall and lanky, like my father. My mother was short and curvaceous, with a bust that stopped traffic and a waist the span of a man's hands. But now that my hair is even greyer than hers, I am shocked, sometimes, to see mannerisms and hear echoes – even roars – of my mother in me.

I told her so once and she laughed out loud, smug: 'The apple never falls far from the tree.'

Later, searching for reassurance, I asked Bob, 'Do you think I am turning into Esther?'

He barely raised his eyes from the notebook where he was sketching a new idea for goodness knows what. 'No.'

'That was a bit too quick for comfort,' I responded. 'Tell me the truth.'

He sighed, looked up and took refuge in a familiar line. 'Asking me a question like that is the same as asking me whether you look fat in a dress. No matter what I say, it's going to be the wrong answer.'

'Don't be such a coward – and if I look fat I want to be told.'

'No, you don't.'

'Well, told in a compassionate and complimentary way, of course.' He raised his eyebrows. I refused to be deflected. 'But my mother – are we alike?'

'You are nothing like your mother at all.'

'Marybeth reckons the reason we don't get along is because we're so similar.'

Bob put aside his notebook. 'Your mother is vain and selfish. She has a sharp tongue. In many ways, she's ruthless.'

'Yeah. But. Am I like her?'

'No.' A glint appeared in his eye. 'You mother is also tough, very funny and a shocking flirt.'

'And?'

'That's as deep a hole as I'm going to dig.' He resumed sketching.

But sometimes, when I made a gesture, acted impulsively, invoked a certain dictum, I felt the influence of my mother as powerfully as if she were standing right beside me. Sharp and shocking as a lightning strike. It made me wonder: With a different mother, would I have been kinder or meaner, an optimist or pessimist, more – or less – inclined towards self-destruction? Are our personalities programmed in the womb or learned outside it? Are we better off being ignorant of the random ingredients that go into the creation of each one of us? Or would learning the recipes give us the power to change outcomes in positive ways? Whatever the driving forces, they were there, those echoes and lightning strikes. How could they not be? We'd shared nearly sixty years of history. She was the one constant and inescapable factor in my life.

After a while, Bob said, 'Your mother always puts herself first. So far, I've never seen you do the same.'

'You haven't known me for long enough,' I said, recalling a long list of drawn-out sequences of scorching self-interest. Shades

THE HOUSE ON THE HILL

of my mother? Or was that little personal trait purely my own adjustment?

Almost ten years ago, and long before we decided to try to accept our mutual shortcomings without (much) comment, I moved my mother from her distant home to a nearby retirement village. She was eighty-two years old, she'd had a couple of falls in quick succession, breaking first one wrist and then the other. She had begun to show signs of barely coping – nests of unopened mail piled around the house, dust an inch thick, a backyard littered with pots and pans burned beyond salvation. She had begun to ask strangers to reverse her car out of shopping centre car parks before she felt able to drive off. She locked herself out of her own house so frequently her neighbour cut a hole in a window so Esther could climb in and out without calling on him for help. She'd begun faking more and more serious illnesses in a bid for attention and, as a result, was seriously putting her health at risk from swallowing drugs for phantom symptoms. Small and large acts that, seen together, were too disturbing to ignore. Unthinkably, my mother, whom I'd always regarded as indestructible, was no longer getting old – she was old.

She looked at me with rabbit-scared eyes when I suggested a retirement village. 'I know where everything is here, so forget it,' she said, but changed her mind in a single moment when I walked her through a small white unit set in rainforest gardens with a cheeky water dragon to greet her from the balcony balustrade. Not that she ever sat outside at the table and chairs, put there so she could enjoy the view. She barely moved off the sofa. Her environment may have changed, but ingrained habits were dragged along intact.

When I packed her home, I was shocked to find piles of the magazine I'd once worked for, stacked inside cupboards. Shocked, because when I'd occasionally ring her to mention a cover story and ask with a little pride (which she always said came right before a fall) if she might like to read it, she was never interested.

'I don't read that rubbish. Anyway, the magazine is too expensive. People will stop buying it soon.'

I learned not to alert her. And yet, when I called into the local grocery store, the Greek owner told me, 'Your mother is proud of you, she . . . busts with pride!' I smiled politely, not believing a word – until I found those old magazines. Every cover story I could remember and other less flamboyant assignments had been thumbed through and then hidden from sight like pornography.

Maybe my mother thought a little praise might go straight to my head and ruin me forever, but she could do no harm by boasting out loud to others. Like her own mother, she'd always been a deeply superstitious woman. Don't walk under ladders. Never cut your fingernails on a Friday. If a painting falls off the wall someone will die. New shoes on the table bring bad luck. Saying goodbye means you'll never meet again. Lilies in the house bring death to your door. *Don't tempt the gods by praising those you love or they will take them from you.*

One day, when I visited her in her new home, I tackled her about the stash of magazines. 'You told me you never bought them because they were too expensive.'

'People insisted on giving them to me,' she snapped.

'Did you actually read any of my stories?'

'Oh, I can't remember,' she said, as if a compliment might kill her. It was the first time I ever wondered whether she might envy instead of cherish (as parents supposedly do) my small achievements. But perhaps more accurately, she failed completely to understand how the ugly, charmless kid, who she was sure was destined to become a withered and bitter old spinster, had somehow succeeded in having the life she'd dreamed of for herself. It puzzles her to this day. And yet, when we discovered I'd somehow lost all the family photo albums in the move, she merely nodded.

'I know you didn't do it deliberately,' she said.

My mother has always been a mass of contradictions. Loving. Brutal. Generous. Mean. Tough. Unstable. Realist. Fantasist. Optimist. Pessimist. Kind. Cruel. No different from most of us, just more extreme, with one overriding impulse: come out on top at any cost. She has only lately begun to admit that her instinct to win meant she was often her own worst enemy in the ups and downs of her life.

'Our relationship could have been so different,' I said, sad, recalling a thousand small destructions, like piles of burning embers, down long distances of memory.

'You're all I've got now,' she replied in a rare moment of vulnerability. She brightened, her lip curled in a way that used to make me flinch. 'So you'll just have to do!'

—

As a child, I believed old people were born old. It was inconceivable to think they'd once been babies or fit young adults. It was more shock than surprise to find, when still very young but old enough to be cognisant, that when I shuffled through my mother's collection of old shoeboxes stuffed with ancient (so it seemed to me) black-and-white photos taken in the days of the Brownie Box camera, those blurry but nevertheless glamorous-looking young people standing slim-waisted and straight-backed were now plump, arthritic Aunt Mary, bald Uncle Bob and . . . my mother? That blonde bombshell?

'It was way before I married your father,' she'd said, in a tone that hinted at blame. 'People told me I looked like Jean Harlow. Mind you, I never thought she was very attractive. Quite a hard face, don't you think?' Even as a child, despite her disclaimers, I could tell she'd been flattered by the comparison.

There were a few formal hand-tinted studio portraits, too. My father as an army captain. Bizarrely pink-cheeked and ruby-lipped, as though the tinter might have been slightly colour blind or a frustrated Rembrandt. My nan, a dark-haired, smooth-skinned beauty in her wedding portrait. At the time I'd stared in disbelief and wondered: what kind of lackadaisical inattention to personal detail allowed youth and beauty to be gobbled away so effortlessly? It never occurred to me that there was no choice beyond a premature death.

In my late twenties, I remember quite clearly reading an interview with model Cindy Crawford, who told a journalist no one stayed young forever and that she, too, would age like everyone else. I was torn between the anguish of realising that someone so divinely favoured was nevertheless unable to hold back decline and being uncharitably appeased by the knowledge that in the end, favoured or not, the same fate awaited every one of us.

My father's parents died before I was old enough to toddle. 'Cancer,' my mother said. 'You and your brother got it from his side of the family. Nothing to do with the Parkers.' My mother's mother, my grandmother – kind-hearted Nan who read the Bible for pleasure – was aged 63 when she died suddenly. 'She ate Bex like lollies. Ruined her kidneys.' My mother's father, my grand-father – an amoral, barrel-chested rum drinker – lived another decade. 'Dodgy heart,' she said. 'My side can take the blame there.'

When I was kindergarten age, my nan embodied comfort, wisdom and patience. She was a stalwart comrade who never failed to take my side against parents who wanted me to go to bed: 'Five more minutes won't hurt, Jean. Leave her be for a little.' If I was solidly in the wrong, though, she stepped aside: 'No good coming to me for help.' And for a while I'd feel unloved and betrayed. Nan died when I was thirteen years old.

After that, when old age was unwrapped from love and came in the form of strangers, I became conscious of details. Particular stale smells, like mouldy bread. Clothes spotted with spills. Tea served in stained cups. Plates gluey with hints of yesterday's fried egg breakfast. Cobwebs strung like garlands from smoky ceilings. Eyes cloudy with glaucoma or cataracts, or milky-eyed blindness. The clicking of ill-fitting dentures. I was revolted by the whole filthy, decaying shebang. Using as a yardstick, whiskery, almost blind, hobbling Old Mama with her livid hands and blotchy skin, who shaved the whiskers on her chin for special occasions and every Friday lunchtime sat in the kitchen of our country pub for a schooner of beer or two, I once insisted during a silly schoolgirl discussion, 'I don't want to live beyond fifty-three.' Old Mama could look quite glamorous when she was all dressed up, and although from this end of my life I see her as a marvel, in my shallow, young years it was not one I wished to replicate.

We had an Uncle Edward (Ted) on my father's side. He visited for a two-week holiday and never left. It was quietly understood in those days that when family members came knocking on the door, you never slammed it in their faces. He was a decent man, an inspired gardener, and every night he did the dishes after dinner. Which endeared him enormously to my brother and me. He also mended our shoes, taught me to play draughts and tried to instil a wide-ranging vocabulary in my lazy young mind. To this day, I remember a mysterious word he revealed like a sorcerer. 'What has seven letters, no vowels?' he asked.

'Every word has a vowel.' I was probably seven or eight years old.

'Not every word.'

The word was syzygy. It means a constellation of stars. Saying the letters one by one was quite delicious, like a nonsensical rhyme designed to challenge lispers. Over the years that word has tipped the balance from loss to victory in many Scrabble games.

Uncle was a hoarder, though, and not fond of showering more than once a week. His room stank of many things: old sweat, old leather, old wool, old clothes. Odours I came to call 'old man smells'. In the end, my mother had a garden entrance to his room built and insisted the interior door remain shut at all times. I was fond of him, even if he did insist on steel tips on my school shoes and maturing blue cheese in the toe of an old boot. The same place he hid his cash.

Esther told me once that he was besotted with her. When she and my father owned a country pub on the outskirts of Melbourne, he paced up and down outside her bedroom window every night, in case she needed protection. From what or from whom, no one was ever quite sure. 'I never realised, of course. Had no idea. Can't remember who told me. One of the boarders, I think, who'd caught him a few times.' I never thought to ask what the border was doing outside her bedroom window.

'Didn't he have an affair with the cook for years?' I said.

'Yes, but he was insanely jealous if anyone came near me. Once, I hugged a mixed doubles partner after we'd won a tournament. Uncle tried to punch the poor man. It was entirely innocent, of course. The hug. Not the punch.'

Still, when dementia overtook him, he must have forgotten his passion. He hid behind his bedroom door with an iron bar raised above his head and tried to kill her when she stepped in with his breakfast tray.

Dad found a nursing home to take Uncle in. We kids never visited. Not once. He just silently melted into oblivion, eventually becoming another Duncan to reside in the Brunswick cemetery. Mostly, I felt glad the sad, shambolic, deeply repugnant and useless tragedy his life had become was over. We all did. Once his room was cleaned out, his treasures consigned to the tip (who nailed steel tips to heels and toes of shoes anymore?), the dreadful years quickly faded from memory. I wonder sometimes if that's where I learned a horror of the impossible demands made by old age when it turns rotten.

'If I reach the stage where I'm a filthy old crone leaking from both ends and there's no hope, turn off the switch,' I once said to

Bob. He grinned. I immediately back-pedalled. 'But get a second opinion, ok?'

I always thought my mother would abhor the idea of being reduced by the embarrassments and indignities of a failing body. That vanity, her long-time soulmate, would win out. As I watched her slide further into dependence and helplessness, I often asked myself what choices I would make in her circumstances. It's an open-ended question. Walk the walk first, as they say. Either way, to see a parent reduced in painful increments to little more than babyhood skews the natural order. It also gives you time to mull and dissect the past. Chase down history, nail down blame. And live forever with the consequences. As I eventually did.

3

THE SPOTTED GUMS HAD SHED THEIR BARK and another summer was on the wane when Michael Baker next phoned.

'He's in Sydney,' Bob said casually. 'Agreed to meet him at The Point for a quick chat on his way back to Wingham. Keep it simple.'

'No, no. Bring him here. I'll make scones. There's not enough time to bake a cake.'

'He's with his wife and son.'

'Even more of a reason to send them off with full bellies.'

An hour later we were sitting on the verandah with steaming mugs and a plate of rather flat, sad-looking scones. I'd added sultanas in the hope it would give them a lift. Turned out Michael didn't eat dried fruit so they were wasted on him. Michael's son, Fletcher, about nine years old with just enough meat on his bones to stitch his wrists and knobbly knees to the rest of him, had the energy of a rocket and took his cues from his dad. He gave the scones a miss, too. Adele, Michael's wife, reached for one and politely complimented them. She had a lovely, no-nonsense face, curly blonde hair and a warm smile.

'They're pretty awful,' I said. She burst out laughing. 'Well,

I've had better but they're ok.' To prove her point she reached for another.

'No need to be kind,' I said, pushing my chair back from the table. 'Leave that awful scone and let me show you around. Fletch! Come and see the chickens.'

We women strolled the perimeter of the house under blue skies while the men talked business. Fletch darted into the scratchy bush, burst into the chook pen, ran along the track into the National Park, flushed out a brush turkey, giving them both a fright. But his speech was slow and deliberate, at odds with his body. Close your eyes and it could have been an old-timer rabbiting on in ancient slang about hard-learned wisdoms. 'Picked it up from the old fishermen he hangs out with when we go on holidays,' Adele explained. 'Seems to have stuck.'

She told their story simply. In the background, a hail of hard little seed heads shaped like bonnets fell from the spotted gums, making tapping sounds on the tin roof of Bob's shed. A few tinnies roared past. A yacht glided gracefully under sail. 'If we don't make changes at the brickworks,' she said, 'we'll be lucky to have a future. Five generations of Bakers in the business and nothing left to show for it.' The bottom line was survival.

We returned to the verandah and said our goodbyes. Fletch bolted down the steps to the pontoon, eager to be gone. Despite his bond with the old fishermen, his family ties to the brickworks, according to his mother, cattle were his greatest love.

'Would you like to see him running the brickworks one day?' I asked.

Adele shrugged, non-committal. 'If that's what he wants. Ready and waiting for him.'

'If we can save it,' Michael added, his voice rich with a father's love and pride. Bob ferried them back onshore. The water was mirror smooth. Autumn seemed a long way off.

—

In the early evening I stood at the kitchen bench chopping onions, ginger, chilli and garlic, making the base for a chicken curry. Through a window festooned with webs, the air, trees and water stilled, settling for the night. The yellow glow of lights shone across the bay in long gold streaks. Bob poured a glass of wine and handed it to me.

'So . . . are you going to take it on?' I asked, taking a quick sip, the strong smell of onions on my hands clashing with the wine.

Bob shrugged. 'Family business. Family politics. No money. A dream they might be able to get some funding from somewhere. All adds up to a nightmare.'

'They're good people. Work hard. Don't expect much. Just want to keep going. Maybe pass it all on to Fletcher one day. Five generations. Imagine that!'

'What they're after has never been done before. It's risky. Very risky.'

'But. Could you make a difference if you had a go?'

Bob sighed. Added another slosh of wine to his glass. 'Two women together. Lethal,' he said. And he walked off to find his notebook. Humming.

It was all in the timing, of course. Most of the choices we'd once blithely taken for granted would be emphatically ruled out forever when we took that step from middle to old age. By then, even replacing our old dog with a new puppy would require a large degree of optimism, blind faith or flat-out denial. And while each day on Pittwater unfurled with the comfort of certainty and security – as much as there ever is – a few gentle jolts out of our comfort zone might lend inspiration to the long, cold winter nights ahead.

After the August winds had hammered the bay and spring was shaping up to be as temperamental and frisky as ever, Bob said, 'Time to do a site visit. Want to come along?'

'You bet!'

—

Around a final bend on the lumpy Wingham Road, Lincoln Brickworks sprawled haphazardly. Wonky old brick kilns. Rusted corrugated iron roofs. Three tall, redbrick chimneys, each one slightly off-kilter and belching black smoke, foretold a limited future under increasing government pressure to reduce pollution. All jammed between paddocks of fat cattle grazing on knee-high pasture. Up the neat driveway and past a carefully tended garden of roses, camellias and crepe myrtles, a scabby old petrol pump with a sun-faded Mobil sign was a relic of a more profligate, energy-rich era.

Michael met us at the car, flanked by two tail-wagging border collies and an overweight, flirtatious corgi he introduced as Hyacinth (known forever after as Miss Flirty Girl). In what I came to learn was standard country style, he enquired about our trip, our health, family life in general and remained happily unconcerned while Chippy fell ravenously on whatever was left in the dog bowls. Eventually, at a leisurely pace, he led the way inside a ramshackle collection of shed-like corridors housing forklifts, conveyor belts, mixing tanks, a chaotic array of clay-dusted machinery and masses of miscellaneous but essential tackle that looked like a mangled scene out of a *Mad Max* car crash. After a short while I left them to it and wandered off on my own.

'See?' said a lanky, white-haired bloke who'd silently popped up beside me. He pointed to a platform above the staff lunchroom where a couple of ancient timber barrows with battered wheels had been chucked amongst anonymous mechanical detritus, no doubt to be cannibalised – in the way I remembered of frugal country men – for a quick fix-it sometime.

'Once upon a time, we used them to ferry bricks up narrow ramps to stack the top of the kilns. You had to push hard, I'll tell you that. Then we'd bring 'em down when the bricks were cooked, holding tight so you didn't lose a load overboard. I'm Old

John, Michael's father. How do you do.' Dressed in what I came to learn was his weekday uniform – faded blue bib and brace overalls (over T-shirts in summer and checked flannel shirts in winter) and heavy work boots – he withdrew a work-reddened hand from a pocket and held it out. The calluses were like steel bolts.

I soon discovered Old John patrolled the yard with the stealth and curiosity of a cat at all hours of the day and, if there was a burn on, night. He had an encyclopaedic knowledge of brick-making from the days when men pushed those unwieldy barrows and stoked furnaces by hand, gauging temperatures by feel and the time it took until your eyes were peeled by the heat. But he was almost eighty years old. And while he was fitter than many men his age, it didn't take a genius to work out he had a pathological fear of technology. I got the feeling the most ambitious electronic innovation he'd ever embraced was the shift from one-armed bandits to push-button poker machines at the local RSL Club. We were kindred spirits, in a way. Technology flummoxed me most of the time.

'I helped Dad in the brickworks from the time I was twelve years old,' he told me. 'Cleaned the flues. Dirty work. I'm a bit short on education, y'see.' His knowledge, though, was far-reaching and profound. Hewn from handed-down lore and a lifetime's experience of good, bad and indifferent seasons, he told me he'd witnessed the local landscape evolve from brush to cattle country, the townscape adopt and drop fashion fads.

'Brush?' I asked.

'Bush so thick and dark and vast a bloke could go in there and never find his way out. Good soil. Leaf rot, y'know. That's what does it.'

He'd felt the visceral thrill of making big money in boom times, but also witnessed small businesses die on the back of a single badly examined risk. 'Soon as you borrow money, you're in trouble,' he said on another day. 'Tough times sneak up on you. By the time you recognise they're on your doorstep, you're buggered. Only way we've survived, y'know. Never borrowed money. Not till now. No right-thinking bloke ever puts his future in the hands of a bank.' He looked into the distance, where a handful of steers he raised for pocket money grazed peacefully, riddled with anxiety.

In front of us, Fletch, achingly young and willing, expertly cut the lawn on the ancient ride-on mower. Generation five, if there was anything left. It was written on Old John's face like a scripture. And where would an old man, who is able to smell the moment a batch of bricks was on the brink of being overcooked or pick at a glance the quality (or lack of it) of a truckload of dirt destined for kilns, find a crucial niche in a new regime of electronic panels and knob-controlled thermostats? Seventy years' experience suddenly rubbish and turfed like a useless, bloated brick. All this written loudly in anxious eyes.

'We won't have to worry about the economy, Dad, if we're shut down,' Michael replied bluntly on another visit on another day in another month, worn out by the yammering that change was a written invitation for disaster to step in and wreak havoc. Old John went silent and shuffled off, shaking his head like a doomsayer.

It was 9.30. Time for smoko. His wife, Barbara, he told me, had set out an extra cup. He thought she had some shortbread handy, too. I nodded thanks and followed down a laneway of bricks lying crookedly from the heavy tread of many boots and shifting soil. We passed the kilns, like a row of glowing pizza ovens, to be hit with a knock-you-flat kind of heat pulsing from deep vaults massive enough to roast a whole pig with room to spare. Burners Skip and Dave, wet with sweat and black with soot, wearing nothing but shorts, singlets, long leather gloves and industrial boots, were feeding timber offcuts from the local sawmill into the blaze at a steady rate.

'Hot, eh?' I said, which barely began to describe the hellish inferno.

'No better spot in winter,' Dave said, grinning, 'but summer sucks.'

Skip, who's married to Old John's daughter, Toni, a journalist who manages a group of local newspapers, mumbled he'd rather be catching waves. Old John peered into the fiery depths. On familiar ground and satisfied, he continued towards the house. But fear of the unknown seemed to seep out of him like the dirty brown wisps of smoke escaping through the decrepit brick walls. If it all ended in calamity, how could an eighty-year-old man, no matter how tough, find the strength to begin again? *That* was engraved in his rounded shoulders.

'Do you ever feed that dog of yours?' he asked, sliding open the door to the kitchen. Chippy was raiding the dog bowls. Again.

———

In the end, the entire project hinged on successfully applying for a federal government grant that would contribute to but in no way cover the cost of the new kiln. The forms were filled in and sent off long before the cut-off date. Everyone was anxious to get started, but no one wanted to plunge in before fully understanding the risks. Applying early turned out to be a stroke of luck. A note came back from one of the assessors. 'While the technical information is detailed enough, I'd suggest a little more history and background when you make your case. You have time to reapply.' Have another go, in other words.

'You're the writer,' Bob said. 'How do we do this?'

'Keep it simple. Keep it brief. Don't be afraid to be passionate.'

He nutted out a new approach. And everyone waited.

Finally, Michael was contacted. Success. Old John shook his head in dismay but Michael grew taller. All those years slogging away anonymously and here, at last, recognition: bricks were worth investing in. Small brickworks had a future. Family businesses could survive if they kept up with changing times. Sweating over fires on stinking hot summer days, frazzled and dehydrated, almost burned through to the marrow and going home to lie on cold bathroom tiles until the heat seeped out of you, now a horror of the past. A new generation. New rules. The reinforcing power of a positive outside opinion meant validation in the face of Old John's endless worries.

When the whooping died down and it was business as usual, Bob disappeared into his study and basically didn't emerge for a year. At one stage, feeling neglected, I grumbled. He confronted me over morning tea with a hard look: 'You have to understand, Susan. If I get the calculations wrong, someone could end up dead.'

4

A WEEK BEFORE CHRISTMAS IN 2009, the phone rang. 'We've called an ambulance for your mother. It's on the way.' She'd fainted in the reception area of the retirement village on the way to her Friday morning hairdressing appointment. 'Nothing broken and she's sitting up having a cup of tea now,' said the receptionist, 'but she agreed to call the ambulance. She looks alright, but it's better to be sure.'

'Of course,' I agreed. 'I'm on my way.'

I didn't panic. I wasn't even much concerned. Every year, as traditional as the season, the script played out with only a few variations on the theme. It would be another near-death experience engineered to attract attention or enjoy a short holiday in hospital or deflect from some looming financial calamity that I would ultimately be forced to resolve. Impossible to ignore but also impossible to take too seriously. I felt a stirring of anger. Remembered a few ancient doozies when I'd fallen hook, line and sinker for a con.

'I have breast cancer,' she told me when I was a cadet reporter on the *Melbourne Sun*.

'Where are you?' I asked, stunned.

'A payphone in Collins Street. Outside Georges.'

'I'm on my way.' I was saving to travel the world, as we did in those days, but I took her to lunch, a favoured Duncan response to most calamities. Something about being looked after by waiters, eating fancy food washed down with a soothing glass of wine, reduced shock and fear to everyday ordinary. I blew a third of my budget on lunch and a designer silk scarf from the most expensive store in Melbourne. Expensive gifts were another Duncan family remedy for my mother. I remember I didn't begrudge a cent. My mother was the centre of my universe. I loved her. Relied on her. Never questioned her judgment. Trusted her with the dangerous naivety of most children and, later, thanked whatever self-protective forces kicked to render me blind to her flaws until I was old enough to flee them. Although she had never raised a hand to me, never shrieked, threatened or even punished me, on some unexplainable level I also feared her, or perhaps feared disappointing her is closer to the truth.

When I felt she was calm enough to drive home, I went back to work. Banged away at some story I don't remember, one paragraph per sheet of paper. Plenty of Tipp-Ex for the typos. Struggling to meet the deadline. My mother and her illness crowding my mind.

At home that evening, she told me there'd been a mistake. 'Cysts,' she said happily. Years later, when I began to question her motives in all things, I wondered whether the cancer story was true or whether she was bored or whether she'd seen my dollars mounting in the bank and thought – because I was still living at home and cavalier about paying board – that she was entitled to a few. And why did she call me? Why not her husband, or her son whom she adored? And yet. Despite a history littered with similar events, I have never found the courage or confidence to call her bluffs. Always, in the back of my mind, the awful fear: What if this time it's all true? What if this time, she's in serious trouble and perhaps dying?

So, as I'd done for decades, I collected my handbag, car keys, found Bob in his shed and explained where I was going.

'Call me if you need me,' he said without looking up. He knew my mother well.

I set off, guilt and responsibility, the two knotted tightly from the beginning of memory, flooding through me. Anger, too, if I'm being strictly honest, because she'd always been able to con me royally.

The sun was hot. Light bounced off the water like knife blades. I mentally scrolled through possibilities, keeping the boat speed low through the moorings. Nothing big, I was sure of it. Neither life-threatening nor horrible. My brother and I didn't call her Sarah Bernhardt for nothing. She'd probably forgotten to take her blood pressure pills.

At The Point, where offshorers gathered to collect the mail, catch the ferry or sink a frigidly cold beer at the end of a hard day, I pulled up short. Took a deep breath. She was on the cusp of eighty-nine. Nobody lived forever. I dredged through images of her the week before. We'd driven for our weekly picnic lunch to the beach at Mona Vale. No signs then of anything potentially ruinous. We'd even talked about death. She had no fear of it, she said.

'Hah!' I retorted, not believing her for a second. Who doesn't fear death − or the eternal mystery of it − at least on some deeply primal level? And why would anyone put up with the increasing indignities, frailties, involuntary leakages and outright agony of old age unless they dreaded what she would call 'judgment day'? My mother believed in God. She believed in heaven and hell. She believed in the power of prayer and the certainty of eternal damnation for committing a mortal sin. And she hadn't led a blameless life. Not that she'd given me anything more than a sanitised version, but I could connect dots, disregard red herrings, sniff out lies as competently as the next person. It still didn't add up to much by today's standards. Unless there was something much more sinister buried way back in time.

That day, the conversation about death continued for a while. 'John will be pleased to see me. And your father has been waiting a long, long time. He spoiled me rotten, you know. Never realised it. Not till years after he died.'

Dad was a heavy drinker. Later a functioning alcoholic. When he and my mother owned the pub, he began the day with what he called a 'heart starter' – a double brandy. My mother, citing illness at least once or twice a week, reached for a *medicinal* pony-sized glass of port with a dash of brandy. In her youth, it was a common tonic for upset stomachs so she got away with it. They were hangovers, of course, but I didn't cotton on for years. By then I'd had enough hangovers of my own to recognise the symptoms in a blink.

By the time I reached the hospital, I'd convinced myself it was another attention-seeking false alarm. I casually announced myself to the triage nurse in emergency. She checked the screen, clicked a few buttons on the keyboard. 'Intensive care,' she said.

—

Her heart was failing. The hideous irony. After faking cardiac arrests for decades, this time it was genuine. As I stood beside her bed, she turned her head towards me: 'I've had a heart attack.' Her voice was surprisingly strong, filled with amazement. Her watery blue eyes wide with disbelief.

'Well, you're in the right place,' I responded, matter-of-factly to hide the shock. 'They're experts at all that stuff here.'

'They'd better be,' she said, already on the attack. *Not ready to give in or give up*, I thought.

After a while a nurse came in, her shoes squeaking on the shiny clean floor. She was neat in a white shirt, navy trousers.

Turquoise spectacles that snapped together on the bridge of the nose hung around her neck. She checked the tubes and wires streaming from Esther's wrist and chest. Pumped the IV line.

'I used to be a nurse,' my mother said, slyly.

'Nurse's aide,' I muttered under my breath.

'You're one of us then,' the nurse said, smiling at her kindly.

'It was during the war,' my mother said. 'I was in Darwin when the bombs were dropped.'

'A few days *after* the bombs were dropped,' I muttered.

'Must have been pretty scary,' the nurse said.

My mother made a limp-wristed gesture: 'Oh, you just got on with it.'

The nurse patted my mother's arm in approval, assembled her glasses and wrote notes on a clipboard hooked at the foot of the bed.

'Great specs,' I said.

'Yeah. Got them in Palm Beach over the counter.'

'Gorgeous. Colour works with your hair. So. What happens next?'

'We'll keep her here for a day or two. See what the specialist decides.'

'When is he due?'

'The heart guy? Tomorrow. Couldn't tell you whether it will be morning or afternoon, though. He's a law unto himself.'

So. Not critically in danger, I thought, relieved. She'd be fine.

I went back to the slippery vinyl chair next to the bed. Sat heavily. The cushion collapsed with a sound like a final gasp. 'You landed in Darwin *after* the bombs and you were a nurse's *aide*, not a fully qualified nurse,' I said. 'Why do you lie?'

'You get better attention if they think you're one of them. And anyway, I worked just as hard as the nurses in those days. When there are wards full of wounded men, no one cares if you've done the exams or not.' She closed her eyes. I watched the monitor — steady but you couldn't call it strong. Could she really be seriously ill? You're not admitted to intensive care for a headache. And even my mother, a consummate actress, couldn't be *that* good.

———

The next morning at the hospital I rang the buzzer, gave my name and relationship to the patient, and marched in. Book in hand. *My Brother Jack*, George Johnston's classic. I planned to read to her. I'm not sure what I thought I was doing. Filling in the silence, probably. Afraid the accumulated bile of the last couple of decades would come bubbling out when, for all I knew, my mother could be dying. No. Death was unthinkable. She wouldn't let me off the hook that easily.

I found her awake and alert but oddly shamefaced. 'Did a poo,' she said, sounding furious. 'In bed.'

'Expect they're used to that here.' Fussing about with the chair, the book, my handbag, swallowing compassion and pity and tending only to the business directly at hand. Afraid I'd howl. 'Right, chapter one.' I began to read.

Soon, she interrupted: 'I wouldn't mind a kiss.'

'No need. No one's said you're dying.'

'It wouldn't hurt you, you know,' she said.

I leaned forward, the book slipping off my lap, and patted her hand. The one without cannulas and tubes inserted into the vein.

'I don't think I was such a bad mother,' she whispered.

And there it was, a golden opening. I took a deep breath, moistened my lips, looked directly at her. I'd expected to see challenge in her eyes. There was only pleading. It was shattering. My father's words rang in my ears: *Never hit a man when he's down.* So all I said was, 'You weren't.' It was all I could bring myself to say. Later, to explain, I added, 'It's just . . . we've never been a family of kissers and cuddlers.'

'Weren't we?' she said, frowning, trying to remember.

'Can't change now,' I said, almost airily.

And yet, one of the few photographs I have of my mother and me shows us locked in a strong embrace. We both looked happy. It was taken in the late 1980s, after she'd sold her Melbourne home and moved to New South Wales to live a few doors along from me. Within a year or two she was doing her best to break up my marriage. She wasn't a match for my first husband, though, who years later told me what she'd been up to. I hadn't had a clue.

A tall, lean man with a shaggy surfer's haircut, wearing blue jeans, a crisp cotton shirt and loafers, loomed in the doorway. 'Your mother needs heart surgery if she's going to survive,' he said, loudly enough for her to hear and in a prosecutorial tone directed fair-square between my eyeballs. I hated him in an instant. Anxious to discuss the situation out of earshot, I asked if we could talk elsewhere. He looked me up and down like I was my mother's assassin and forced me to ask every fraught question as we stood by her bedside. He didn't trust me. In a way, I didn't blame him. There was a part of me – not small, either – that wanted to be free of the obligation to look after a dribbling, incoherent wreck, if that's what the future held for her.

'What is the downside of major surgery for a woman of my mother's age?' I asked in a rude voice.

'There are risks.'

'How big?'

'Big.'

'What does "risk" mean?'

'She could have a stroke in the operating theatre. She may emerge from the anaesthetic with dementia. She may die under the knife.'

I swallowed. Glanced at my mother. She seemed to enjoy being the centre of attention but oddly dissociated from the fundamental issue – her life or perhaps death. We might have been discussing a stranger. 'What's the upshot?'

As I recall, he fudged that answer. Instead, he said, 'If we don't operate, she'll die.' Or perhaps that *was* the upshot. She'd definitely die in the short term, not long term. Surgery may not ensure a pretty survival; statistically it probably wouldn't be pretty, but she'd still be breathing. The cynic in me wondered if my mother's private medical insurance, which I'd been paying for decades, was a contributing factor to his attitude.

As if he'd heard me thinking, he added, 'Your mother lives independently, she's bright and aware. If she failed on any of those levels, I wouldn't recommend the surgery.' He turned to Esther, a slightly evangelical look in his glittery blue eyes, and asked, 'So, shall we operate or not?'

'Go for it!' Esther said, sounding almost excited, as though she was about to embark on a holiday of a lifetime. 'Your brother and dad will just have to wait.'

And I will have to pick up the pieces if it all goes awry, I thought. Then I asked myself what I would have done in the same situation. Grab the lifeline. Of course, grab the lifeline. Even a saline drip would have to feel like nectar if you knew that when it ran out you faded forever. She may have believed in God but not enough to trust Him on the big issues.

That afternoon she was transferred by ambulance to North Shore Private Hospital. Nobody told me. When I returned the following morning to see her, she'd been erased from the system. I thought she'd died. For the two minutes it took to sort out details, I was afraid I might sink quietly through a great maw in the floor.

—

On Christmas Eve, the bay foamed white. Mutts – well-bred, under-bred, in-bred, broad-shouldered, chicken-chested, long-legged, stumpy, brindle, red, blue, brown, black and white –

their heads straining to stay above the water, battled for honours in the annual, completely shambolic, Scotland Island to Church Point Dog Race. Entry fee a longneck of beer and a can of dog food – any size. Hundreds of people lined the ragged shore, cheering, shouting, barracking. An armada of boats hung off, out of the way, loaded with people cheering wildly. During the years I'd lived offshore, the race had changed from a quirky little tribute to an offshorer's best mate to an event that attracted dogs and crowds from all over. I resisted the temptation to mourn the loss of the intimacy of community. Times changed. As I joined in seeking out friends and neighbours to wish them health and happiness, a surgeon I'd never met sliced open my mother's chest, plunged his hands into the cavity where her purple heart throbbed amidst ropy veins and arteries, and held the balance of life or death in his hands. *Not a vegetable*, I thought. *Please don't let her come out utterly ruined.*

I rose very early on Christmas Day and drove along almost-deserted highways to the hospital. The emptiness was eerie, as though someone had sounded an alarm. No one walked city side-walks. Shopfronts stared blankly. Even the cardiac ward, when I found it, seemed deathly still.

'Only a few patients and a skeleton staff over Christmas,' a pleasant nurse told me, leading the way to a waiting room with kitchen facilities. It looked like the small, private space where I knew from experience grieving families gathered to be told terrible news.

'She's ok, right?' I heard the note of panic in my voice.

'Yes, of course she is. I'll just check on her before you go in.'

My mother lay in bed. Wires like strands of spaghetti rested on her dry, papery skin. A corrugated tube was thrust down her throat. Winking green and red lights flashed and occasionally emitted a high-pitched squeal. The room was bathed in a sombre yellow light. Her eyes were closed, her breathing wet and ragged through that awful tube. I stood and wept. Glad I was there and wanting desperately to be elsewhere. Happy to see her alive, terrified for her future.

I placed a small ornament of a Christmas fairy with golden wings on her bedside table to acknowledge her enduring passion for the festive season. I'm not sure whether it was a clumsy gesture meant to prove – more to me than to her – that I cared deeply. Or perhaps it was a distraction from the distressing truth that, even now, I could not bear to touch her. Unable to identify whether it was her oldness I struggled to love or forgive, or the woman I knew her to be.

Her eyelids never flickered. Not even a finger twitched. I vaguely heard the nurse tell me Esther had had a triple bypass as well as the scheduled heart valve replacement. I was devastated. She'd been perched on a fatal edge – days, perhaps only hours, from death – and I'd missed all the cues, too busy nagging her about small white lies. I sat for a short while, struggling to remember our good times. All I felt, though, was the endless burden of her. Since my brother died, hadn't she always told me, 'You're all I've got.' It was a noose that grew tighter every time I tried to pull away.

At Lovett Bay, I tied the boat and climbed the sandstone steps, instinctively dodging one or two splatters of wallaby poo, a spider's web, taking care not to brush the foliage on either side to avoid ticks. Where the pathway turns left and the steps are steep and uneven from time, I paused. Remembering. When she was much more mobile and before she became constrained by walkers and untrustworthy legs, my mother tackled the steps but looked up to say something at a crucial moment.

'Watch out. Focus!' I yelled, too late. Her eyes widened in surprise as she fell forward, her legs failing to catch up with the rest of her. She came down on a mossy boulder. Flat on her face. 'Jesus, Esther, I told you to focus,' I said in the angry tone that partners with dread and fear, one that I have used many times to stave off grief. She lay there speechless. Unmoving.

'Esther?' I bent over her. She twisted her head to face me.

'First time I've ever been grateful for my water wings,' she said, laughing, probably because she was still alive, though definitely in shock. 'Cushioned the landing,' she added.

I sat next to her on the rock and we laughed and laughed. Congratulated her foresight in arranging a forty-eight-inch bust to be useful on an occasion such as this. Then she held out her hand. 'Tore a fingernail. Ruined my manicure. Now I'll have to cut them all short. Damn.'

'I'll leave you for a minute. Get Bob. You ok?'

''Course I am,' she said dismissively. Not for the first time, I wondered at my mother's ability to rise above catastrophe. She'd faced major heart surgery as though she was off on a cruise or booked in to a flash resort for a few days. Nearly broken her neck but mourned a broken fingernail. *It's the child in her*, I thought, *the child who cannot see beyond the moment*. That's how she gets through dire straits. She refuses to look beyond the instant. I see all the angles, good and bad. Always have. Is that why we had an uncanny ability to step off on the wrong foot? Her Pollyanna optimism in the face of life or death decisions clashed violently with my instinct to focus on threatening issues and ways to solve them? And yet, hasn't she always told me, 'Laugh in the face of adversity.' And hasn't that single anthem saved me more times than I care to remember? But isn't it also the same anthem that drives me to despair when her world is crashing and she's headed for ruin, and all she does is wave a hand as though it's of no great import and some angel of mercy will step in at the last minute to avert disaster? And yet, here she is, aged eighty-nine and a survivor against all odds.

Inside the house, I rolled up my sleeves and began to prepare Christmas dinner. My mother was absent for the first time since

I'd returned to live in Australia nearly thirty years ago. The day felt less lustrous, as though constant traditions had been spuriously waived and left us all poorer. I could never have predicted the loss.

———

The following morning, she opened her eyes when I entered her room. There was a faint glimmer of the old shine that flooded just before she aimed the point of a knife at you. The tube had been removed from her throat.

'They've guaranteed me ten years,' she croaked. I pulled up short. I must have looked shocked. She stretched her dry, cracked lips in a victory smile. 'But I reckon I'll be able to push it to fifteen.'

I counted the years on my fingers. 'So I'll be looking after you until I'm seventy-five,' I said with a mock groan.

She managed a real grin. 'I win,' she said hoarsely. And we laughed together.

After two weeks in rehabilitation at a private hospital high on a hill in Dee Why, with views of red-gold beaches and crashing surf, my mother was ready to return to civilian life. I booked her into respite care at the Village to ease the transition, expecting her flashy, witty, acerbic self to re-emerge, reinvigorated by a strongly beating heart and blood fizzing with oxygen. A fantasy, as it turned out.

Heart surgery did not magically transform Esther into the fit, healthy femme fatale of her youth that I believe she'd envisaged. It saved her life but it did not restore her to even half the level of fitness she'd enjoyed pre-surgery. It made her vulnerable. It made her weak. Worst of all, it made her fearful. Now she worried: Would a single reach too far for the television remote control trigger a rip in her flesh that might dislodge her new valves and end her life? Would negotiating a high gutter with her walker push her physical limits too far and result in another heart attack?

Would a stroll of more than ten feet without resting every few steps send her spiralling into the final void? She switched from a woman carrying her age well, into a fearful, grey-faced old woman too afraid to spend a week, a day or even an hour without help available at the push of a button.

'Give her time,' Bob said. 'She'll get more confident as she goes along.' At least, I thought, she had all her wits, bright, shiny and with the requisite number of points sharpened in ancient and recent skirmishes.

'You must have done something good in a former life,' I joked. 'Or maybe you've got a direct line to God.'

'Both!' she quipped straight back. But her stay in assisted care stretched from weeks into months. Eventually the manager told me it was time for her to go home or arrange a permanent move. Would I have a talk to her?

—

In her respite room – bed, bathroom, closet and minuscule kitchenette – I carefully explained that she'd come through surgery magnificently, without any hideous side effects. I explained that her renovated heart was beating strongly. The follow-up appointment with the Rottweiler, as I called the specialist, had confirmed it. I explained she'd been given a Get Out of Jail Free card, and it was up to her to make the most of it, to vindicate the faith shown when she was slipped onto the tail end of a busy operating schedule on Christmas Eve. She was a very, very lucky woman. Then I explained it was time to return to her unit.

'Your health is as good as it's ever going to get. You'll have to go home sometime,' I said as kindly as I could. 'Might as well make the break now.'

I stocked her pantry with cans of her favourite soups, stews and plenty of the beetroot she craved when she felt crook, in the same way I longed for canned tomato soup and buttery toast.

Filled the fridge with mountainous stacks of her beloved crème caramels. Paused midstream. Should a woman who'd had a heart attack, open-heart surgery and three heart valves replaced eat creamy sweet desserts? *Oh hell*, I thought, *she's nearly ninety. She can have whatever she likes.* So I made sure there was a restorative bottle of whisky within reach, as well as a bottle of gin for drop-ins. If you were reduced to existing instead of living, you might as well give up.

But after less than two days and just one night alone, she asked to be returned to respite. The manager called me for instructions. When I arrived at her unit to suss out the situation, Esther said, 'I'm not well enough to manage on my own.' She reached for a cup of tea on the coffee table with a violently shaking hand. I looked away. *Losing an argument? Fake a shaky hand. Get caught in a lie? Fake a shaky hand. Make a mistake? Fake a shaky hand. See how frail I am?*

'You're not ill,' I said firmly. 'Technically, you're fitter than you've been for a long while.' She put a hand to the centre of her chest, just below her neck. A single puce vein, no more than a thread, snaked and pulsed under skin, still bruised yellow and blue.

'Look,' she said, opening her shirtfront. A raw scar, about eight inches long, like a symbol of initiation, ran down her sternum. 'The pain. You have no idea.'

I crumpled instantly. 'Ok,' I said, 'we'll organise more time. But one day soon, Esther, you're going to have to face up to living alone.'

'Where are you and Bob at the moment?'

Puzzled, I replied, 'At Tarrangaua. Where else would we be? Why?' She gave a little shrug, inviting me to work it out. 'Ah, I see. You wouldn't make it across in the boat, Esther, let alone up the track. You'd be back in hospital in a flash and I'd be accused of inflicting grievous bodily harm. Imprisoned with a life sentence for cruelty to mothers. Then you'd really be on your own.' Hopelessly joking, trying not to sound as bad a daughter as I felt.

'Bob would look after me, wouldn't he?'

Was she serious? I frowned. My mother had always flirted with the boyfriends I brought home. Lunched with them when I was away on jobs or overseas. Tagged along to parties when I was a cadet journalist. Looking after me, she explained. At the time I never questioned her. From this end of my life it seemed curious at the very least.

'Not sure about that. He's a good man, but . . .' Thank god, I thought, for the moat between us. Thank god for the difficulty of offshore living. Thank god I do not have to feel guilty for failing to move her into our home and our lives. I played the trump card: 'If anything went wrong you'd be long dead before the paramedics made it across the water. I'll see if I can organise a bed tonight, but you might have to wait a couple of days, ok?'

She nodded, but it probably felt like a lifetime to her.

Half an hour later, I said, 'You're in luck. Let's go. I'll bring your stuff over when you're settled.' I helped her off the sofa, put both her hands firmly on her walker. 'Follow me,' I ordered.

We proceeded to cover a very short distance at a stop-start snail's pace with enough theatrics to warrant an encore. Was I being mean? Cynical? To test her, I pointed at the sky: 'Could rain any minute. Your hair will be ruined.' She galloped. I laughed silently. But the spurt was brief. A funny white band appeared around her mouth, crept along the bridge of her nose and reached into her forehead. She looked like she could collapse. 'Hang on. I'll run back and get an umbrella.' She nodded. Unable to speak.

Three months later, I asked her one last time if she was ready to return to her unit.

'No,' she said, pouting.

I held my hands up in surrender. Spelled out the future for her: 'Once you've officially quit your old unit you can't go back. Are you sure that's what you want?'

'I'm sure.'

I gestured around the small space. 'Four closed-in walls from now on, a single room.' She nodded. I tried again: 'If you're worried about coping on your own, we'll find a way to make it work.'

In effect, the *independent* life she'd described to the heart specialist outside my hearing was moot. I did her shopping, a cleaner came once a week, I took care of her bills and finances. We went out to lunch regularly. If Esther didn't feel like cooking, she called the village restaurant or the takeaway Chinese in Mona Vale and arranged to have lunch or dinner delivered. Or she met the *girls* in the dining room. A carer dropped by to chat with her twice a week at twenty dollars an hour; a good woman, whom my mother referred to as *a real daughter.* A comment I eventually let slide straight through to the keeper without reacting. Eventually.

'I'm well looked after here,' she said, indicating her little space. 'It suits me.'

I gave her a long, severe look. Was she frightened? Did she crave company – staff – popping in and out all day? Was she truly incapable of doing anything at all beyond shuffling to the bathroom or making a cup of tea in the tiny kitchenette? But nobody's health improves if they lie anchored to a bed. I gave it a final shot. 'If you don't use it, you lose it,' I said, resorting to the kind of language my mother understood best.

Her eyes flashed. 'I do my exercises every day,' she snapped. 'Look!' And from a supine position she raised first one leg and then the other. 'See?'

I sighed. Stood up to go. 'You have to make an effort, Esther. For your own sake.' She threw me another dirty look. 'Ok. I'll get things moving,' I said. 'For what it's worth, I think you're putting yourself at even greater risk.' She closed her eyes, locking me out. I hesitated, wondering if I should try to bully her into trying harder. Gave in and gave up. Her life. Her choice. But it's never that simple. It was impossible to shrug off the idea that somehow, because you were younger, fitter and sharper, it was your responsibility to try to make the best choices for a vulnerable parent. Even the tough ones.

As I left, she called after me: 'It's like living in a hotel, you know. They wait on me hand and foot.' And there it was. The underlying thrill and attraction. My mother found what I considered the ignobility of dependence to be a luxury. Or perhaps in a spin worthy of a crooked politician, that's how she rationalised her situation so she could live with it. As always, it was impossible to know.

I began unravelling the legal rigmarole of her unit. Meanwhile, she was well looked after. It was a phrase that became a catchcry of self-congratulation. As if having someone zip her trousers, button her shirt, wash her, was a singular and great achievement. Years later, I read a book by Atul Gawande titled *Being Mortal: Illness, Medicine and What Matters in the End*. He argued: a person has a right to make her own decisions. If they end in catastrophe, so be it.

My mother had exercised that right.

5

IN BETWEEN MY MOTHER'S HEALTH ISSUES, Bob attempted an interim quick, cheap fix for the kiln that didn't work.

'I'm sorry,' I said, feeling guilty, 'I pushed you into all this.'

He grinned, slipped an arm around my waist: 'I was ready for a challenge.'

After more than a year of hard slog and in the depths of winter, it was time to install the new brick kiln. We rented a basic redbrick house in Killabakh, a blink-and-you-miss-it locality at the tail end of a sealed road and about twenty-five minutes north of Wingham. Tidily arranged on a gentle hill, the house had views across deep green valleys swathed in fog that burned off by mid-morning. Way below in a cold, almost sunless nook, smoke spiralled lazily from a cottage chimney, but I never saw anyone moving about. Every day, like a gift from the gods, great slabs of golden heat poured through the kitchen windows. Free. Renewable. No nasty side effects or far-reaching impacts on the planet. An impossibility at Pittwater, where soaring spotted gums allowed only a tepid dose of light to penetrate, and our heating bills were beginning to prompt outrage and disbelief. Unfurnished except for a mattress on a legless base, a few cooking utensils, a couple of chairs and a foldaway table, it was a perfect camp for three or four weeks while the new kiln was being built and tested.

I raided the disorderly and musty second-hand shop behind a garage roller-door shopfront in Wingham for a few cheap necessities. Scrounged and bargained my way to a retro, three-legged coffee table, two dodgy lamps and a bedside table by promising to donate them back at the end of our stay. Then blew the budget on a totally impractical set of Grindley art deco side plates and a serving platter. They civilised a simple slice of cake in that spartan environment. That had to count for something.

Every morning, Bob lit the wood-fired heater in the kitchen, fixed a breakfast of porridge, fruit, yoghurt and milk. Let Chippy out for a run. Showered, dressed then brewed a fresh cuppa to bring me in bed before heading off in the chilly predawn light.

'Watch the tricky bend,' I'd murmur, the earthy fragrance of tea inducing half-wakefulness. 'And the speed humps on the bridge.' Repeated over and over. Afraid if I forgot them just once, fate might seize the opportunity and deal a mortal blow. As if any of us controlled fate.

At weekends, when the brickworks were closed, Bob and I explored the countryside. Steering clear of suburbanised coast-lines, instead following winding dirt roads. On a single journey, the sun might shine, rain pound, wind shift from a breeze to a gale, sleet fall. The bush was never still. It trembled, swayed and swung to a rhythm and song while sunstruck raindrops hung like strings of beads. Everywhere, avenues of tree ferns wafted dreamily like giant, feathery fans. Colours collided. Blue. Yellow. Grey. Every shade of green. Dense. Soaring. Glistening. On high plateaus where the country opened up and the pewter sky seemed within touching distance, piebald cattle, their swollen udders at bursting point, patiently filed towards the dairy for relief.

Once, lured by the smell of the sea, we surfed the corrugations of Crowdy Bay's bush tracks and saw a thousand-strong flock of budgerigars take to the sky, turning it green like a lawn. For a second or two, the world was reversed. We laughed, the two of us, for the luck and privilege of being there.

In a high, cold town called Comboyne, we followed our noses to an honest café where a fire burned cosily and ordered hot chocolate and scones with jam and cream. Real cream. We were in some of the best dairy country in Australia. Patting our stomachs with pleasure and a hint of remorse, we returned to the car where, warm in her bed on the back seat, Chippy slept the agitated sleep of the old. Twitching and whimpering, as though, like my mother, death was tapping her on the shoulder. But we'd made a pact, my old dog and me. She would live to be twenty years or even older. I may not have trusted her to ignore a wallaby or a rabbit, but I trusted her on this.

'Who's the best little doggie in the whole wide world?' I said, rubbing her ears. She snuffled her way to wakefulness, looked greedily for a treat. 'We ate the lot, little doggie. Next time.' She huffed in disgust, buried her snout in the softness of her bed and closed her eyes once more.

'This landscape,' I said to Bob. 'I'd never have guessed at all this. So fertile. Green. Not what you'd expect from a sunburnt country.'

'There's a waterfall they claim is the second longest drop in the world. Want to take a look?'

———

Very early in our stay, Michael and Adele turned up in their ute with two enormous armchairs from the brickworks office.

'They might look a bit crook but they're comfy as hell,' Michael said, sitting down to prove his point. The kettle went on. Cake came out. The Grindley plates shone. The faint cloud of brickworks dust from Michael plonking in the armchair settled quickly.

'Did you hear about the home invasion?' Adele asked. 'In Cedar Party Creek. Woman in her eighties, living alone. Had to walk to the main road to wave down a car for help in the middle of the night, poor thing.'

'Awful!' I responded, settling for a long chat.

A couple of days later, the Wingham Hotel, known as the Bottom Pub and established in the late 1800s, burned to the ground. The town went into shock. Wingham was a quiet little backwater, they lamented. This sort of stuff happened elsewhere. Soon after, a woman was shot dead by her husband for reasons known only to himself. Wingham? Sleepy?

—

After close to two years of intense work – triggered by a phone call from a stranger – a new, low thermal mass kiln, which released just one-third of the maximum particle emissions allowed for this type of business, was up and running. From henceforth, when Lincoln Brickworks did a burn, the wide blue skies of Wingham would remain crystal clear. Despite setbacks, delays and Old John's fears and stubborn lack of faith, the results, ticked off by an independent tester, went beyond expectations.

'Knew you were a genius,' I whispered in Bob's ear.

'Genius? Nah. Like luck, it's where hard work meets opportunity.' But he was pleased with the result.

Old John, who'd prowled the brickyards through long winter nights during test runs, made a confession in a white-flag moment. '*My* father,' he said, 'he would've gone for this in a flash. Anything new, and he'd have a go. Long as it made sense to him. He was a modern man.'

Michael walked away, unable to trust himself to speak. Then turned back, managing a smile: 'By the end of the year, it will have been Dad's idea all along. How about we order some pizza to celebrate?'

Ironically, the new technology extended Old John's working life. As the hard physical yakka of hand-stoking was no longer required, he was easily able to drive the forklift to pick up and deliver timber to the firebox. Before anyone realised what was going on, he'd taken over the graveyard shift between midnight and six and learned the secrets of the flashing red and green lights in the spiffy new control room. Digital read-outs no longer blurred like hieroglyphics. Not that he'd ever entirely trust their accuracy. Once or twice a night, he climbed a ladder, pushed aside a viewing panel and checked the glow. As he'd done since he was a kid.

——

On our final morning at Killabakh, the sun shone warmly. Our cosy winter, borne comfortably in a north-facing house, was almost over. We packed the car, finding a safe corner for the carefully wrapped Grindley plates.

'Why don't we rent a little apartment in Cooktown and spend winters there from now on?' I said. Winter warmth, I was thinking, was a game changer for our aging joints.

Bob pulled his head out of the rear of the station wagon. 'Cooktown?' he repeated, as though he must have misheard.

'Yeah. Cooktown. We could bypass Lovett Bay winters forever.'

'What's wrong with Lovett Bay winters?' he asked, genuinely puzzled.

'Nothing. It's just warmer in Cooktown.' Still a bare-bones frontier town when we'd last visited, it was civilised enough to be comfortable but not so civilised it had lost its heart or character.

'Cooktown,' Bob said again, frowning now. He closed the hatch with exaggerated care. 'Are you serious?' I nodded. 'But what would I do there?'

'Go fishing . . . Remember the huge tuna and snapper you caught? And a mackerel too? Go exploring . . .' I continued. 'Remember the birds in Lakefield National Park? The huge crocodile that waited and waited?'

We were on our honeymoon and camped on Twelve Mile Lagoon, a muddy expanse of water that was home to courting brolgas, magpie geese and light-footed jacanas. Every afternoon, flocks of whistling kites, wings outspread, elegantly surfed the thermals like newspapers swept up by the wind. On our second day, the old couple from a neighbouring campsite about a kilometre away slid past us in their boat to shout a warning. A big croc, they said, had stalked the previous inhabitants and we should be wary. Two days later, as we put-putted under the power of our puny eight horsepower outboard in our tiny fragile tinny, leaks patched by Bob with glue and gauze from the first aid box, we saw an evil-looking corrugated spine waiting amongst the lily pads in the shallows at the bottom of the old couples' campsite. 'Watch out!' we yelled, pointing. The ridge sank silently, stealthily, scarily, without making a ripple.

'All I remember about Cooktown is Chippy scurrying off to the caravan park with the other two Jack Russells from the B & B and returning stinking of bacon every morning. Her stomach hard as a bullet. Thought she was going to explode,' Bob said.

'Cooktown was great!' I insisted.

'And?' Bob asked.

'It's the shed, isn't it? You'd miss your shed. Yeah, bad idea. Let's forget it.'

We locked the door, delivered our goods for recycling to the second-hand shop and drove past the brickworks where the decommissioned furnaces, already growing frail with disuse, were sheathed in moss and sprouting tufts of grass. How quickly, I thought, the present turned into a barely remembered or recognisable past.

We'd said our goodbyes earlier. Michael, grinning, commented, 'You weren't here long but you sure stirred things up. There was the home invasion in Cedar Party Creek, the Bottom Pub burned down, and a bloke shot his missus. If you'd stayed any longer, we were going to pass around the hat to send you on your way. No offence, mate, but Wingham hasn't been this volatile since the war. The first one, that is.'

The local volatility, as it turned out, was only the beginning of a much more widespread descent into madness. A bunch of greed heads on Wall Street and from the international banking industry – unable to do the most basic arithmetic despite their chosen professions – had criminally placed the world financial system in such jeopardy it was on the point of collapse. The building industry screamed to a halt, orders for bricks dried up. The tough times Old John recalled were back. Only tougher.

A few months later, on a follow-up visit to check the kiln, the brickworks cat, an effective and much-valued mouser and ratter, was found dead in the garden. 'Snake got her, that's what we think,' Old John said in the matter-of-fact way country people discuss death. 'Grey cats. They're good cats. Shame.' As it happened, there was a burn on and the firebox was roaring. With a mumbled, 'See ya later, Kitty Kat,' she was swung into the flames.

'Ashes to ashes, eh?' Michael remarked.

'Well,' Old John responded, rocking back on his heels, hands in his overall pockets, 'there might be a new business opportunity here.' Michael, Bob, Skip, Dave and I looked at him blankly. 'Pet cremations,' he said, nodding to himself. 'The vet reckons it's a growth industry. It's got me buggered, though, how you'd pick 'em apart when you cleaned out the box.'

'Same as people, Dad, probably,' Michael said. 'Never been able to figure that one out, either.' Old John sloped off, dogs at his heels. 'Least he didn't say *I told you so*. Might look into pet cremations. You never know . . . Nah. Steady on. Just kidding. As you were . . .'

Vale Kitty Kat. What a send-off.

6

BACK AT PITTWATER, I began organising my mother's transition from independent to assisted living. It involved unravelling the mind-bogglingly complicated legal minutiae of the conditions of the lease on her old unit and negotiating a price for her new home. After the entrance fee and an annual accrued interest fee of two-and-a-half per cent on her investment, which was also part of the deal with her independent unit, there was a flat monthly fee, four times the amount she'd been paying. Additional services, such as help with bathing, pill giving, laundry and meals delivered to her room instead of eaten in the dining room were extra costs. Worth every cent. Retirement villages provided a service that took the worst of the load off families, although it paid to read the fine print very carefully.

At the last minute, Bob noticed a subtle detail even our lawyer failed to pick up. Essentially, it meant she'd be paying an annual interest of two-and-a-half per cent on the cost of her entry into the independent unit, even though her new unit entry cost was less than half that amount.

I explained the arrangements to Esther. She shrugged, as if dealing with the dirty business of money was beneath her.

'I want you to understand,' I said, frustrated. 'You need to know what this entails.'

'How's Bob?'

'Don't try to change the subject. We're discussing your future here and how to plan so that all the bases are covered.'

'Pish tush,' she said, reaching for the television remote control.

A nurse knocked and came in with the new regime of pills rattling in a thimble-sized plastic cup. 'Medication time,' she sang. Esther opened her mouth like a hungry baby bird. A look of complete submission in her eyes.

'What, you're too ill even to lift a couple of pills to your mouth,' I said, ashamed of her. The nurse dropped the pills on her tongue and handed her a glass of water.

Esther swallowed and pointed dismissively in my direction: 'Meet my accountant,' she said. I shook my head. Disgusted. The nurse laughed, let the screen door slam behind her.

'I'll be packing up your unit in the next couple of days,' I said, giving up.

Discussions about money with my mother had sometimes ended in blood – mine. Her lifelong trick, when all else failed, was simple: 'I'll kill myself,' she'd say. 'That'll fix everything.' And my brother and I, and certainly my father, would buckle immediately.

'Think about what you want to keep,' I added, fighting hard to remain pleasant. 'There's not much space here. Most of your stuff will have to go.'

Immediately, a suspicious, accusing look crept into her eyes. Since Esther had turned pilferer, she'd begun to suspect everyone of the same crime. Once, in complete frustration and fury, I pointed out that it was hardly likely I would steal from her when I'd been silently picking up bills for her for years – medical insurance (decades), groceries (intermittently), clothing (at the start of every season), birthday parties (decades), car repairs (decades).

'I always paid for all that myself,' she hissed furiously.

'Whatever,' I said, giving her a hard look. We both knew the facts. She backed off.

'Everything I have will be yours when I'm dead, anyway,' she said.

I took a deep breath. I knew what came next. She'd launch into a well-honed script about how much money she planned to leave me. How everything she ever did was for my benefit. How all she ever wanted out of life was to see me happy. As always, I would nod, playing the game. As if I couldn't see through the self-interested carrot-and-stick routine. As if I didn't understand that she'd trample over me to save herself from a speeding bus. That when she ran out of money – as she had when my father's careful financial planning blew up in a way my brother and I could never quite understand, when the money from the sale of her Melbourne house was frittered away on clothes, costume jewellery and god knows what, when the small amount of money remaining ran out – I'd be expected to step in with an open cheque book. It was a lifelong pattern. It sent my father into desperation. 'One hundred pounds for a dress?' he'd shout, red-faced with fury and disbelief. 'Sixty pounds for a pair of shoes? Another sixty pounds for a second pair of shoes?' It was a fortune in those days, the equivalent of thousands of dollars. He always sorted the problem, though, found the money somewhere, sidestepping debtors' prison by the skin of his teeth. As my mother knew he would.

At one stage, on what could have been a whim, my mother went job hunting. She said it was to boost family income. I suspect it was to escape the house. To everyone's surprise, she got a job catering for a local council, using the pub days as proof of her experience (my mother helped in the kitchen when she was needed, but we had cooks for the hard slog). Turned out she was good at it. For big functions, she reeled in as waitresses a few women from her tennis team who were as bored with their predictable suburban lives as she was. My father said her job drained his bank account. My mother said he refused to acknowledge all the bills she paid. My father's version is probably correct. When he died, my mother didn't have a clue what to do with the household accounts. Years later, she still relied on the women at the post office to do the paperwork for her. When she moved to the retirement village, I organised her bill-paying.

———

It was a grey, drizzly day when I knocked on the door of her temporary room in respite care to begin shifting her belongings into her own freshly painted room in assisted care.

'Come in if you're good-looking,' she called gaily, over the top of the clamour of the television.

'Heading up to your old unit to pack things,' I said.

She patted the bed. 'Sit down. Talk to me.'

My heart sank. It was a routine precursor to a bout of emotional blackmail. I remained standing, reached for the remote and hit the mute button. 'On a mission. Can't hang around. Too much to do. I'll call in to say goodbye when I'm done for the day.'

Out of the blue, she swung her legs to the floor and reached for her walker. 'I'm coming with you,' she said with a hint of her old feistiness.

I held up a hand: 'Stay where you are. You'll get wet, catch pneumonia and die.'

'Fiddlesticks,' she retorted, rocking back and forth on the bed, gathering momentum for lift-off.

I helped her stand, feeling with shock the soft emptiness in the flesh of her arms. She wobbled for a moment, closed her eyes and took a few deep breaths. 'If you die, don't blame me,' I only half-joked.

'Lead on, Macduff,' she ordered, struggling upright. Outside, hunched with determination, she shuffled up a gut-busting hill (stop-starting but nevertheless at a quite impressive pace for a woman who was too ill to throw a few pills down her throat only a few days before) and landed wheezily but triumphantly on the sofa.

Mistrust oozed out of every pore. If it weren't so sad, I would have laughed. 'This is the plan,' I said. 'I'm going to pack whatever you don't need in boxes and store them in Bob's shed. If suddenly you want something, all you have to do is ask. I'll find it and deliver it. So you don't have to discard anything you love.' I'd discussed the strategy with Bob, worried that if I tossed out even a single chipped glass or cracked plate I'd be accused of theft or abuse. Held accountable forever.

She flopped back against the sofa, as though she'd won a significant battle and foiled a dastardly plot with her presence. I went to the fridge. Searched the freezer for an ice-cream. 'Here,' I said, irresponsibly handing her a Magnum but thinking, *what the hell, carpe diem*. 'You've got some whisky, too. Let's make this a party.'

She unwrapped the ice-cream. Bit into the chocolate. I found a towel and gave it to her to dry off the drizzle. Roughly wrapped a crocheted afghan, standard issue for the aged, around her shoulders. Set the heating on high. Watched a piece of chocolate drop on her shirtfront and melt. Decided whisky was a bad idea.

In a switch worthy of Machiavelli, she waved an arm around: 'I don't have much space in the new place. Tell me what you want and it's yours.'

'Nothing,' I said, sighing inwardly. Her face fell. *Play the game*, I told myself. *Make her feel important for a while.* 'Anyway, you've already given me all your good stuff. And I gave you most of this stuff.' The sofa on which she was planted (given to her after the pink chintz snapped in the middle while she was sitting on it). The table for the television. Pots and pans to replace the ones she'd burned beyond repair. Clothing I'd handed over when she admired it, even though we both knew it wouldn't fit.

She pointed to a storage cupboard. I crossed the room and opened it. It was stuffed with glassware that hadn't been shifted since I'd unpacked it five years earlier when she moved from her four-bedroom home into the unit. I shook my head. 'Nope. Have more glasses than I need now. I'll pack them. You might want them later.' Ridiculous. We both knew it. But it was meant to sound hopeful instead of hopeless.

'What about the dining table and chairs?' I asked. 'They'll take up too much space.' She thrust out her bottom lip. 'Ok, ok, we'll store them in case you need them sometime,' I said, giving in immediately and refusing to think about the effort involved in shipping them across the water, getting them up the hill and then finding space in Bob's shed where the bush rats would have a field day.

Without warning, she suddenly shrank – collapsed – into the sofa, her face gloomy and despondent: 'No point, is there? Not really. Not unless *you* want them.' I was about to shake my head but her quiet acknowledgment of a limited future stopped me. Did she really need me to tell her that the possessions she'd fought so hard to acquire had no value to anyone else?

'Dad's old writing desk, the watercolour of the Murray River. Do you want them?'

'No. Let's get rid of the lot,' she said, reverting to the boom-or-bust mentality that had so often brought her undone and that rears up in me more often than I like to acknowledge.

The writing desk was falling apart but, like the unsigned watercolour, had been part of my life since I was born. 'I'll look after those, then,' I said, appalled at the idea of sending them off to Vinnies. The gloom lifted from her face, replaced with sunny smugness. She'd set the trap and I'd fallen into it head first.

'All your paintings? What about those?'

She perked up. 'I'll take them with me. They're much admired, you know. Everyone comments when they see them.' There were about twenty left from an original stock of about eighty, the result of a one-year art course where the cost of framing every single painting emptied her bank account.

'Right.' Thank god, I thought, she'd given most of them away.

In a sort of bandy-legged shuffle like a toddler, one hand on the walls for support, she followed me into the bedroom, carrying the dripping ice-cream out in front of her like a chalice. She fell on the bed, signalling thumbs up, thumbs down as I exhibited one item of clothing after another. 'Chuck that. Keep that. Ooooh, chuck, no, keep that. And that.'

'What about your fur coat?'

'Your father gave it to me as a thank you when I nursed his mother through cancer.'

'I didn't know that.'

She shrugged: 'There's a lot you don't know.' Her comment made me hesitate.

'There's a lot *you* don't know,' I said in a hard voice.

She gave me a funny, half cross-eyed look. 'You're my daughter. I know you inside out.'

Now, I thought, *ask her now about her father, my grandfather, and what she knew or didn't know about the man.* Butterflies took flight in my stomach, I felt short of breath and, in the end, I couldn't find or form any words. Esther waved the ice-cream stick. I took it from her. Placed it in a bin in the kitchen. I returned with a damp cloth to wipe the stain, telling myself that to question her would achieve nothing anyway. Life is life. You play the hand you are dealt. No one escapes a share of tough times and, hopefully, good times. But some things eat away at you no matter how often you slam the lid on them. They rise like demons if you let down your guard in a weak moment. Dirty little secrets gain power from the very act of keeping them secret. The deeper you try to bury them, the more alive they become. But I waited for the butterflies to quieten. Kept on sorting clothes. *God forbid I should rock the boat now or ever.*

'Keep it?' I asked, picking up the fur again and giving it a shake to attract her attention.

'Yes. I promised to give it to Lisa. Make sure she gets it when I die.' Curly-haired Lisa from our Christmas lunches who untiringly wooed Esther with flattery and humour.

'Ok. I'll make a note. I'll tell her not to hold her breath, though.'

———

It took three days and about forty trips to the clothing charity bin, conveniently located next to the high-care nursing home, to reduce Esther's possessions to necessities. Two sheet sets. Two duvet covers. Two duvets. Two pillows. Four towels. Seven summer outfits. Seven winter outfits. Extra shirts and trousers. Five pairs of shoes. One set of fluffy pink slippers. Low storage drawers that could double as a coffee table. A large chest of drawers that would fit against a wall.

'What about the bed?' I asked her.

'No. I'll take the sofa.' My mother had slept on sofas round the clock for as long as I could remember. I'd always believed it eliminated the need for bed-making ('If the beds are made and the dishes done, a house always looks clean and tidy') or justified her claim that the birth of my brother and me ruined her sleep forever ('Never slept a wink after you two kids were born'). But in the old days, people died in bed instead of a hospital, and perhaps it was a risk she wasn't prepared to take.

'I think a bed would make more sense,' I suggested.

'The sofa cushions snuggle into my back,' she snapped, ending the discussion.

Bob and I dismantled, lifted, carried and transported what my mother had chosen to take with her into the next stage of a rapidly compressing life, including my father's writing desk and the Murray River watercolour. Which turned out to be the only two things she really wanted, after all. Apart from her own paintings, of course.

Three weeks or so later, she asked me to return some grape-festooned silver-plated goblets I'd packed away and stored in the loft. 'The writing desk looks bare without them,' she said.

I mentally raised my hand in a high five of victory. 'Easy. Can you wait a couple of days?' She looked vaguely disappointed. 'Anything else?' I asked, angelically.

—

During those three days of packing and sorting under the watchful and suspicious eye of my mother, her carer had knocked on the door. 'Your mother asked me to come and help,' she'd explained. I'd glanced at Esther, her body hunched forward over the coffee table, playing with a bowl of rings as though they were dice. She'd looked shifty, as though she'd been caught out. I'd realised she still didn't trust me.

'Great!' I'd said. Then I'd marched to the glass cupboard, thrown open the doors. 'I'm sure Esther would like you to take whatever you want.'

I'd seen my mother flinch. 'Well, I'd like to keep the crystal,' she'd said quickly. 'And the red jug. And –'

'How about these?' I'd interrupted her, holding up a set of frosted glasses and dessert bowls.

'No! Not those!' she'd yelped.

I'd begun wrapping them. 'There's no space where you're going. They have to go.'

The carer, embarrassed, had put up her hands to say no. But I'd grimly insisted. Esther had backed off.

Knowing she was unhappy, a petty little victory, nevertheless, gave me a momentary thrill followed very quickly by shame.

Each night, I returned to Pittwater and lay awake, counting on my fingers all the ways in which I'd been fortunate, matching them against the ways in which my mother had been unfortunate. If it were a competition, I would have emerged the undisputed winner.

A long time later, I asked myself if *unfortunate* was the correct term for the form my mother's life had taken. Disappointing was more accurate, and strongly littered with self-destruction. Even when she was handed the one thing she insisted would bring her unbridled joy, it was never quite right, never added up to her expectations, never quite good enough. So many gifts over so many decades resulted in disappointment. It was years before I realised that, even though my mother's ego was boundless, her self-esteem was rock bottom. Her bucket could never be filled because why would anyone give her anything unless it was worthless? Thinking back, there *was* a single gift that gave her unadulterated pleasure.

On a trip to New York, Bob suggested buying her a gaudy red feather boa from a magic shop. She adored it and pushed aside the little blue box from Tiffany's with the remark, 'Did you get that from the cheap third floor?' She flung the boa around her neck and preened, chin raised, looking down her nose, in a sort of 1930s screen siren-ish way. I could've whacked her.

Each week, as was our custom, I continued to collect my mother from the hotel-like reception area of the retirement village to take her to lunch. Each week, from a bent position over her walker, she eyed me up and down and asked, 'Is your iron broken?' Or: 'Is that shirt meant for going out or have you been gardening?' Or: 'Why don't I ask my hairdresser if she can do anything about your dry hair.' A thousand more little digs too pathetic to even make an effort to recall. I'd hoped that after heart surgery, which was said to soften the toughest individuals, we'd manage moments of gentle, even honest and accurate conversation. I longed to crack through the fantasy-laden accounts of her life to reach into the roiling mess of experience that had made her. And, in the process, understand what had moulded me. Instead, we slipped straight back into our traditional combative habits.

One day, to break the monotony of our lunches, I suggested a shopping expedition to buy a couple of armchairs to go on either side of my father's writing desk, so visitors to her unit would have somewhere comfortable to sit. 'Let's go!' she said enthusiastically. 'I can do anything.'

In the store, my mother charmed the sales staff. Coming up with a heap of witty one-liners, cracking jokes, bursting into short sprints to check out one chair after another. I would have thought her amazing too, if she'd belonged to someone else. But out of sight of an audience, she fell apart, her breath coming in short bursts, her face grey. By the time I delivered her back to her room she could barely speak.

'They look great,' I said when two red leather chairs in a streamlined style you might find in a club in Cuba were delivered. 'This could be a swish studio apartment in New York.'

She looked pleased. Shuffled around the coffee table/storage drawers in the new, tippy, arms-outstretched-for-balance, toddler-style waddle she'd adopted since surgery. Delight and anticipation scrawled on her face. She lowered her backside, dropping the last couple of inches heavily and with a loud grunt. In a blink, she slid to the floor, like a kid on a slide.

'Slippery little suckers, aren't they?' I said, trying not to laugh.

'Might stick with the sofa in future,' she replied. I went to hoist her upright. 'Not that arm, that's my bad arm.'

'Yeah, ok, sorry.'

Bob installed her paintings. I bought her a new kettle and toaster in red to match the chairs. Left enough space near the sofa for the walker. Vital for her to make the six- or seven-step journey safely to the bathroom. Her meals – cereal and toast for breakfast, sandwich for lunch, hot dinner – were delivered to her room. She was not ready yet, she told me, for the physical effort involved in reaching the communal dining room. *So death still sits cross-legged on her lap, holding her captive. Her choice*, I thought, *her choice*. If I'd run into the specialist with the bedside manner of the Rottweiler, I would have hugged him. None of this was my doing.

7

ESTHER'S HEART ATTACK turned into my own wake-up call. *Do it while you can.* It jumped around in my subconscious like a flea. Move the goalposts, I told myself. Rearrange old horizons and set new boundaries. Every time I squibbed, an image of my mother repeating *I'm well looked after,* as though it was something to shout proudly from the rooftops, appeared like a haunting.

Feel tired and frozen instead of exhilarated and romantic when crossing the water in a tinny on a cold dark night? *Do it while you can.* Want to wait for a sunny day to do the shopping instead of thumbing a nose at drenching rain? *It's only water.* Feel fear when the wind blows hard and the boat burrows deep enough to sink? *It's a short swim to land.* Can't carry heavy loads anymore? *Split them into smaller lots.* Can't fling a dinner party together in an afternoon? *Plan and prepare ahead.* Can't remember why you walked into a room? *It's not life-threatening.* Hot flushes driving you nuts? *They're not as bad as they used to be.* Sixty is the new fifty. *Only it isn't.*

My libido was sinking. Sex had become painful despite an apothecary of unguents. Intimacy, the exquisitely complete condition that coexisted naturally and effortlessly with love and friendship in a good marriage, was under threat. No wonder my mother's generation referred to menopause as *change of life*. Although, to me, on some days it felt more like I'd been felled by a coup. Violent, subversive, with the enemy invisible. *Do it while you can,* I'd mutter. And for heady, delusional seconds I'd convince myself I could still throw a change of underwear in a backpack, leap into a car and drive north, south, east or west and begin again. Be that same young risk-taker fuelled by dreams and hopes and damn the consequences.

Then a young woman would walk past with unblemished legs and firm upper arms. Or I would baulk at a minor physical challenge, such as leaping for a rope. Or my stamina would ebb by mid-afternoon instead of midnight. Or I would turn away from Bob at night instead of reaching for him. As it turned out, there was only so much spin a mind could take before collapsing under the weight of reality.

Bob couldn't fail to notice the big shifts in my behaviour, but he let them pass without comment, stepped in with support when he saw me struggling. But it was the subtle, inadmissible shifts that gave strength to uncertainties, had the potential to do the most damage to our relationship. I no longer initiated sex when once I'd dragged him to bed, a cognac for each of us, in the middle of a summer afternoon. I found reasons to retire early or read a book very, very late, so we fell asleep at separate times. And while I yearned for the feel of his hands on my skin, his body alongside mine, I also sometimes dreaded it. Sex had become complicated. It required thought and an almost clinical preparation that did more to douse than kindle desire.

As the intervals when my body behaved and responded became rarer, Bob inevitably opened a dialogue I'd been dreading. 'I know something is wrong, but I don't know what it is,' he said, looking into his wine glass, avoiding my eyes. We were on the verandah.

It was the end of another summer. Although I have an almost ency-clopaedic memory for meals on unforgettable occasions, I cannot remember a single ingredient that passed my lips that night. I recall pushing my chair back from the dinner table in a way I was aware he could have read as panic or anger when all I meant to do was flee, to dodge making the hardest of confessions. That I was getting old. But he reached across and wrapped his fingers around my wrist without pressure, more to signal that even if I ran off, this was a conversation I couldn't avoid forever. 'People who care about each other communicate with each other,' he added.

'Yes,' I answered. He waited. The night spun out. In the corner, a mosquito coil smouldered, the musky scent all-enveloping. Stars shone through a lacy arbour. Somewhere across the bay, voices muddled. I thought of the two of us. Our short history. We lacked the bond of successes and failures, tragedies and triumphs – children – to fill the gaps with rich memory and shared experience as one stage of life faded and another began.

From the beginning, I'd believed that underlying the basic human need to love and be loved, sex was the primary force between us. Without it, I could imagine only cool, empty spaces, widening chasms until we might as well be strangers living under the same roof. So I made a weak excuse, began to clear the table, offered dessert. Left him sitting alone. Returned and held up the wine bottle in query, filled his glass. 'You mean everything to me,' I said, hoping it was enough. He nodded. We left it there, but we both knew it wasn't over.

A week later – well, maybe a few days, perhaps two weeks, I don't remember more than the fact that we'd been carefully tiptoeing around each other as though one of us was mortally ill – I slid a question across the kitchen bench that I knew was pure dynamite, but I couldn't stop myself. 'If we never had sex again, how would you feel?'

'Never?' he said, after a long pause.

Nervous, unable to speak or quiet the roaring in my head, the nerves in my stomach, terrified I'd put the two of us in irretrievable emotional jeopardy by going to the extreme end of the issue, I shrugged, pretending it was a casual question. He wasn't fooled for a second.

'I've told you before, Susan, that if relationships depend on sex they're doomed.'

'But no sex. None at all,' I insisted, unable to back off, testing him and the foundations of his love, wanting to know the answer and bite out my tongue at the same time. Expecting him to respond with the defensiveness that often conjoins with hurt and confusion when a man's sexuality is threatened. I'd forgotten he was one of the few grown-ups I'd ever met.

All he said, very calmly, was, 'If you're saying you never want to have sex again, you need to tell me the reason why.'

'I'm not saying that,' I said, 'but I'm terrified the day will come. Nothing to do with you. My body. It's changing. Changed. My head, too. God, nobody ever tells you about all this stuff. Everyone lies. I'm certain of it. As if admitting you no longer have regular sex is high treason, a hanging offence. Am I the only one who feels like this at my age?' Adding, in a softer voice: 'Is there something terribly wrong with me?'

Was I damaged in ways I didn't understand, is what I meant. One way or another, sex abuse defines your life, no matter how skilfully you learn to compartmentalise. I'd told Bob about my childhood, as I'd told my first husband and, once, an ill-advised lover. When Bob asked me to marry him, he had a right to know. Ghosts. Demons. Wounds. They shape your image of yourself. Influence outcomes. Skew fragile moments. I told him carefully and in a way that left him a graceful exit if that's what he felt was necessary.

He'd said nothing. Then he'd disappeared into the kitchen to make a cup of tea. 'It's all in the past,' he'd said eventually. 'That's where we'll leave it. It doesn't change who you are.'

'It's best there are no secrets,' I'd said. He'd nodded.

Bob took my hand. I loved his hands. They were big, safe, warm on the coldest day, rough but not hard. Capable of intricate engineering or pulling apart rocks. With my hand in his, I'd follow anywhere. I held the heat of it against my cheek for a moment, eyes closed. Briefly considered making an offer I knew I couldn't keep: have sex anywhere you like but come home every night to eat dinner and sleep. So I stayed silent.

'There's no point or pleasure in sex if both of us aren't enjoying it,' he said.

'So you don't want a divorce,' I replied, trying to manage a grin.

He looked to see if I was serious, and I believe I was. 'Sex doesn't mean much in the long run and I'm not the kind of man who gives in at the first barrier.'

Bob understood what it cost me to have that conversation. I understood the gift he'd given with his response. Uncertainties, insecurities dissolved into nothing. We would redefine the quick, effortless, thoughtless, impulsive and compulsive emotional responses of youth that we'd carried into middle age, believing they would go on forever. Outlive particular desires. Find new ones to explore and develop.

———

When the stars of late autumn were thick and bright across the sky and the dew settled by early afternoon, soaking forgotten washing so it had to be left for another day, Bob agreed to help friends deliver a yacht back to the west coast of the United States. While he was cruising the louche tropical islands of the South Pacific for six to eight weeks, possibly longer depending on the whim of winds and weather, I would finish my fourth book. If time allowed while Bob was still on the high seas, I dreamed of walking a section of the ancient Christian pilgrimage of the Camino de Santiago de Compostela. *Do it while you can.*

'You're a terrible navigator. You'll get lost before you even get started,' Bob said when I told him my plan.

'Hah! I've made my way around the world plenty of times and always ended up in the right place.' He raised an eyebrow. 'Eventually,' I admitted. 'Look, I'll be fine. There'll be plenty of signposts, and I'll just follow the long line of pilgrims heading from south-west France to the coast of Spain. Easy.'

'Where in south-west France?'

I looked at him blankly. 'Well, wherever I choose to start.' He gave me the same look I'd given my mother when she told me she planned to trailblaze from Sydney to Darwin on a motorbike to celebrate her 70th birthday.

'You don't own a motorbike,' I'd said dismissively.

'I'll buy one.'

'You've never even been a passenger on the back of a bike,' I'd said, alarmed.

'I won't have any bad habits to unlearn then,' she'd replied airily, with her trademark flick of the wrist.

I'd been about to argue the absurdity and danger of the whole concept when my first husband, Paul, took me aside. 'She's baiting you,' he said. 'Tell her it's a great idea.' So I did. And motorbikes were never mentioned again.

She never liked Paul, not even when he was dying of a brain tumour and helpless as a baby. He saw straight through her. The Compostela idea, I realised, was a whim worthy of my mother. I let it go, shamefaced, aware my fitness level was questionable and I may well have taken taxis from one section to the next at the first sign of a blister. As my mother probably would have if she'd ever attempted anything so foolhardy.

Bob and I eventually agreed we'd fly into Rome on the same day, rent an apartment for a week, hit the high spots, catch up with someone I hadn't seen since I was a journalist on the *Melbourne Sun* and then meet the Alans x 2 from Elvina Bay, who would join us on a trip to the wilds of Morocco. We'd compromise on the Compostela idea by returning to Italy, where we'd make our way to Umbria to walk through sunny vineyards, follow the crumbling remains of ancient Roman aquifers, traverse mountain tracks and explore medieval villages. Not quite the Compostela but much more realistic than trying to walk seven hundred and fifty kilometres on my own.

Our adventure would culminate with a week savouring the magic of Venice. 'Pittwater will be Venice in a thousand years,' I predicted, after I'd booked an apartment built under heavy oak beams in the renovated attic space of a fourteenth-century building overlooking one of the smaller canals.

'Only thing I can say for sure is that we won't be around to see it,' he replied. I fell silent. It happened more and more, this out-loud acknowledgement of the finite.

'The building doesn't have an elevator,' I explained after a while, 'but the boat slipway still exists on the ground floor. Lovely to think of mysterious boatmen sliding through foggy waters on romantic assignations in the dead of night centuries ago. Faded frescoes on the walls, too, if we can believe the pictures on the website. Six flights of stairs, but worth it, don't you think? And we're used to steps. It will be a doddle.' *Do it while you can.*

For the first time in decades I could leave my mother without a twinge of guilt. The carer, whom she adored, would do her shopping when she needed anything and continue to call in twice a week. Everything else was covered by her assisted care status. Even the doctor was just along the corridor. There were absolutely no grounds for her to complain.

'How long will you be gone?' she asked, when I told her about the trip.

'Two months.'

'I'm well taken care of. Everybody loves me. You needn't worry.'

THE HOUSE ON THE HILL

'Yep.'

'Phew!' I said to Bob. 'She never once asked what would happen if she died while we were gone. She didn't mention funerals or ask where we'd scatter her ashes. I'm beginning to wonder if she's decided she's immortal.'

'So am I,' Bob said. 'A world first, eh?'

At the end of March 2011, Bob flew to New Zealand to join an all-man crew on board a sixty-four-foot yacht called *Van Diemen.*

'If you meet someone gorgeous and willing on an island of swaying palms, don't tell me about it,' I said, half-serious, when I delivered him to the airport.

He looked at me thoughtfully. 'So you wouldn't mind?'

'Oh, I'd mind. But I'd understand. At least I think I would.'

'A bunch of old blokes on a boat way out at sea? Doing four-hour shifts around the clock? All we'll want in port is a cold beer and an eight-hour snooze.'

'Yeah. Right.' I knew I sounded cynical.

Bob shook his head from side to side. 'I'm in clover. Why would I mess with what I've got? Can't you understand that?'

'Not really,' I said honestly. Without another word, he got out of the car. Hauled his gear from the rear. Started towards the terminal. Afraid we'd part feeling bad and shaky and unhappy and insecure, I chased after him, catching him by the arm.

He turned towards me and dropped his bag. 'Love you,' he said, putting both arms around my waist.

'Yeah. Me too. Sorry.'

'Nothing to be sorry about. I'll call you from Auckland.'

'Stay safe.'

'Always.'

———

I locked myself in my office to finish work on my book. It was my first attempt at fiction and I'd approached it with an airy and totally unfounded confidence. Discovered it was a weirdly topsy-turvy way of thinking for a former journalist who'd been trained to chase facts, stick to the truth, simplify and never exaggerate. Fiction upended those rules. Very quickly, I felt overwhelmed, out of my depth and deeply afraid that I would fail spectacularly, letting down publishers, booksellers and the whole gamut of people who'd had enough faith to offer a contract.

'Wear it away,' Bob had advised, over and over. But from the beginning I'd felt almost disoriented. As confronting as it was to write emotional truth in memoir where there was nowhere to hide, I found it more difficult in fiction where there was everywhere to hide. In memoir, even though writing about real people meant using words carefully and with consideration, it was less fraught than creating believable characters out of thin air. Plot followed fact in memoir, whether it was interesting or boring. In fiction, plots were limited only by imagination. I sank into one clichéd scene after another, bamboozled, in the end, by my own dastardly twists and turns. Ditching the doctrine of journalism, it turned out, was like being forced to swap religions or speak in a foreign language. But each day I sat at my desk in my office with views through gum trees of boats, birds and bays, and persevered to the point of exhaustion. At some point, I can't remember when, I suddenly realised fiction was a revamped version of truth and heavily disguised. It was like an awakening.

When I'd finally put together a beginning, middle and end, Caro, a friend and neighbour who'd been instrumental in the previous three books, came and sat beside me while we dissected every page, paragraph and word until it was finished. But instead of setting off with a box filled with typewritten pages as I'd done five years earlier with my first book, I pressed a computer key and, in seconds, one hundred thousand words landed deep in the heart of a cubicle in a skyscraper in North Sydney. It was like letting go of a child without having a clue whether you'd ever see her again, or even being sure where she might end up. I missed the personal contact, ceremony, and celebration of delivering a manuscript by hand. And yet, if I had to go back to using a typewriter, I'd probably give up writing books. Like Old John at the brickworks, technology had unquestionably extended and broadened my working life.

On the high seas, Bob emailed when he could and called when the boat slid into port in Tonga, Samoa and Christmas Island (in the Kiribati Line of Islands). Then there was silence for a week. I emailed: 'If you don't get in touch soon I will keep shopping.' There was no response. I began to worry. I called the wife of another crew member.

'Their communication system has broken down,' she explained. 'They're all fine, but the winds aren't helping and it's slow going. They won't reach Hawaii on schedule.'

Two weeks after their due date in Honolulu, the phone rang. Before I even picked it up I knew it was Bob.

'How are you? How was it?' I asked, relieved and happy to hear his voice.

'Good.'

'And?'

'Oh yeah. Good.'

'Ok, tell me all about it when we meet.'

He went on to explain the timing was too tight for him to complete the last leg to Los Angeles. He'd leave the boat in a day or two, visit his son in Pittsburgh and meet me in Rome. He'd found a flight from New York that landed forty-five minutes after I arrived from Sydney.

The day before I was scheduled to fly to Rome, the bank sent me a notification that my credit cards had been hacked and they'd been cancelled. 'But I'm going overseas tomorrow,' I said, horrified at the thought of travelling without the security of plastic money.

'We'll issue new ones. They'll be waiting for you when you arrive.'

Fat chance. I didn't even have an apartment number, just a street address. The plan was to meet the owner at a café in the Campo dei Fiori for the key handover.

8

BOB WAS TANNED ALMOST BLACK, hair bleached white. There was a lovely, loose, muscly fitness in his stride. I picked him out of the crowd at the airport in Rome in a second and waved him over. He took my hand in his. Laced fingers. Held on. *The balance. It's back*, I thought.

At Campo dei Fiori, the famous market hummed. Food. Flowers. Crafts. Clothes. Set out like artwork. We breakfasted on pastries and strong coffee, waiting for our contact. She appeared typically, unhurriedly, Roman-style late, wearing a low-cut black linen dress with a scarf tied casually at her neck. Magnificent cleavage. She was incredibly sexy in an understated way. I felt a pang of envy. *We're still breathing and we're here. Get over it.*

We followed her swinging hips, her rope-soled shoes, slim brown legs smooth as silk, along cobbled lanes to an ancient door that swung open on rusted hinges to reveal a small courtyard. Inside, a courier stood searching mailboxes in vain for a name that matched the envelope. He asked our guide for help.

'For you!' she said, not quite sure what was going on.

'Our new credit cards. Bloody miracle,' Bob said.

'Fantastic,' I responded joyfully. We signed a form. The courier took off. Without offering to help with our bags, our guide led the way up four flights, while we followed dragging, grunting, puffing. After a quick tour (one bedroom, tiny bathroom, well-equipped kitchen, small but adequate living area), she left us alone.

We showered, slept for an hour and hit the street with an address on a piece of paper. As it turned out, my former colleague lived about two blocks from our apartment. And another colleague, a woman I'd once shared a house with in London and who once baked authentic Spanish tortilla to temp my chemo-bastardised palate, was her house guest. Instead of feeling like a tourist, I felt as though we belonged.

—

Lorraine was thin, stylish, apparently ageless, and she lived in one of those fabulous apartments with frescoes painted on the walls and terraces that overlooked angels, gargoyles, warriors, chariots, spires, domes, terracotta roofs and the whole extraordinary cacophony of two thousand years of architecture. Another quick pang. But I'd trade a thousand Romes for Pittwater – no matter how heretical that sounds.

We dined on sweet, dripping rockmelon wrapped in tender prosciutto. Melting slices of fresh buffalo mozzarella sitting dreamily on thick slices of ruby tomatoes, topped with a single green basil leaf. Tangy and creamy all at once. Fragrant salamis. Robust meat loaf. Crisp salad greens. Clean Italian white wines. We yabbered on and on about the old days. Funny stuff, mostly. Then inevitably: 'What ever happened to?' A rollcall. So many dead. We looked at each other around the table. Does everyone wonder, as I do, at the quixotic nature of fate?

Two days later, we joined the Alans x 2 to wander through the treasures of the Vatican. Followed English travel writer Georgina Masson's beautifully detailed Roman walks. Under her guidance, we found tucked-away treasures, understood nuances in a staircase, a lintel, a dark and gloomy painting in a church. We dined on good, and once awful, food.

At the end of every day my feet yowled and my back felt poleaxed. *Do it while you can.* I'd once loved travel for its freedom. But there was nothing in my life anymore from which I longed to be set free. Occasionally, prompted perhaps by exhaustion or cultural overload, I wondered what we were doing handing over another fistful of euros to visit yet another monument when the one we'd just investigated was already a fading memory. As I write now, the moments I held dearest were the ones spent with friends. I needed to flick through photos to recall nearly everything else.

—

A few days later, Bob and I, the Alans x 2, boarded an afternoon flight for the *souqs, kasbahs* and exotic wildness of Morocco. Our goal was Amassine, a village so remote it barely registered on the most detailed maps but renowned amongst dedicated rug lovers as the home of very fine, traditional Berber weavers. I am, I confess, a rug nut. Not in a sensible, knowledgeable, investment kind of way. It's pure instinct. Some rugs make my heart beat faster. Some rugs I can gaze at for hours on end and never get bored. Some rugs make my spirit soar. I blame a visit to Afghanistan and Iran in my early 20s, when I went to my first rug bazaars. The noise, smells, dusty light and darkness. The haggling, hard-eyed men in flowing shirts, faceless women in long robes tying knots at looms. So seductively mysterious to a little Aussie country kid. I've been spellbound ever since.

I once even travelled to Turkey to find the weaver of a colourful rug on the floor of my office, her initials woven into the design. A mad whim (worthy of my mother?) but it was a great trip. My weaver, whom I'd envisaged as a wild nomad with flashing brown eyes and flowing robes, turned out to have the cutthroat instincts of a goat trader and was middle-aged, plump and desperate to find a husband for her daughter. She'd skinned me alive during a trade for some embroidery I've long since misplaced. Or perhaps the fiancé existed and the money was for a wedding dress. I've forgotten the details. Remember only laughing uproariously when I handed over the money. You've got to respect determination and grit.

After a short flight, we landed in Casablanca. Instead of finding the city imbued with the romance of Bogart and Bergman, it was noisy, ugly and soulless. Over the next few days we moved on to Rabat, Meknes and the wonders of ancient Fez, following a well-worn tourist trail. On a sharp, clean day, and after a bone-shaking drive along winding dirt roads through high-mountain passes, with tea stops in mud huts in desolate country, I said, 'Such a bleak landscape. Nothing could ever grow here.'

'You're wrong,' said one of the Alans from the back seat. 'Once these barren mountains were covered in forests. They've been worn down and out by goats and people over millennia.' Bob disagreed from the front seat. An enthusiastic debate ping-ponged. Every so often a lone tree appeared, clinging precariously to an almost vertical mountainside. 'See!' Alan said, pointing, feeling vindicated. 'Evidence of the struggle to regenerate.'

Finally, our four-wheel drive came to a halt outside the village of Amassine. It could go no further. Inside the walls, roads and pathways were donkey-cart wide. We'd just stepped back one thousand years. Hoisting our bags on our backs, we began walking to our accommodation.

'It's not exactly throbbing with life, is it?' Bob said, looking around. The streets were deserted. 'You'd have to love rugs to come here,' he added in a tone that hinted he'd never understand my passion. A couple of kids, a girl and a boy, under the age of ten, materialised out of nowhere. Smooth-skinned and beautiful with huge brown eyes framed by lashes that touched their eyebrows, they smiled widely, revealing a mouth full of decayed and missing teeth.

'So sad,' I muttered to our guide.

He shrugged. 'We have tried to help. The imam is against toothbrushes.'

'And that's the end of it?' I said in disbelief.

'That is the end of it.'

We stayed in a large rendered house with a warren of rooms that spread out on different levels. It belonged to the tall, thin, gently mannered headman of the weaving cooperative and had been modified to suit dedicated, rug-loving tourists who travelled from all over the world to meet the weavers. Not only did we have a squat toilet when most of the villagers used the open fields to perform their more basic ablutions, the house also had a *hamam* powered by bottled gas.

By day, we met the weavers, nimble-fingered, cheerful women who shared their dirt floor living space with orphaned lambs, roosters and bossy hens. In the evening, we sat on benches on a narrow balcony and ate various meats, spices and grains cooked by men. Mopping the juices with tough flatbread. At night, we slept on rugs on the floor, covered by rugs, with more rugs hung as room dividers. It was raw and real. To me, worth a thousand visits to the Vatican.

At the end of a cold but sunny day spent walking along beautiful valleys thickly carpeted with purple wild orchids and blue hyacinths, Bob and I sat naked in the candlelight of the *hamam*. The warmth and humid cosiness eased our aches and pains. Better than a large, restorative cognac, we agreed as we washed each other's backs with bowls of stingingly hot water and, feeling deeply soporific, sat on small timber stools to idly debate how long we'd survive in this kind of primitive settlement where there were no supermarkets, no doctors, no dentists, not even a chemist where a pack of basic painkillers could be purchased to ease a nagging headache. A place where, all year, chill winds funnelled down from the barren peaks of the High Atlas; where, in winter, snow fell thickly and a bundle of firewood to supply a meagre, transitory heat cost more than a pinch of the precious saffron grown in a nearby village.

'The squat loo,' I murmured. 'It's agony going down and getting up. I feel like someone's sticking red-hot screwdrivers through my knee joints. Not sure I could take it for too long.'

'You'd get used to it,' Bob replied, tipping another pitcher of exquisitely hot water down my back.

Not in a million years, I thought. But I immediately regretted disclosing the deteriorating condition of my knees. The impulse to hide, deny and even fib to preserve an illusion of youth was still instinctive. Sitting naked with just one breast and a long, ugly scar after a bout with breast cancer that even candlelight failed to soften, I was fully aware Bob had seen, experienced and understood the worst of me and in me. But somehow adding bad knees to the ailment list of the aging felt like inflicting yet another potentially mortal wound to the relationship.

So I lied. 'Yeah. 'Course I'd get used to it.'

By the time we stepped into the frigid starstruck Moroccan night in our pyjamas, ready to dash upstairs to our bed, we'd concluded that the choice between living sustainably and just plain unbearably was going to be eternally tricky, even impossible for we pampered Westerners.

The next day, we moved on from our quiet rug weavers to chaotic Marrakech. We stayed in a luscious *riad* run by a sophisticated French woman. Our room had a large ensuite, flushing loo, a shower and thick white bathrobes hanging behind the door. The sheets were heavy cotton. A cool, blue pool of water shivered in the shaded central courtyard. Every morning we ate flaky pastries and fresh fruit on a rooftop. Dodged and weaved through thick crowds and noisy motorbikes to lunch on the perimeter of the throbbing *maidan*, where snake charmers, storytellers, monkeys in frilly red dresses and tasselled hats, henna tattooists, food vendors and whirling dancers performed as they have for thousands of years. Dined on ten-course dinners in restaurants as old as the city.

It was vibrant and exotic but somehow, after the simplicity and frugality of our rug weavers' village, the excess niggled. Where was the balance, I wondered, between too little and too much? Hadn't I just been told somewhere in Italy (or read somewhere), that when Galileo pointed out the absurdity of calling jewels and gold *precious* and soil *base*, that if soil was as scarce as jewels a prince would spend a cartload of gold to have enough soil to sow an orange seed? That poor man was convicted of heresy when he should have been granted a sainthood for common sense. But I asked myself, not for the first time, should we all be trying harder to live more sustainably on an overburdened planet?

—

It was high summer when we returned to Rome. We farewelled the Alans x 2 over an extravagant, six-hour dinner at the home of a couple of their charming expatriate friends. Bleary-eyed the following morning, we fended off gypsies at the railway station and bought train tickets to Venice. We arrived tired, hot and hungry in the middle of the afternoon, unsure whether the woman who held the keys to our apartment would be waiting to meet us, or not. Like most things Italian, emailed directions were enthusiastic but confusing and I'd received no reply to my queries.

I will never forget the moment we emerged from the station. I burst into tears. Felt a wave of homesickness that made my knees buckle. Water. Boats. Seagulls. 'This *will* be Pittwater one day,' I said to Bob in a voice broken by emotion. 'Different but the same. As long as no one is ever allowed to touch the great lung of the Ku-ring-gai National Park.'

A few water taxis, all long-nosed with gleaming timber, sparkling chrome and cushiony white vinyl seats, were tied to bollards. We headed straight for them.

'Not quite the same as our shabby old pink water taxis,' Bob said, 'but they will have to do.'

We leapt on board and sat back, feeling like Grace Kelly and Cary Grant. The driver began to tell us boat rules. We held up our hands to halt him, said we were good with boats – he needn't worry we'd do anything stupid. He stowed our bags, we showed him the piece of paper with the name of the piazza where we were to meet our contact and set off. The tears kept coming. Venice was overwhelming. Nothing, not even the water and boat link with our Pittwater life, could have prepared me for it. It delivered what big-city travel rarely did for me anymore: inspiration.

There was the usual confusion but eventually we found our contact, received the keys, opened a heroic old door to the entrance and puffed up twelve half-flights of decadently wide, beautiful marble steps to our attic apartment. It was glorious. Old beams, views of a canal, a good kitchen, a weird little hip bath no adult could possibly use but in Venice – it was perfect anyway. We parked our bags and took off exploring. Ate pastry here, drank a coffee there. Later, a cocktail while around us a band played and people – American tourists, I suspect – danced with Broadway skill and kept us spellbound. Wine with dinner. Afterwards, we negotiated the stairs slowly, tipsily, to the peace and quiet of our own space. We stood side by side at a window, gazing at the tiled rooftops of Venice spread before us.

In the morning, Bob set off to find coffee and more pastries, and returned to present breakfast in bed with an Italian flourish. Two days later, the American holiday season began and the weight of so many visitors must have sunk the waterlogged island further into the sea. I also received word from the publishers that my book needed more work and the deadline loomed. I opened the windows to the sights and smells – occasionally putrid – of Venice, and worked solidly for the rest of the week.

Work made me feel like a local, added a depth that went beyond a simple holiday. I ran out at lunchtime for melon and prosciutto, fresh mozzarella, the first peaches of the season. Prepared lunch in the kitchen, sat at the table to eat. Bob explored the maritime museum, investigated restaurants to take me to dinner, took boat trips to other islands. It was a lonelier time for him, but he didn't complain. Then it was all over. The work. Our two months away from Pittwater. I'd seen Venice at last. I yearned for nothing more from travel. We returned to Rome to catch our flight home.

Looking back, I sometimes wonder if the juxtaposition of the excess of Rome and the Vatican (vow of poverty?) and the simple frugality of Amassine was the unwitting catalyst for what turned out to be radical reform for us. And even though we were ignorant of the fact, we'd already half-committed to set life-changing events in motion. Or maybe it was more basic than that. Perhaps we were searching for manageable challenges to sidestep the uncomfortable, even disquieting sense of becoming increasingly irrelevant as younger minds shaped the ground of the future. More and more, it felt as though my feet were sinking into the quicksand of the past, where none of the old reference points held true. Overnight, it seemed, I'd crossed an invisible border. Woken in a world so changed that every nuance, skill and truth I'd busted a gut trying to learn and understand was suddenly worthless. No one cared what I thought. No one was interested in what I'd spent a lifetime discovering. No one even wanted to seat me at a table with a view. Only my oldest friends were willing to put up with me. Even more alarming, I was less and less curious when once I'd been a shameless stickybeak eager to learn.

To be on the cusp of sixty was so infuriatingly humbling, it was tempting to radiate disgruntlement purely as a defence mech- anism. I consoled myself with the thought that, with nothing to lose, I didn't have to give a damn anymore. The key to freedom and clarity. But some days, I simply asked: 'Is there a twelve-year- old lurking anywhere who can explain how this works? Or even a five-year-old?'

9

Sydney was a cold, jet-lagged shock. It took me nearly a month to overcome the nausea and empty-headedness brought on by too many time zones in the space of too little time. I tried to remember how I'd coped when I went on overseas assignments and vaulted straight from the airport to my desk. Recalled a horror, sleepless flight from the Philippines, after peering into the vast wardrobes of Imelda Marcos and the death room of Ferdinand following their fall from power in 1986. All that theft and corruption and he ended up in a bare cubicle on a single bed with an oxygen tank alongside. A man screamed and ranted through the night flight, hallucinating or about to run amok with a machete, who could tell? None of us slept a wink. We all sat quiet as mice, afraid even a sudden movement might launch him into a violent spiral that could bring down the plane. At my desk just before 7 am, I was so wiped out I couldn't even speak coherently. I always bounced back in a few days, though. The resilience of youth. But I was no longer young and, at this end of my life, even an hour of feeling off-colour felt like a waste of precious time.

When I called my mother to say we were home, she didn't miss a beat: 'Where have you been? I've been frantic.'

I ignored her. 'Picnic or restaurant?'

'Picnic!'

And we settled into our routines without further comment.

———

'Spending winter in Cooktown might be a bit radical,' I said, one cold night after our return from the heat of the European summer, 'but if we could find somewhere warmer within easy reach of Pittwater, maybe we should give the idea some serious thought.'

We were sitting in a small room we called the Snug. Lined with books and housing Bob's late wife's early Australian pottery collection, it boasted the television and an insanely comfortable armchair with plenty of room to put your feet up and accommodate the dog. It was Sunday night. The heating was on high. Chippy and me, pressed up against a wall of soft cushions, were cuddled under a rug. She was twelve years old now, with a snout more grey than tan, signs of glaucoma and the beginnings of arthritis in her legs. She, too, felt the cold more keenly.

'A winter bolthole,' Bob mused, his feet encased in sheepskin boots and raised on a footstool. I'd expected him to poo-poo the idea again, but he reached for the spiral notebook he kept handy and drew a line down the middle of the page. 'In an ideal world, what would you like?'

I didn't even have to think: 'Flat land. Enough for a good garden. Power attached. Town water or a permanent water supply.' Bob added north-facing. No more than a four-hour drive from Pittwater, we agreed, or it would entail a flight – difficult to organise with the dog. And there was the issue of my mother. We needed to be within reasonable reach in case of emergencies.

In the background, architectural guru Kevin McCloud (that man has a lot to answer for) was wrapping up a program on a young couple that had gone out on a mind-boggling financial limb to build a dream house, risking every hard-earned penny, even bankruptcy. At the end of the program, the couple revealed an anonymous benefactor had essentially saved them from debtors' prison.

Madness, we said, shaking our heads and sanctimoniously telling ourselves we'd never take unreasonable risks. At some point, we nodded to each other, they should've stepped back from the dream and been content with what was realistically feasible. But sitting in judgment from the safety of your sitting room is easy. In truth, none of us knows what follies we're capable of committing until we're put to the test. Our heads filled with plans that neither of us thought for a moment might be beyond us. Not so different, then, to the foolish dreamers we'd scorned.

'It would be an investment, too,' I said dreamily. 'Holidays are like standing next to an open fire and chucking in your cash. Nothing to show for it when you're home except a few mementoes there's not enough space for anyway. We'll be spending money wisely.'

A search began for five to twenty gently undulating acres with power and water connected on an easy access (bitumen road), north-facing site. A pre-existing house would be great, but if the land was suitable, we were prepared to build from scratch. With careful planning, we might eventually live off-grid. A minuscule contribution to the planet, but every little bit helped. Why not investigate Wingham, we said?

The town was built around a huge grassed square sporting a de Havilland Vampire fighter plane from the Korean War, and a great log to remind locals of the days when timber was the main game. The still-working post office was built in 1884, the courthouse (defunct) in 1934, and the police station (also defunct) in 1909. You could always get a park in the main street (except during funerals). A wonderful fruit and vegetable shop called Granty's featured local organic produce. There was also a butcher shop, a few bakeries and a selection of excellent coffee shops that ranged from traditional old country town (crustless cheese and tomato sandwiches cut into precise quarters) to slick new-age (walnut, fig and blue cheese salad) and hippy organic. A chemist, newsagent, clothing shops, shoe shop, op shops, white goods store, knick-knack shop, homewares store, rural produce stores and a pump and irrigation specialist ensured you could buy everything from an egg cup to a tractor without leaving town. A large supermarket took care of the basic necessities. By the standards of our remote Moroccan village, Isabella Street was the equivalent of the Champs Élysées. The countryside, which we'd explored earlier, was stunning. Flourishing. Green. Gentle. Rugged. Creeks. Rivers. And within a short drive, beaches and a clean blue ocean.

Choosing the Wingham area had the added advantage of knowing a few people, and it had a sleepy Old World charm. Big business had bypassed it in favour of nearby Taree, a regional centre with a greater population density. We also knew that if weather patterns remained true, we could expect warm, sunny, dry winter days balanced by clear, cold nights. The pace was also idyllic.

'You need to keep your eyes open,' Michael told me early in our Killabakh stay. ''Cause if someone waves and you ignore them, your name goes on a list.' List? 'Yeah, you're a snob.' Oh. 'Or you need new specs . . . '

At the much deeper and possibly unacknowledged heart of the decision was a desire to avoid the trap of dissolving into a convenient but unchallenging future until we, too, reached the day when being 'well looked after' summed up our daily existence.

———

For the next few weeks, I trawled the Wingham real estate websites without much success. Properties were either too big, too small, badly sited (for us), too far from town (in the best of all worlds, we'd stipulated a maximum of ten minutes from the heart of Wingham) or too close to town. We were heartened by prices, though. They were well within our budget, probably as a result of the Global Financial Crisis, as it was now labelled. While I wasn't keen to profit from someone else's problems, the alternative was to stay home and do nothing.

'But we won't haggle if someone's doing it tough, ok? No one likes to profit from another person's misfortune,' I said to Bob.

'Let's wait and see what happens,' he replied.

As it turned out, I needn't have worried. Anyone who buys and sells cattle in endlessly fluctuating markets driven by drought, floods, over-supply or under-supply or the whims of governments who make decisions from their often self-serving, short-sighted inner sanctums has to know the value of a dollar to the last cent. It's mostly the dreamy-eyed city slickers like us who really need looking after.

When the net failed to throw up anything interesting, we booked a room at the local dog-friendly B & B and walked through the door of one of two real estate agents located in town. We settled on a bloke called Peter, primarily because he didn't flinch at allowing a white-hair-shedding old doggie in his nice, clean car. While he wasn't even remotely rough-edged compared to the more slippery and opportunistic members of the species who dealt in Sydney's boom-or-bust housing markets, he exuded a reassuring earthiness that inspired trust and confidence. He ferried us around (at a speed we found alarming on narrow country roads but that we later learned was legal and normal) with endless patience and good humour.

Each night, we lobbed back at the B & B to dine on a sumptuous feast highlighting local produce. Comboyne cheeses, locally grown vegetables, relishes from a Wingham café called Bent and German-style smoked meats from a Taree butcher named Rudi, famous for his streaky bacon, sausages and salamis. A fire blazed warmly. Chippy was tucked comfortably and quietly in her own soft bed. The wine was excellent. It seemed like all the signals were pointing in the right direction.

One thing we'd learned, though, was just because a place was called Flat – as in Dolly's Flat, Wherrol Flat, Cundle Flat or Caffrey's Flat – the term had no bearing on the actual landscape. At best, it meant *comparatively* flat or referred to small areas of river flats. Mostly, the terrain was a roller-coaster of hills – high, fat, steep, rocky, wooded, cleared. But climb them, and we found that the views were spectacular. Hills, we decided, *could* be tolerated. The right hills, of course. Nothing too steep. Nothing too wild. Nothing too difficult.

But as winter drifted into spring and then summer, nothing appealed. We were in danger of losing our enthusiasm, wondering if the whole idea had been crazy from the word go. But neither of us voiced that thought. Not out loud, anyway.

—

On cue, the silly season engulfed Pittwater. For some reason, I idly thought it would be lovely to have an offshore Christmas choir. Bring together people who liked to sing Christmas carols, on-key, off-key or even tone deaf, it didn't matter. No pressure, Pittwater style. It would be a salute to the holidays, community and our environment. It would be lovely to perform on a barge, I thought, anchored in Frog Hollow, where the acoustics of a small bay backed by a steep escarpment would help give our voices volume. If we could find a choirmaster as well, to instil a little musical cohesion and finesse, it would add to the mix. Offshorers could prepare a picnic, throw out an anchor, get comfy in a tinny and join in the singing as the sun went down and the nocturnal wildlife of the Ku-ring-gai Chase slowly woke. And while voices carried across the water, the pulsing sea under the hull would lull, soothe and settle spirits worn ragged by the rush of Christmas. Restore and, in a gentle way, ready us for the big day ahead.

'What do you think?' I asked Bob.

'I'll do what I can to help but don't ever, ever ask me to sing.'

It didn't occur to me until much later that it was precisely the same sort of hazily considered idea my mother might have come up with.

When Toby Jay and Dave Shirley agreed to let us sing on their muscly lighter, the *Laurel Mae*, I knew the idea had legs. I began searching for a choirmaster.

'You'll never get Doc Lloyd,' everyone said. 'He's been asked to establish a community choir heaps of times. Says outdoor musical events are a nightmare, he can't condone the presence of alcohol at any performance, and he has an aversion to wobbly women's voices.' *Strike three*, I thought, *but you've got to ask, don't you*?

John Lloyd lived on Scotland Island. His CV included Director of the Centre for Research and Education in the Arts at the University of Technology, Sydney and conductor of numerous university and community choirs and orchestras. He had a stellar reputation as a serious classical musician. He was way out of our league, but I called him anyway.

'We want to sing carols at Christmas,' I blurted. 'On a barge in Frog Hollow. Have locals rock up in their tinnies with a picnic to join in. Pure Pittwater. Nothing flash. Not sure the singers will even be able to hold a tune. Will you help out?'

There was a second's hesitation, then a light but gravelly voice replied, 'How many people do you think will come?'

'Ten. Maybe a few more.'

'When do you want to start rehearsals?'

'As soon as we find a piano.'

There was a longer hesitation. 'John Marshall has one. Perhaps he'll let us borrow it.'

I disconnected and shouted: 'Yay! It's a goer.'

John Marshall and his wife, Melanie, own and run PMC Hill Real Estate, specialising in offshore sales. They are both kind-hearted and generous in the ways that matter – with their time and their effort.

'When do you need it?' John Marshall asked, as though it was no big deal to load a piano onto a small tinny to cross choppy waters to Lovett Bay, unload and get it up eighty-eight steps.

'Tomorrow?'

'Yeah, ok, leave it with me.'

'Bob will help.'

'Nah, we'll be right.'

And so, in the magic-wand tradition of offshorers, Carols Afloat was born.

We recruited singers through our local information networks, *Brigitte's Bay News* and *Pittwater Offshore News*, and asked all volunteers to assemble at Tarrangaua at 6.30 pm for a 7 pm start. Bring whatever your tipple to grease the vocal chords, we said, and a light supper will be provided after rehearsal.

It was an enthusiastic but slightly shambolic beginning – not enough word sheets, a few carols none of us knew and, given the wetness of the season, plenty of leeches to be picked off legs and feet. But somehow, John Lloyd, who has Welsh blood running through his veins and a streak of authority none of us were bold or dumb enough to question, inveigled a group of close to thirty larrikin spirits to stop chatting and focus.

'Now,' he said, tapping a baton on the top of the piano for attention. 'Who can read music?' Two hands hesitantly went up. 'Ah,' he said, perhaps truly aware for the first time of the challenges that lay ahead. He ran his fingers over the keyboard, hit a few chords and, it seemed to us, resigned himself good-naturedly to our motley lot.

We warbled thinly and with muddied tones through 'Once in Royal David's City'. Limped on through a repertoire of twenty-two traditional carols, growing a little more forceful.

'Ok,' John said finally, 'that wasn't bad.' We all laughed, grinned and slapped each other's backs in congratulation. The baton tapped the piano once more. Silence fell. 'Now,' John added, 'let's try to turn it into music.'

John effortlessly transposed keys in his head so we could (almost) hit the high or low notes. Patient, always patient. A little testy only when we dropped the 'h' from 'heaven' or failed to crisply finish words ending in 't' or 'd'. When we'd sung our lungs out and felt limp with exhaustion – singing for a long time is much harder physically than you'd think – we found places at tables on the verandah to share food, wine and conversation. Which is at the heart of all that is our offshore Pittwater life. Nothing could ever equal it. So why, I wondered, were we searching elsewhere for a place to call home? It was temporary madness. We'd recover soon and ditch the plan completely.

As our performance date drew closer, someone came up with the idea of including onshorers in the celebration. There had been long-running, heated debates between both sides about changes to the car park and commuter dock. We could ride the barge from Lovett Bay to The Point and sing again for anyone who wanted to stroll from mainland homes to the jetty and ferry wharf to join in. There was only one ironclad rule: 'Don't fall overboard on the trip from Frog Hollow to The Point. We won't turn around to pick you up.'

———

While the choir warbled along with small improvements and much raucousness each week, the turbulence between my mother and me only increased. Esther complained about seeing double. Used little foot-tapping gestures, like a blind person, before stepping forward. And yet, in a restaurant, she read the menu without difficulty. As usual, I had no idea how to extricate truth from attention-seeking play-acting. Each week, I heaved her walker into the back of the car. Scooped up the papers that fell out of the under-seat carrier. Mostly out-of-date flyers announcing village activities. Christmas and birthday cards from friends who made the effort to stay in touch. Some of them years old.

'Bum first,' I ordered, 'or you'll end up in a tangled mess.'

'I know, I know,' she replied, making small, hesitant movements, her feet at weird angles as she twisted her body to feel her way towards the car seat.

'Do you want help?'

'No! I can do it. I can do anything.'

It played out identically every time.

There were changes in her, though. Her ankles were so swollen that flesh spilled over the edge of her shoes. Her fingers looked like fat sausages, the rings so tight I worried they might cut off circulation and I'd find her one day, sitting fingerless on the sofa, her digits lying on the floor where they'd dropped.

'Have you seen the doctor lately?' I asked.

'He comes to my room every week. All the others inmates have to make an appointment to see him in his surgery. I'm special.'

'What does he say?'

'About what?'

I sighed. Out of the blue, she said, 'I think I was jealous of John's wife. He was my son, after all, and I found it difficult to see him with another woman.'

'Blind Freddy could have told you that,' I responded.

Our father, by the time John and I were teenagers, had descended so deep into the bottle he would never find his way back to daylight. For all that, he was an easy drunk. He strove for oblivion, not confrontation. So my brother was the one who took my mother to glamorous restaurants, bought her expensive clothes, whipped her away for weekends in Sydney or Adelaide and sent her shopping while he went to the races. When he married, the whirl that lifted her out of the dull flatline of her beer-sodden suburbia came to an abrupt end. Outraged, my mother tried so hard to foul the marriage that my brother banned her from the house until Esther came to her senses. It took years.

'He loved me, though. He really did. I know he did,' Esther said. I squirmed in my seat. The words were somehow un-maternal. Unfitting. Should I remind her how she tried to undo my first marriage? I didn't see it, of course. I never saw her self-interest so rat cunningly disguised as maternal concern. Not even after my late husband spelled it out in words of one syllable.

'She wants the best for me,' I insisted.

'She wants the lot for her,' he retaliated. But still, I couldn't reject a lifetime's conditioning that, in all things, my mother must come first and that, like most mothers, she held my best interests at heart.

At her most generous, she wanted my brother and me to excel because she planned to tag along on our coat-tails. It all went screwy because as much as she desired our success, when we achieved any small measure, she envied and, occasionally, even tried to sabotage it.

One day, I pulled into our habitual park at the beach. Reached for her coffee, resting on the dashboard. She tried to remove the lid. 'No, no, remember? You drink through the slit. That way nothing gets spilled.'

'We didn't have things like this when I was young. A cup was good enough.' For some reason, the conversation turned to death. 'Your brother will be pleased to see me. Your father, too.' A familiar refrain.

We talked about the Bonegilla days. 'Wish I'd known that was as good as it was going to get,' she said. It was the 1950s, she was the beautiful blonde and extroverted wife who shone brightly in the small pond of Bonegilla Migrant Camp, where the Australians were at the top of the social order and treated like royalty, which suited my mother perfectly. Good, though?

I remembered kindergarten. Another kid whacking me in the sandpit on my first day and the reeling shock of it. I remembered weekend movies – mostly swashbuckling comedies. The kindness of a teacher who took me home and fed me frankfurters cooked on a bar radiator. I remembered my father drunk at the club. The fear of him swerving all over the road on the short trip home. I remembered my mother playing weekend tennis. My brother selling soft drinks at the tennis club to make pocket money. I remembered migrants rioting. The Italians about the quality of the food. The Hungarians over a soccer match. Shutting ourselves inside our house until the furore ended. I remembered my mother nagging my father to get us a billet in Block 21, which had more social kudos than Block 23. Or was it the other way around? I remembered my mother being called to look at my finger paintings in preschool. Black and white shapes. Pages and pages of them. Never a skerrick of colour.

'Is there anything you'd like to tell us?' the teacher asked, her voice comforting and full of concern.

'No,' I replied.

'Has anyone done anything to you? Hurt you?' the teacher asked.

'No,' I said, again. I seem to recall my heart pounded. That I shook with fear and shame. My grandfather was two hundred miles away and I was still terrified. I recalled I wore a smock in finger-painting class to keep my clothes clean. Recalled my mother wore a dress with large buttons down the front. How did she miss the clues?

I changed the subject: 'I've been trying to find a couple of leather chairs like your red ones. They don't make them anymore.'

'Well, it won't be long before you get mine,' Esther replied, gearing up for a round of emotional blackmail.

I pounced hard and fast. 'They're the wrong colour. And anyway, it'll take a vet's needle to see you off once and for all.'

Caught out, she laughed from deep in her belly. 'You realise we've both got a shockingly black sense of humour?' she replied, still grinning.

'Who said I was joking?' We laughed long and loud but one day, I promised myself, I will ask her if she knew. Soon, I thought. Because time was running out and if she died I would spend the rest of my life wondering.

'We're singing carols on a barge this year,' I said. 'Why don't I pick you up a couple of days earlier for Christmas so you can be part of it?'

Esther's eyes lit up, the little toe-tapper in her rising to the surface. 'On the barge? With you?'

I shook my head. 'Don't think we'd be able to get you on board. I meant you could watch from the chair in the garden. It looks directly at Frog Hollow. You'd have a prime spot.' Wreaths of disappointment engulfed her face. 'Sorry,' I added, 'too risky. If you went overboard you'd be a goner by the time we managed to rescue you. Mind you, those water wings of yours would probably keep you afloat.' But she didn't even smile.

On the night of the carols, the choir gathered at the Lovett Bay Boatshed, decked out in red, green and white, wearing silly reindeer hats and flashing earrings and neckties. The piano was carried out of Tarrangaua and lifted into the back of Bob's toylike but grunty red truck, where it was tied down firmly to survive the thirty-five-degree descent on a bumpy sandstone track. John Marshall and a wonderful photographer, Chuck Bradley, who'd been a tireless organiser at every rehearsal, set up speakers and microphones. Mick Morris provided a generator for power. Toby Jay kept track of wires, cords and ordered us to stay clear of the edges. John Lloyd, his white hair frothing, ran his fingers lightly over the keys. Outdoors, the sound was like magic conjured from air in the trees, zephyrs skimming the water. He asked where the piano stool might be hidden. There were blank looks. Then the youngest one amongst us ran up the steps to retrieve it.

While we waited for the final technical details to be sorted, the choir took up positions in three sections (soprano, alto and men) and sang a few scales. No one noticed black clouds rising on the horizon until they blocked the evening light. 'Is it going to rain?' we asked each other, appalled, unwilling to believe that six weeks of rehearsals might end in a cancelled performance.

Someone said loudly, 'What we need is a Christmas miracle.' And bizarrely, a few moments later, the clouds broke apart and scudded away to the north and south. Sun poured down from the heavens. Blue filled the space above our heads. The choir sent up a loud, triumphant cheer. John launched into 'Jesu, Joy of Man's Desiring'. We opened the wine earlier than we'd intended and raised a toast to unseen beneficent forces.

Toby steered the *Laurel Mae* into Frog Hollow with a feather-light touch, deftly and skilfully dodging million-dollar boats on moorings and a flotilla of tinnies already anchored with picnics underway. It was a wonderful, quintessentially Pittwater sight. I looked up at the chair where I'd suggested my mother sit and listen. It was empty.

10

Out of the blue, Esther announced she had a new boyfriend. 'Well, friend, really, but he's very fond of me. We met on a blind date.' My mind reeled.

'Blind date?' I croaked. I was seated in one of the red leather chairs in her room, waiting to take her out to lunch.

She smiled in a dreamy, smitten way: 'His name is Stefan. We've already been on a bus trip together.'

'Bus trip?' I was struggling. My mother loathed buses. The only public transport she approved were taxis. 'He wants me to convert to Catholicism so I'll be able to find my way to life everlasting. Told him I already had a religion.'

'Bus trip?' I repeated, flummoxed.

'One of those outings organised for old people,' she explained.

'And, um, who organised this blind date?'

She gave a casual little wave, as though it meant nothing. 'His carer. The one who helped me before I had my heart attack, when I lived in my unit.'

'Oh.'

She went all dreamy again. 'He has skin like a baby. Smooth and soft. Not a wrinkle anywhere.' I couldn't think of anything to say. She continued: 'It may sound strange but we enjoy each other's company. And he's very, very fond of me. Which doesn't hurt a girl's ego a bit.'

'Jesus, Esther, I thought you were past all this sort of stuff.'

'Hah. You're never past it. Trust me on that one, kid. He gave me a painting the other day. Christ on the Cross. Well, a print. Not a painting. Gruesome. I hid it.' She pointed in the direction of the chest of drawers.

'Why don't you throw it out if you don't like it? Or give it to someone who'd appreciate it?'

'Can't. He comes to my room occasionally.'

'Eh?'

'Pish tush, hold your horses. I know what you're thinking.' *Nightmare* summed it up. Quickly replaced by, *Maybe they'll get together and she'll be off my hands.*

'How old is he?' I asked brightly, but also fearing something I couldn't quite define.

'Ninety-nine.' The dizzy notion of freedom evaporated in a flash.

'So, um . . .'

'I invite him for a meal and have it sent up from the kitchen,' she interrupted. 'Mostly, his carer takes us both to lunch at the RSL.'

'Ah, great. Sounds like terrific fun.'

'She plays the pokies while Stefan and I talk. We have a lovely time. He's a real gentleman. He insists on paying for me. Although I pay my way, too. I'm like that. I never take without giving back.'

'Of course not. Wise move.' I was catching up. 'So he's mobile, then. That's amazing for his age.'

'Oh no, he's in a wheelchair. But his carer takes care of all those details. She's very good to me, too. A wonderful woman.' I waited. 'Just like a real daughter.' Snap.

'Right. Sounds excellent,' I said.

I couldn't deny there was a new lilt in my mother's voice, slightly less of a shuffle in her step. She took more care with her lipstick. Smelled again, of Red Door – her favourite perfume. She was more rigorous in her choice of jewellery and clothing. Plus, her health seemed to have improved remarkably. She'd shed the tippy-toddler walk, the shaking hands, little grunts, brow-smoothing gestures of distress. But it wasn't until she told me she needed a dentist's appointment and new shoes that I understood this new romantic attention had lifted her out of the doldrums and given her a reason to make an effort. I should have been thrilled. I was furious. I felt I'd been conned again.

——

Towards the end of January my mother launched her campaign. It began, as usual, with: 'I don't want a birthday party this year. Just a phone call will do.'

'Yeah. Right. How many people and where do you want to hold it?' I asked. She fluffed girlishly and made self-deprecating noises. I quickly added: 'No more than twenty and how about we have it in the sitting room of the village? It's a gorgeous spot.'

'Boring. We see it every day. And there'll be about eighty guests, as long as we're all still alive come March 21. Should fit on your verandah easily. The eighty includes your Pittwater friends, of course. We need some young blood around to balance it out.' Young blood? Us? I sighed. It's all relative. As American millionaire Bernard Baruch once said, old age would always be fifteen years ahead of him.

'You're sure you want to have the party at Tarrangaua? It's not the easiest place to get to and you're not exactly fit.'

'Piffle. The ferry trip is delightful. And you've got the truck for anyone who can't manage the steps.'

'Like you, you mean.'

'I'll have you know that most of my friends are quite fit.'

'I've met your friends, Esther. Remember?'

———

The logistics of holding a ninetieth birthday party at Tarrangaua for a group of thirty octo and nonagenarians, including Stefan, were terrifying. My mother, in typically Pollyanna fashion, insisted it would be fine. Bob and I fought hard against the plan and then capitulated.

'It might be her last big bash,' I said.

'As long as no one ends up leaving in a body bag,' he responded. He wasn't joking either.

Two weeks before the big event, during lunch at the restaurant at The Point, my mother sipped a bourbon and cola. 'Finger food is best,' she said. 'Old people like to have lots of different treats but all of them small. After a certain age, you don't eat much, you know.'

'Ok,' I said.

She ordered the seafood pizza. Tackled it with gusto. I had the kid's spaghetti bolognese. The waiter made an Italian-style fuss of her, kissing her on the cheek, flirting outrageously. A stream of offshorers walked past, on their way to pick up their mail.

'Have you met my mother, Esther?' I said. They showed an interest in her age, her health, complimented her skin and hair. Her outfit. Jewels, of course, and plenty of them. She fluffed like a broody hen.

'I'm doing ok,' she told me in an almost flirtatious aside. 'Not bad for almost ninety.' In a quiet moment, she asked, 'What band have you booked?'

'Band?' I asked, failing to get her meaning.

'Music. For dancing.' She used her fingers to try to break threads of melted cheese. The last piece of a pizza meant for two disappeared down her throat in a tangled mess.

'Well, I hadn't thought of a band. What would you like? Rock and roll? Jazz? A string quartet?' I was being sarcastic. It skated way over her head.

'As long as there's a singer.'

'Right,' I said, exhaling on the word.

A week later the phone rang. My mother asked, 'What florist have you booked?'

'For heaven's sake, Esther, who do you think you are? The Governor-General?'

'No carnations or lilies. They bring bad luck and death.'

I found a local singer and accompanist who lived on Scotland Island and were savvy about the challenges of offshore living. Decided to arrange the flowers myself. Worked out a finger food menu that was easy to eat – smoked salmon sandwiches, sausage rolls, bite-size quiches, chicken sandwiches, smoked trout pâté, and then little lemon curd tarts, lemon cake and a chocolate birthday cake so rich it was guaranteed to whack up the blood sugar levels to rock-and-roll levels for anyone with a hint of hubris left in them. All the bases, I believed, were covered.

—

Late March is generally a soft, autumnal time of the year, but my mother's birthday dawned with a clap of thunder powerful enough to rattle the house. Quickly, a storm and seas of such ferocity developed that even the ferry service considered cancelling. Coupled with a very low tide, the party was turning into a life-threatening event.

'Let's shift the venue,' I said in an early-morning telephone call. 'Bob and I will transport the food and wine to the sitting room in the village. I'll get someone to light the fire and we'll have a cosy, safe and easy time.'

'No!'

'God, Esther. Just think about it for a second. Stefan is nearly one hundred years old and in a wheelchair. Everyone else is almost as vulnerable, including you. If the ferry trip doesn't damage them beyond repair, getting soaked to the skin will.'

'No way! People our age don't get the chance to have many adventures,' she said, cutting short the call. *Running true to form and blind to the long-distance picture and horrendous ramifications.* It wasn't until the smartest guests rang to say they couldn't make it that my stress levels dropped. *Only the really tough and strong ones will attempt the trip. It will be ok.*

At the height of the storm, Bob and I stood on the verandah and watched the ferry loom out of the spume and rain, riding whitecaps side-on. Almost corkscrewing. 'There'll be blood on the decks,' I mumbled, unhappily. 'And that's if we're lucky. Otherwise, broken legs and arms. It's a full-on catastrophe.'

Without a word, Bob pulled on his wet-weather gear and headed off. I caught sight of a tinny skimming the white caps. Almost airborne. Tarps flapping. The musicians were on their way. In that moment, I loved offshorers with a passion I couldn't begin to express. *Don't let the weather hold you back.* A local maxim.

Rainwater gushed down steps from the clothesline like a fountain, flowed onto the driveway and found its way into a long ribbon of spoon drains. Broken branches, fallen cabbage palm fronds, twigs and leaves were banked up, creating rubbishy little dams. 'Bloody hell,' I muttered to no one but myself. Bob backed our truck – no roof or even canopy – on to the track. Deep, rutted and so steep people sometimes screamed involuntarily travelling up or down. Once, Esther was almost catapulted head-first into the bush when the truck hit a ditch – dubbed forever after, the 'Esther Bump'. And that was on a fine day.

A few good, lean men with weather-beaten faces, wearing shorts, boat shoes and red, yellow and blue jackets slick with rain, swept past cheerily and grabbed umbrellas. I apologised for sending them out into hard conditions. They laughed, those friends who'd come to help. Wild storms were the oxygen, the lifeblood of boatmen.

In the kitchen, Lisa and Fleury assembled neat trays of smoked salmon sandwiches, easy on the horseradish cream to accommodate tender stomachs.

'It's bedlam out there,' I said, shaking my head. 'Someone's going to be dead by the end of the day. I guarantee it.'

Lisa laughed from deep in her belly: 'You're not going to get rid of your mother that easily. She's made of iron, that woman.'

My mother and her boyfriend copped a drenching that would have felled weaker spirits, but as soon as they arrived at the house, Esther left him in the capable hands of his daughter and her husband. Soaked, her skirt clinging to legs, her newly styled hair dripping wet, her eyelashes heavy with droplets, she scurried through the kitchen to the sitting room, furiously ripping her walker out of the way of obstacles.

'She's checking on the flowers,' I whispered to Fleury.

Esther reappeared minutes later: 'I'd get rid of that florist if I were you.' I caught Fleury's eye, raised an eyebrow, and we both bent double and guffawed.

The first guests appeared on the verandah, wet through to the skin. I rushed to find towels to dry them off. *Insane*, I thought, *this is completely insane. I am nearly sixty years old. It's time I learned to say no to my mother.* Bob, water running off his jacket in thick rivulets, went to check the radar and returned with a worried face. Worse was on the way. Due around departure time.

My mother's two hairdressers, practical women, went into immediate damage control. 'We need hair dryers,' they said. They manned the hallway hosing hot air over wet clothes. As soon as word of their rescue operation spread, the queue became quite long. Meanwhile, a freezing wind whistled the length of the verandah. Cane chairs and cushions, sad flapping tablecloths, were all sodden. The idea of a gentle, civilised party in the balmy open air was well and truly a washout. The musicians set up in a cramped corner of the sitting room and made the best of it.

We wrapped the almost centenarian snugly in a faux fur blanket and lifted him from the wheelchair to an armchair by my mother's side. The new outfit she'd bought for the day couldn't be quickly dried, so I found a red satin Chinese-style jacket that fitted her quite well and striped red trousers that needed to be rolled so she didn't trip on the cuffs. Considering I am five feet ten inches and she has shrunk to barely five feet one inch, she looked quite resplendent.

A fire roared. The heating was turned to the max. The singer sang old jazz numbers. A few creaky hips swayed. The sandwiches were scoffed in minutes. There was a run on tea and coffee, which we're not used to on Pittwater. Pink returned to grey cheeks. The sausage rolls, a warm concoction of lamb, cumin, coriander, mint and pine nuts, disappeared in two circuits.

'God, we might run out of food,' I wailed.

Lisa looked at me as though I was mad. 'There are three more courses of savouries and three desserts. You'll be fine.' I learned that day, that even though my mother bucks the trend, most elderly people scoff in a rush but peak quickly on very little. It's as though their blood sugar drops and they need a quick hit to prevent them from hitting the floor.

'Are you going to make a speech?' I asked Esther when the musicians were having their lunch. She shrugged, just a little coquettishly. 'Come on,' I urged. 'Everyone's made a huge effort to get here. This is your big moment.'

So we hoisted her from her chair, dusted the crumbs off her chest and positioned her in the centre of the room. A still silence descended. I said a few utterly inadequate words. Unable to waffle on sentimentally, even though I knew she'd adore it. I stuck to the truth: despite our often difficult relationship, love abided and always would. 'Your turn,' I said, giving her the floor.

My mother, always the entertainer, the master of slick one-liners, who lived to be the centre of attention, shrugged her shoulders and held out her hands with the palms facing the ceiling: 'Thank you for coming. I love you all.'

'When were the best times?' I prompted, to get her rolling.

Like an actress who'd momentarily forgotten her lines, she suddenly launched into long, rambling stories about my brother. The good times they'd shared. The bond between them. The same brother, I thought with a cynical smile, who'd banned her from his house after he married. The same brother who, on his deathbed, begged me to promise to keep my mother out of my life. 'She's evil, she'll destroy you if you let her,' he whispered. It was the morphine talking, I thought. But afterwards, I was never again as oblivious to the sly digs and put-downs as I'd once been.

She mentioned unforgettable times in her ninety-year history. Her wild accounts of traipsing in Africa, tap dancing in London and tantrum-throwing in Rome, coming on assignment with me to document the relocation of over-friendly polar bears in Churchill, Manitoba. Stories the other inmates had already heard but had treated with suspicion. Today, though, I was there to lend credibility.

As it turned out, she wasn't a good storyteller. Left huge gaps. Made nonsensical leaps. After a while, the room grew restless. I brought the speech to an end. 'We still have dessert to serve, the birthday cake to cut, and a ferry to keep track of,' I said.

'I wasn't finished,' Esther grouched when she was back in her chair, scrunched down deep in the feathered cushions like a gnomish clown in my clothes.

'I saved you,' I said.

'Oh,' she replied, understanding flooding her face. It was a rare moment of humility. My mother, I realised, rarely put herself on the line. She preferred to criticise from the sidelines. That way, she never lost the upper hand.

We brought out the cake with a blizzard of sparklers (that melted the chocolate icing), singing 'Happy Birthday' at the top of our lungs. Even Edwina's black-and-white spotted mutt, Moe, joined in. Off-key but enthusiastic.

Two hours into the party, the oldies conked out and began heading for the ferry wharf. The rain was still torrential. The wind icy. In the south-west corner of Lovett Bay, the waterfall was a foaming white curtain. I suggested Esther spend the night with us and go home when the weather eased in a day or two, but she refused. She wouldn't desert her guests. Still wrapped in the white fur blanket, we loaded Stefan into the truck. He looked radiant. So did my mother. They'd be soaked through again by the time they reached the ferry. They didn't seem to care. Bob and Michael from the Lovett Bay Boatshed stayed onboard to help offload at the other end. The ferry was already running one-and-a-half hours behind schedule and the day wasn't over.

From the verandah, we offshorers watched the ferry surfing the seas back to The Point. No body bags. Relieved, we bolted inside, filled our wine glasses and settled in front of the fire.

'Is he really your mother's boyfriend?' Edwina asked. I grinned an assent. 'She never mentioned you once,' Edwina added. 'Not even a thank you for throwing a great bash.'

Hah, I thought, *payback for not waxing lyrical about her devotion as a mother.* I hadn't even noticed. Later, I regretted my behaviour enormously. It would have cost nothing to recall her good deeds and thank her for them.

—

The same week, two guests died (in their sleep) and one was hospitalised with life-threatening pneumonia (his family was called to say final farewells but, mercifully, he survived).

In a phone call to tell me the news, my mother, who didn't even suffer a sniffle, twittered: 'Better to go out with a bang.'

Surely she meant it was better for *other* people to go out with a bang? Who'd risk open-heart surgery at her age unless they had an iron grip on life? I heard a faint cough, clearing of the throat, as though she'd recognised the double standard. 'Oh, by the way, I like the jacket you loaned me, so I'll keep that. But your trousers were too long. You can have them back.' Attack – always the best form of defence.

On our next lunch date, we made our way to the car.

'Picnic or pizza?' I asked.

'Picnic.'

Taking the walker from her to store in the boot, I said, 'Why wouldn't you let us move the party venue to the Village?' She tackled the car seat from an angle that would end in disaster. 'Bum first, remember? Bum first when you get in the car.' A groan. Grunt. Plenty of wincing. *So she hadn't escaped her birthday celebrations completely unscathed.* Her bottom sank at the wrong angle. 'You need to move further forward.' She made little sobbing sounds. 'Are you alright?' I asked. With that, her bottom found the seat. She flopped back, eyes closed. 'You're not about to die, are you?' Using a joking tone.

"Course not.' She managed to get one foot inside. The other refused to move. After a while, I lifted it for her. Closed the car door. Went around to the driver's side and attached her seatbelt.

'I hope that party was worth it,' I said grimly.

Her eyes still closed, she said, 'I wanted a wake while I was still alive. It was such a pity your father was dead for his wake. He would have enjoyed it enormously.' And there it was. The subplot. My mother couldn't cope with the thought of missing her own farewell, even if it meant risking her life. It all made sense now. Every wake has music and flowers.

11

On a grey, drizzly day, damp but not cold, Bob and I sat on the verandah nursing our cuppas. Our mood was flat. Out of the blue, Bob suggested a visit to the US to see his son and wanted to know what I thought about tacking on a trip to the Galapagos Islands. Maybe spend a couple of weeks exploring Chile as well.

Within seconds, sweat was pooling on my upper lip, under my eyes, running down my spine, my thighs and the back of my knees. Anxiety, I have learned, conjoins with menopause and, in my case, had resulted in a strangely altered mental state – a new fear of flying. The prospect of spending long periods folded painfully in the prison of economy while my disobedient head spun horror scenarios that included engine failure, terrorists or, at the very least, deep vein thrombosis, was horrible.

I dumped my cuppa, pushed back my chair from the table and, mustering every ounce of self-control at my disposal, walked casually to the rail to look out over the soft green water of Lovett Bay. Gathering in the peace and serenity until the snivelling, flaccid menopausal alter ego, who lurked like an evil spirit waiting to pounce in a weak moment, shrank back into her fetid hole.

Gave myself a silent pep talk. I was a woman who'd once travelled fearlessly into countries flagged unsafe by foreign affairs. I'd
backpacked and hitchhiked and stared down hardship, discomfort
and even threat. So when had the certain knowledge of inevitably
being ripped off, mugged, sick or hopelessly lost been upgraded
from an irritating fact of foreign travel to an insurmountable
deterrent? Was it experience that had dulled my appetite for
the unknown? Or fear that I may no longer have the physical
and mental resources to survive even insignificant hurdles? Or
perhaps I'd once felt the unmitigated terror of being handed a
life-threatening diagnosis and had no stomach anymore, even for
minor physical risk.

There was another factor. I'd done my share of travelling.
Lining up for another round of antiquities, buildings, art works,
medieval towns, stuff that at home I wouldn't give a glance, had
the unsettling whiff of time-filling. Without realising it, I'd
begun to think of travel as pointless voyeurism, that we tourists
were no better than fly-in fly-out workers in remote areas. We
come, we see, we conquer and we move on. More bad meals.
More language difficulties. More rip-offs. More downtime at
train stations, airports or on buses. But all I said was: 'I've always
wanted to see the Galapagos.' Denial? Bravado? Yes, but mostly
a morbid fear that once I began admitting defeat I would quickly
spiral down into the *well looked after* zone and never crawl out. 'I'll
check out flights and accommodation this afternoon.'

Bob grinned. 'Get busy then,' he said, coming over to slip
an arm around my waist, visibly energised by the prospect of an
adventure. I made a silent vow never to narrow his options for
want of a stiff backbone. At the same time, I lamented the hideous
inequity in the aging of men and women.

'Do you ever fear flying?' I asked, genuinely curious.

He gave me a sideways look, not sure where I was coming
from. 'You mean in a plane?'

'Of course I mean a plane,' I replied, slightly exasperated.

'Nope.' He paused. 'Do you?'

A slick arrangement of lies sprouted on the tip of my tongue. 'Yes,' I admitted instead. He was silent for a while.

'I switch off. Can't you do that?' Mental toughness, is what he meant.

'Not anymore,' I said.

'You'll be right,' he said. 'I'll hold your hand all the way.'

I smiled: 'Yeah, that'll do it.' Picked up our empty mugs, stacked them in the dishwasher and walked down the long hallway to my office. It was strewn with tribal rugs that once graced the backs of the camels of Iran's Bakhtiari nomads on their seasonal migrations. What happened, I wondered, to their old women who could no longer make those difficult journeys? Were they left behind to die, as they were in some cultures? Their bones picked over by hawks so that by the time their families returned the following year, there was nothing left to show they'd ever existed?

Through the window, I watched a small tinny, miniature in the distance, cut a line through dead flat water, scissor sharp. Chippy harrumphed and settled in her basket at my feet. I typed 'Galapagos' into the computer.

———

A few days later, the phone rang.

'A property came on the market yesterday,' Peter said. 'It's not exactly what you're after, but if you've got time you might want to take a look.'

'How far out of town?' Bob asked.

'About fourteen minutes.'

'What's the road like?'

'Bitumen with about two kilometres of dirt at the end. But it's a road, not a track. Kept up by the council.'

'Aspect?'

'North.'

Bob ended the call. We packed a change of clothes, booked the B & B, scooped up Chippy and, with heightened purpose, hit the cavalcade of trucks and sun-seeking grey nomads escaping the southern winter. We both sensed we were either on the verge of something big – or calling it quits.

We arrived in Wingham around lunchtime. Peter and another man we'd never met were waiting for us in a bog-standard office with a desk covered with stacks of advertising flyers and two rows of demountable cubicles on either side of a hallway. We'd never stepped beyond reception before. To us, it signalled rising stakes.

'This is Tim,' Peter said, introducing us to a shorter, rounder version of Michael from the brickworks. Tim held out a hard, tough hand. 'I'm a dairy farmer in my spare time,' he said when I mentioned his grip.

'Ah,' Bob said.

'I specialise in working farm or agricultural land sales,' Tim added. It was a subtle moment. I missed it completely.

Tim explained that Peter had mentioned we were looking for a block with a north-facing house site and views. He'd checked his own listings and thought a Wherrol Flat property might tick most of our boxes.

'How about we all go together?' he suggested.

'We've got a dog,' I said.

'So do I,' he replied with a shrug.

I sat next to Peter in the back of his mud-splattered four-wheel drive with Chippy held tightly on my lap. As soon as Tim hit the open road, if he was running true to local form, he'd floor the accelerator. In the front seat, Bob asked detailed questions. I listened with a sinking heart. For a start, instead of five to twenty acres, it was cattle country, currently running a herd of forty Red Polls but capable of supporting up to seventy steers in a bad season, a few more in a good year, and it covered a whopping (to us) two hundred and twenty-eight acres.

'It's got a new cattle yard,' Tim said in the warm tone that I soon discovered good cattle yards, decent tractors and reliable log splitters – farming equipment in general – elicit from men who work the land. 'And the paddocks are clean.' An even warmer tone this time.

'Clean?'

'Mostly kikuyu and clover. Not many weeds.'

'Flattish country, is it?' Bob asked.

'Hilly. But there's a couple of sites – one in particular – that might make a good spot to build a house.'

I waited for Tim to get lyrical, launch into a hard sell. But he remained silent. *Can't be that great*, I thought, failing to understand that smart country real estate agents understand that properties sell themselves when the right buyer comes along. It wasn't smart to push a sale when you were going to bump into the (possibly unhappy or even irate) buyer in the main street of town at least once a week when he did his shopping.

I switched out of the conversation. The windscreen wipers batted at the drizzle. The head-clearing scent of eucalypts seeped inside the car. I was heartened by the sight of green river flats. 'Hilly' could mean different things to different people. Up ahead, a sign warned heavy trucks off a one-lane bridge and ordered us to give way to oncoming traffic. There were swerving black skid marks to prove it was wise to heed directions. We began to climb. One hill. Then another. In the distance, a long line of hills loomed high enough to qualify as mountains. I closed my eyes, feeling my anxiety levels rise, a hot flush creeping up from my toes.

The car slowed. Tim pulled onto a clay dirt driveway, turned to custard from the drizzle that hadn't let up all the way from Pittwater. Bob jumped out to open the gate. Outside, the sky was low. We drove past the new cattle yards and bumped up a hill, fishtailing in a wet spot.

'Might be a spring there,' Tim said. 'There's plenty in these hills. More when it rains hard for days.'

There was no hint of even a track for us to follow. He slipped into first gear, engaged four-wheel drive, gave the engine a slight rev. A group of half-grown steers, their damp hides the colour of blood, looked us over curiously. Eyes fanned by long, sexy lashes. A black beast with a blank white face looked at us stupidly.

'What breed is that?' I asked, but not genuinely interested.

'That's a baldy,' Tim said. He came to a stop in a lovely copse of gum trees where cattle had recently camped. There was cow shit ankle-deep to prove it. I shut Chippy in the car and stepped around the dung into the spongy softness of lush pasture. It was a pretty enough spot on a flat-topped hill at the base of much steeper hill. But nothing special.

'Water connected?' Bob asked. Peter shook his head.

'Power?' Another head shake. Given the dodgy access and the fact that we'd have to build a road to a house site, it was fast becoming yet another no-go in a long list of them.

'What's the view like from up there?' I asked, pointing towards the top of the big hill shrouded in dark clouds, misted by light rain.

Peter shrugged. 'There's no way to get there by car,' he said, as if that was the end of it.

'How about a walk?' Bob asked me.

We both felt it at the same time – an indefinable headiness, a lightness of spirit, rising hope. Peter and Tim, perhaps sensing a shift in the atmosphere, tagged along. We worked our way upwards along a wide swathe of grass not long slashed. On either side the vegetation was knee-high and dripping wet. There were bright spots of little yellow flowers.

'So pretty,' I said, 'like tiny daisies.'

'A weed,' Tim said disapprovingly.

I stooped to uproot a few plants without understanding I'd already begun to assume ownership. 'At least it's easy to pull out,' I said, 'not like that hideous lantana.'

''Round here it can take over a paddock overnight, so farmers slash it,' Tim said.

'Of course.'

We brushed the rain off our shoulders and kept going. At the halfway point, we paused, breathless.

'How good's the fencing?' Bob asked. His face had the flat, closed-off look he gets when his mind is racing.

'Most of it's new. Where it's old, you'd need to do some work,' Tim said. We set off, quiet again, until we reached the summit. The real estate agents wandered off to leave us alone. Or perhaps they were anxious to get back to the dry warmth of the car.

'Wish I'd brought the camera,' Bob said, in a whisper, as if to speak loudly might shatter the splendour.

'All this? It's too . . . too big for a camera,' I said, my voice as soft as his. Valleys were draped in white mist from which emerald hilltops rose as islands. Flat against a big sky, mountain ranges flowed like oceans of blue. Towards the east, a storm played out. Sheets of lightning flashed. Fork lightning, white-hot, seemed nearer to where we stood. In the north, heavy rain fell in thick grey curtains. In the south and west, black cauliflower clouds rumbled softly. A wedge-tailed eagle soared elegantly above us. Bob slipped his hand into mine and we stayed there, statue-still, unwilling to break the spell, for a long time.

Hills are so deceptive, I thought. From a distance, they look like they come to a point, but they plateau, worn to flatness by the wind and weather. *If we built a glass shack, here, we could lie in bed and count stars, watching the moon come and go, and in the morning observe the sun thundering up from the horizon until the valleys shone. But: two hundred and twenty-eight acres? We'd have to be mad. And a house on a great hill where the winds must rage? Insanity.*

Just then, way off to the north, a blade of sunlight broke through bruised clouds. Shafts of gold fell out of the sky. One rainbow. Then two. Then a third. The hills and valleys around us were pulsing with light, colour, life. And we were goners.

'How much?' I asked Bob, as rainbows faded and the first fat drops of rain landed wetly on our faces.

'On a clear day,' he replied, 'do you think we'd see the sea from here?'

Later, I likened it to setting off to buy an oriental carpet, knowing exactly what size, colour and design you were looking for, and walking out of the shop with a completely unsuitable, impractical piece because it was so glorious you knew it would give you pleasure for the rest of your life and damn practicality.

'Offer half the asking price,' I said, trying to claw my way back to the real world. 'There's never been a better time to find a bargain.' Bob's eyebrows shot up. 'Business is business,' I snapped. I had the grace to blush.

On the brink of transferring a poofteenth less than the asking price for two hundred and twenty-eight acres of steep hills and deep gullies, my stomach roiled with a mix of nerves and nausea. My father's words spun in my head. 'You need to be comfortably off when you're old,' he'd say while rearranging the stack of bills on the mantelpiece above the fireplace, where he kept them until they were all paid at the end of the month. 'It's the only weapon you've got left.' Then he'd read the obituaries with particular interest in public figures, skipping the plaudits to get straight to the value of the bloke's estate. He had admiration only for those who left a serious amount. 'A life well lived,' he'd say. Or in the case of a few politicians: 'A life on the take.'

But despite every argument against instigating huge changes at this unpredictable and vulnerable stage of our lives, here we were,

Bob and me, acting like a couple of starry-eyed newlyweds and throwing everything at a dream. Or more likely, a folly. At best, we might last ten years before our bodies gave out and our rolling green pastures deteriorated into barren, weed-infested plots.

'Are we mad?' I asked Bob.

'Yes,' he said, grinning confidently.

'Ah. What the hell. Go on.' I pointed at the keyboard. 'Hit the send button.'

In an instant, we'd crossed into a parallel universe so un-resemblant to Pittwater, it was like zipping on a new skin. We were landowners, now, in country where cattle were a religion and boats were about as useful as a bull in a herd of steers. No house, no water, no power – not even a sludgy track to a good campsite. Boom or bust. Shades of my mother. Never far from the surface.

Soon after, we agreed to agist about forty steers for the former owner for three months at a rate of three dollars per head per week. Even at full carrying capacity, if we were vaguely contemplating a return on our investment, we were living in la-la-land.

———

Towards the end of spring, 2011, we loaded the tinny with a tent, grass cutter, fire drum and camping equipment. Shipped it across the water to pack in our newly acquired ute. No more B & Bs. No more restaurant dinners. We were serious landowners and it was time to walk the boundary, explore the gullies, ascend the hilltops and pace the plateaus. Study the sky. Learn rain patterns and the prevailing winds. Sit in country, as a wonderful Indigenous poet, Ali Cobby Eckermann, once said to me.

'What does that mean exactly?' I asked.

'Feel the land,' she replied. 'Listen to what it says.'

Friends and neighbours on Pittwater no doubt watched our departure shaking their heads and wondering what kind of idiots quit a magical seaside paradise for a scruffy bush block. We laughed when anyone questioned us. 'This place is as beautiful as Pittwater, but in a different way. And wait until we bring you fruit from our trees, vegetables from our gardens,' we told them, smugly. 'You'll understand.' We stopped for coffee and pastries at St Ives, a ritual by then, and hit the highway, slapping our knees with excitement.

'We're off! Bring it on! Onwards and upwards!' In the back seat and deaf to our shouts, Chippy didn't stir.

———

They say it is normal for both buyers and sellers to feel remorse when the deal is done. As I walked the paddocks for the first time, it felt like waking up from a fool's dream. Everywhere I looked, I saw work. Not the kind I was used to – sitting at a computer, cup of tea handy, and writing – but hard, physical yakka. Mending fences. Grubbing out weeds. Controlling lantana in ankle-breaking gullies. Cleaning dams. Clearing paddocks of bushfire fuel. The kind of work that couldn't be postponed. That left you stiff, sore and mute with tiredness. The kind that never ended. Remorse didn't quite cover it. Naked horror was closer to the truth.

And yet, despite the awful anxiety that we were at the wrong end of our lives for this kind of challenge, beauty overwhelmed. Wide land opened to the sky. Light poured down in great warm slabs. Wind skated across hilltops until trees sang in furious symphony. Fifteen years of living on the tree-shrouded tidal shores of Lovett Bay quickly felt slightly claustrophobic. It was like letting a cool, fresh wind pulse through heart, head, mind and soul. Brushing away the cobwebs, as my mother would say, to allow in the light.

We picked a mostly level campsite at what turned out to be the halfway point between the front gate and the tip of the Great Hill. Bob shovelled enough cow manure to fertilise an orchard, slashed the long grass, and in the shade of a few old gum trees, we pitched the khaki canvas tent in which we'd once honeymooned. I made up two camp stretchers with clean sheets, pillows and doonas, found a spot for Chippy's bed, and placed our pyjamas under feather pillows. The stale smell of the tent matched the pungent, earthy aroma of cow dung, but we had a clean and cosy shelter to sleep protected from whatever the weather gods chose to throw at us. Bob set out two folding chairs around the fire drum and we wandered off to collect wood. There was enough to set a fire to cook for five hundred within a few paces.

'Remember Amassine?' I said. 'Even twigs were precious.' I held out my arms for Bob to load me up. 'We'll never go short, eh?'

We were surprised to find nine dams nestled secretively in deep hollows. Surprised, because in our smitten state we'd completely overlooked the need for water. Most were utilitarian holes scooped out of gullies. One or two were shaded sylvan glades with deep blue spring-fed ponds thick with tiny white waterlilies. Pretty spots to throw a rug on long pasture for a picnic on a hot summer's day, we thought, naively. One afternoon, tired from a long walk, I sprawled out on the soft grass and quickly jumped up. Too damp. Too smelly. Possibly a cow-poo health hazard. Once I wouldn't have cared. Once I'd walked barefoot in the rain along greasy New York sidewalks. Happy afterwards, to spend an hour scrubbing sticky black grime from the soles of my feet.

Before the sun went down, we sat around the campfire, moving our chairs whenever a gentle shift in the air wafted plumes of smoke in our faces, making our eyes water. Bob grilled loin lamb chops until the heavily salted fatty tails crunched like pork crackling. I added a simple salad – mixed leaves, red capsicum, red onion, avocado – tossed in a fine olive oil and red wine vinegar that I'd brought from Pittwater. The old cast-iron grill, also from our honeymoon days (when I carted exotic spices, condiments, sauces and even cheeses from one end of Queensland to the other, until I realised nothing beat the simplicity of fresh local produce bought from roadside stalls), leaned triumphantly against a gum tree. Age and rust may have wearied it, but it was not yet defunct. *Like us*, I thought.

When a sliver of moon appeared, Bob asked me, as he does as a joke occasionally because he knows my memory for dates is appalling, how long we've been married.

'A lifetime and a minute,' I replied, reaching for his hand. He stood and refilled my wine glass. The sky was thick with stars, the night air clean and sharp.

'Ten years,' he said. 'Any regrets?'

I laughed. 'Ask me in the morning when the wine's worn off.'

'What about this?' He made a sweeping motion circling the dark abyss with his arm. 'Any regrets?'

'Honestly?' Bob nodded. Firelight danced across his face. It was so quiet we might have been the last two people on earth. 'I swing wildly between euphoria and terror.' And then it came to me, from way down deep in my undeserving little soul. 'We're already so privileged, I wonder if this, this . . . wanting more, is somehow . . . obscene.'

We were both silent for a long time. Flames died down. The orange glow of coals shone through the perforations of the fire drum like windows, so it resembled a model apartment building. The wine in our glasses emptied, leaving only a grainy red residue. I thought about doing the dishes. Decided they'd wait until morning. It was too late to boil a billy and, anyway, we needed to conserve water. The dams were a long, long way down in the valleys and no doubt polluted by the cattle. Unless we wanted to make daily treks to the brickworks to refill the jerry cans, washing up would have to be a once-a-day event. Every moment has an upside if you look hard enough.

'Ready for bed?' I asked.

'I wouldn't want to be one of those old blokes who sit around doing nothing day after day. You've got to have a job. Any job. Hours feel like weeks otherwise. Unless you give up completely and watch television. Not much of a life, that. Around here, there'll be a bit to do.'

'Here? If you want to, you'll be flat out until the day you drop dead, hopefully at the age of one hundred and ten. Let's hit the sack, eh? And we need to think of a name for this place. One we can pronounce and spell. Not like Tarrangaua. What about High Point?'

'Sounds like a shopping centre.'

'Ok, Einstein. You come up with one. Where's the dog? Have you seen the dog?' I said, holding down a note of panic.

'She put herself to bed hours ago. Do you want to use the bathroom first or shall I?'

'Hah! Very funny. I'll go left. You go right. Watch out for cow dung. We already smell like refugees from a smokehouse.' I paused on my way to somewhere private: 'My mother told me that when she was a kid, when there was just a single rung of water left in the tank after a shocker drought, she was allowed a mug a day to brush her teeth and have a wash. One mug. That was it until it rained. If she could do it, so can we.'

'Did she drink it then, so it wasn't wasted?'

'Smart arse.' I marched off into the darkness, looking for a decent log to hang my backside over. Going down was bearable, getting up wreaked havoc. *Bloody knees. Bloody body refusing to ride to orders. Who gave it permission to turn rogue?* The horrible knowledge too that, as a rule, after a certain age joints like knees don't improve.

At god-knows-what time, Chippy growled. I woke instantly. Froze. Listened, lying motionless, my hand on her neck to keep her quiet. A whooshing sound, like dry grass swaying in the wind. But it was a still night. Cattle, maybe? Not wallabies. They thump. Scratching sounds on the other side of the window flap. Too close for cattle. Bandicoots. I'd put money on it. I soothed the dog by pulling her on to the camp stretcher and settling her in the bend of my knees.

'Who's the best little doggie in the whole wide world?' I whispered. She huffed and snuffed and spun until she faced the opening. Then stared into the night, my brave old dog, with a low growl. Not bandicoots then. After a while, she dropped her head, sighed heavily and started to snore. My husband's steady breathing never faltered. Whatever it was, it was gone. Slowly, my heartbeat returned to normal. I lay awake for a long time in the stale fug of the honeymoon tent. Seesawing between dread and gameness for what lay ahead. Listening to every slight rustle in the grass. The delicate movement of air whispering through the tall gums of our campsite.

In the morning, we found fresh scats not far from the camp. 'Wild dogs,' Bob said, flatly. 'Better keep a close eye on Chippy after the sun goes down.'

12

ON OUR RETURN TO PITTWATER, I called Esther: 'How about a picnic at the beach?'

'You're on,' she said, sounding bright and cheerful. 'See you at noon in reception.'

'Done!'

The last time I'd collected her from her room, I'd decided to change our routine. Her unit had taken on the glitter and disarray of a backstage dressing-room. Multitudes of necklaces hung from a dusty black velvet mannequin, a collection of watches were heaped in a pile in a ceramic dish. Another dish was filled with rings. Lipsticks lay discarded. Her hairbrush sat on a pile of Village notices and mail-order catalogues. The sofa was piled with blankets: those ubiquitous afghans, the faux fur used to keep her boyfriend warm at the birthday bash, a couple of doonas, a patchwork blanket I'd knitted one winter to avoid reaching for a glass of wine too often. The television blared. The sink was full of dirty dishes. The rubbish bin overflowing.

For a long while I'd tidied up while she checked her hair and lipstick. Then I'd rebelled. If she preferred to sit in a mess instead of making the smallest effort to wash her breakfast mug or plates, it was her choice. So instead of fetching her and feeling captive and claustrophobic in her room, I insisted she wait at reception. Displeased with the new arrangement, she invariably attacked me on my arrival. But I'd become more skillful at fending her off.

'Are you putting on weight?' she asked.

'Heaps.'

'Your face is very red. Have you been drinking?'

'Heaps. Ready? Ok. Let's go.'

Within moments of greeting her, no matter how many times I promised myself that this time it would be different, we got off on the wrong foot.

'Bum first,' I said, as I always did, helping her into the car. I had meant to tell her about the new property, our camping trip, how I'd recounted the story to Bob about her bathing with a cup of water, but I was afraid I might say something irreversible, so I said nothing. At the beach, the wind was strong enough to buffet the car. I reached into the back seat for our food. Placed a tray of oysters on her lap. Her face softened with pleasure. She slid a finger under the milky-grey globule and severed the muscle. Tipped the shell so the meat fell neatly into her mouth.

'How's Stefan?' I asked, deciding to begin again.

'Very, very ill. I don't see him anymore.'

'Oh, that's sad. So hard for his daughter. She's devoted to him.'

My mother gave me a hard look. I wanted to stitch my lips together.

———

One day, I flicked through Esther's bank statements, wondering how she managed to go through so much cash each week when she was unable to get out and about much anymore.

'How much?' Bob asked when I mentioned it.

'Three, often four hundred dollars.'

'Have you made a list of her outgoings?'

'Yep. Far as I can tell, they add up to about one hundred and sixty dollars. That includes hair appointments, the extra money for the monthly Village dinner party and personal items the carer buys for her. Oh, and the cost of the carer.' If she needed anything beyond the carer's reach, I filled the gap.

'Doesn't make sense,' he said. 'Might pay to find out what's going on.'

'You'd better come with me,' I said. 'She loses her manners completely when we have conversations about money.'

We found her lying on the sofa as usual.

'To what do I owe the pleasure of your company?' she asked, sensing a hard note in the atmosphere. She battled into a sitting position. Bob remained in the doorway. I pushed aside debris to clear a seat. 'We're just a little worried, Esther, about the amount of money you're spending.'

She reared up, snake-like: 'It's mine. I'll do what I like with it. Don't worry, you'll get your half-million when I die.'

I felt a ping, like a rubber band snapping somewhere inside my chest. And I lost control.

'First of all,' I said, my voice clipped, 'you don't have half a million. Not even close to that amount. Secondly, throw your money away, if that's what you want, but don't expect me to step in when everything explodes. Those days are over. If you have to move into high-care – and the day will come, because you intend to hang on until everyone around you has died of frustration or fury – I'd have to sell my house to pay the bond, and I bloody well won't do that so you can buy more cheap trinkets to satisfy some greedy little urge. You are ninety-years-old. No necklace is going to cure that.' I know I am shouting. 'You are a selfish, egotistical old woman with delusions of grandeur. Grow up. For god's sake. Grow up.' I stood. Tired. Fed up. 'If you end up in the gutter, so be it. I'll drive right past you without even looking.'

Esther reached under the sofa. Found a long, yellow plastic shoehorn. Held it up like a club. Her eyes were black with fury. She bounced backwards and forwards, trying to get off the sofa.

'If you hit me with that I will hit you so hard you will never get up,' I said, absolutely enraged. A lifetime of letting her snide remarks go through to the keeper and, suddenly, a step too far. Fury boiled over. I wanted her to hit me. Hoped she would strike out. It would be the excuse I needed to walk away and never return.

Without missing a beat, Esther sweetly said, 'I was only going to scratch my back.'

'You're on your own,' I said, past the point of caring. 'From now on, sort out your own life.'

Bob opened the door and I walked through it. Behind me, I heard him say, 'Goodbye, Esther.'

'She doesn't care,' I said, still spitting with fury. 'She doesn't care that her stupid, pointless extravagance could mean I have to sell my house. As long as she can play a rich old lady buying jewels. Favours. Whatever. I have no idea.'

'You didn't bring your mother up very well,' Bob said, opening the car door.

'What do you mean?'

'She knows how to press all your buttons. She's got you sorted.'

'Not this time,' I swore vehemently. 'Not this time.'

'You've got to give her credit. She's so quick. Scratching her back?' And he laughed out loud.

'What keeps her going?' I asked, refusing to see the funny side.

'You,' he said. 'Part of her can't bear to think you'll go on enjoying life after she dies.'

'That is a truly awful thing to contemplate,' I said, but I wasn't entirely shocked.

At home that evening, while Bob watched the news, I considered the new footing of my relationship with my mother. If I felt a skerrick of regret for my behaviour, I whacked it down with the words, *she'd failed to protect me.* I'd first heard them when my head was unravelling under the pressure of a destructive love affair and I found my way to a chair in a psychologist's office. For the first time in my life, I babbled without restraint, unveiling old demons. 'Your mother failed to protect you,' he told me gently. It was a shattering moment. Turned all I believed to be true inside out. But back then I was an expert at shoving aside awfulness. *Compartmentalising*, the shrink called it. An art perfected by children unable to cope with what is happening to them.

Now, that single line had given me the right to hold on to outrage, withhold forgiveness, understanding and compassion. I curled my fist around those words like they held a cure for a fatal disease. I'd crossed a line. Witnessed her feel a tremor in her powerbase. Whereas I – I'd felt the past shaking loose. One wrong word from her, I thought, and I would tell all. I'd let her live with a nasty little slice of family history on her conscience until the day she died. No more protecting her from awful truths, or even minor unpleasantness. I had never felt so enraged in my life. But by morning, after a night of restlessness, I'd calmed down. Turning my back on my mother was impossible. She'd trained me too well.

Three days later, the Village manager rang: 'Esther says she's interested in moving to a two-bedroom apartment. That a fellow called Frank is coming to look after her. We thought we should check with you before doing anything.'

'Pure fantasy,' I said. 'Frank is my Uncle Frank. He lives very happily with his daughter and her family in country Victoria. He's the kindest man in the world but he'd run a country mile.'

———

I let her sweat for a week before I rang to ask her if she'd like to have lunch.

'If you can spare the time,' she said nastily, straight on the attack. A part of me wanted to applaud. She may have lost the high ground but she'd never, ever give in. We sat in a black silence at the beach. I waited for payback and it didn't take long: 'Denise [her carer] is wonderful. More than a daughter to me.'

'Yes, she's a lovely woman. But remember, she's paid to help you.'

'Oh, she loves me. Our relationship goes way beyond professional.'

'Ask yourself, Esther, if she'd be there without the pay cheque.'

'I'm lucky to have someone to care. She kisses and hugs me, you know.'

'That's nice.'

'Most people are happy to hug me.'

Well, I thought, *we're back on track.*

After a while, I asked: 'Why didn't you ever remarry?' I was curious. Her life could have panned out so differently. 'You were a good-looking woman, still young when Dad died [in her early fifties], enjoyed the company of men.'

'Your brother told me he wouldn't approve,' she said. Surprised, I said nothing. It didn't sound like my brother at all. After a moment or two, she added: 'I thought about getting together with your Uncle Frank. But really, he wasn't my type. A little uncouth for me.' But not so uncouth, I thought angrily, that she didn't run straight to him when I threatened to leave her to fend for herself. At that precise moment I couldn't bear being near her for another second.

'Uncle Frank is one of the most decent and wonderful men I've ever known,' I said, my jaw clenched. I grabbed our rubbish and jumped out of the car to dispose of it. Breathe fresh air. Drove her back to the Village in silence.

Uncle Frank, in his late eighties now, with rough hands, tanned skin and buggered knees, could no longer stride the thousand-strong rows of peach, apricot, nectarine and cherry trees of the family orchards, humping a weed sprayer or, in the depths of winter when the first green buds formed and pruning began, secateurs. Instead, hobbling, limping, swinging his legs out wide to avoid bending his knees, he watched over his four-year-old great grandson so everyone else in the family could be flat-out picking, packing and shipping the fruit, earning a decent living some years but mostly surviving through sheer bloody-mindedness. He called Esther every Sunday night without fail to keep family links intact. Until she moved into assisted care, he holidayed with her for one, sometimes two weeks annually. Handing her cash at the end of each stay to cover the cost of feeding him, which my mother accepted without a qualm.

I strode around to open the car door. Let her struggle to her feet alone, afraid that if I stood too close I'd be tempted to slap her. She shuffled off, bent over her walker.

'You might want to take a good hard look at yourself, Esther,' I said harshly. She didn't even flinch. Later, I decided what must have happened: he'd turned her down.

My cousin Jayne, Uncle Frank's straight-talking daughter, told me once that Esther was well-known for embroidering the truth. 'No one pulled her up, though, unless she went too far and someone got hurt. Mind you, she had a habit of going too far, your mother, so she was pulled up a fair bit.'

So at our next picnic, to make a point, I said, 'Uncle Frank handed Jayne every penny he had to help see them through the drought. A good man, eh?'

'Alright,' she said grudgingly, 'there's no need to rub it in.'

—

On my return home after *a mother day*, Bob traditionally made a soothing cuppa and sat down with me while I looked for reassurance that, even though I was far from an ideal daughter, I was not truly as terrible as Esther judged me to be. He called it the Post-Esther Debrief. Said it was a documented fact that children of self-centred, volatile parents were bound more tightly to them than kids from more balanced families, and that there is well-researched evidence that the aged become more self-centred and less inhibited. Something to do with the deterioration of their frontal lobes, which control social awareness and emotion. 'You might as well get used to it.'

'She's never been any different,' I muttered. But I silently wondered if I was rewriting huge slabs of history to suit our current situation. If I was shutting out all but the calumny in order to justify my own gracelessness. This, an awful memory: in the era of posh accents and silk scarves trailing from handbags, of white stockings, beige shoes and fine, pale-blue wool Norma Tullo dresses with innocent white organza collars, when my mother lined up alongside the other mothers on sports day or the school play or speech day, I was ashamed. She tried too hard to hide a lack of what she called 'class', although she meant wealth. She was embarrassing. All these years later, that is one of the hardest admissions I've ever made. One of the greatest shames of my own.

'I lined the holes in the soles of my shoes with newspaper to pay for your education,' she told me once. Her meaning was clear: I owed her. It was a rock-solid defence that could never be breached, no matter how often she pushed my brother and me to the limits. And she did push. For her birthday – I can't remember which one – she told us she had always wanted a croc-odile skin handbag. So we scraped together the money – four hundred dollars as I recall, at a time when my weekly salary was less than thirty dollars and John was a law student making ends meet by working as a waiter on weekends. Her power was built on guilt, and she used it unashamedly. Twisting greed to give the appearance of generosity. 'This handbag will be yours one day,' she told me. It was an absurd remark, but it took the sting out of the cost, as she knew it would. *Everything I do is for you.*

———

After Stefan became too ill to take her to lunch or visit her, my mother physically and mentally kept reducing her world. It meant a single hour unfolded like an unbearable weight. And the years flew.

'I have lived too long,' she said on another occasion at the beach. I'd arrived too late for lunch, so we broke tradition and settled for coffees and pastries.

'Are you bored?' I asked.

'I'm not complaining. Everyone loves me. I have no idea why.'

'You're not a whinger. That helps. And there's always a good supply of chocolates in your room.'

'Larry brought a python to work the other day. Thought the old ladies would enjoy it. He got reported.'

'By you?'

'Me? Don't be ridiculous. I thought it was wonderful. Made my day. Those old girls, they need to step outside their bedroom doors more often.'

'Those old girls are younger than you.'

And in truth, my mother was the one who expected life to knock on the standard metal security entrance to her apartment. Not many – beyond the carer and me – lifted the latch, so her closest relationships were with the nursing staff who showered, dressed and then, at night, slipped her out of her daywear and into a nightie, and – as she described it – tucked her into bed with a kiss on the cheek. 'Like a child.' It was clear she adored it.

In winter, she had a view of a camellia festooned with bright pink, plate-sized blooms. In summer, a few flowers popped up in a bed of annuals. One day, she reported she'd made friends with a frog. After that, a rabbit. I accepted the frog story. Put the rabbit stories down to temporary drug mismanagement (dropping her pills or forgetting to take them).

Outside the car, seas were so calm surfers in wetsuits bobbed aimlessly on their boards. She stared at the water, the sky. I pointed to a couple of people on horseback but she made no effort to look. 'Would you like to get out of the car to see them?' I asked.

'No. I'll take your word for it.'

'Are you feeling ok?'

'I'm not about to drop off the perch, if that's what you mean and, even if I were, I've told you, death doesn't scare me.'

'I think it does,' I batted back, expecting to get a rise out of her.

'What would you know?' she said dismissively.

'I've been hearing you're at death's door since you were forty-nine years old, Esther. For a woman who thought she wouldn't make it to fifty, you're doing ok.'

Again, she failed to take the bait. Instead she said, 'You have no idea how much my body hurts. Even when I lie still, it feels like rats are gnawing at my bones or pushing needles into them.'

'Your choice,' I reminded her.

She brightened: 'I'm well looked after. Everybody loves me.' She coughed. A deep phlegmy sound. Impossible to dismiss as fake.

'Are you alright?' I asked again. She rolled her eyes. I added: 'When's your next doctor's visit?'

'Tomorrow.'

'Ask him to listen to your chest.'

'It's hay fever. I get it every year.'

'Ok. Your body. Your decision.'

———

A couple of weeks later, there was another call from the retirement village. Esther had had a dizzy spell on her way to the hairdresser. An ambulance had taken her to Mona Vale Hospital. I thanked the receptionist for letting me know. Why did it always happen on the way to the hairdresser? Unaccustomed exercise, or was she searching for an audience? I replaced the receiver. Was this to be the routine now? A phone call. An ambulance. A bedside vigil. One increasingly frail step closer to death each time. Doctors keeping her going way beyond her capabilities. She must be petrified, I thought. Feeling her life trickle through her fingers. Powerless to stop old age cashing in the betting slips. I asked myself again whether her heart surgery was a gift or a curse. Suspected that on any given day, for my mother, it was both.

The cough turned out to be a mild case of pneumonia. Old people's friend in another century. For three days I delivered a cappuccino and a pastry for morning tea while a cocktail of anti-biotics and saline was pumped into her bloodstream. I dutifully sat by her side for as long as I could endure it. Not long, to be honest. I was finding it harder and harder to listen to repetitious monologues riddled with self-praise. 'Yes,' I said at one stage, losing patience, 'everyone loves you. I know.'

On day four, the nurse told me Esther was well enough to leave. I began to pack her bag. Suddenly, she developed a wheeze. A long hiss on an exhalation from deep in her chest. The nursing staff grew agitated. Changed the linen and guided Esther back to bed. 'We'll check it out, love. Make sure you're good to go.' Turning to me: 'She'll be here another day. Maybe two.'

It was on the tip of my tongue to tell them my mother's nickname was Sarah Bernhardt and that my brother and I had heard that wheeze many times when she was cornered. But I hesitated. She was old. Recovering from pneumonia. There was a slim chance this might be real. I unpacked her nighties and toiletries without comment.

'I won't see you tomorrow,' I said. 'I've got a full day.'

'I know how busy you are.' Her tone was sharp. Meant to make me feel guilty. As a small child, when my mother reprimanded me I would instantly retort, 'I didn't ask to be borned.' I still felt that way quite often. I made my way down a long and chaotic corridor littered with trolleys, transfusion poles, blood pressure kits, mobile toilet seats, heart monitors, canvas bags stuffed with soiled bed linen. Walls were a collage of rubber glove packs, paper towels and dispensers of antiseptic handwash. A therapeutic arsenal with a backdrop chorus of coughs, groans, cries and, once or twice, mad, unintelligible hysteria from a man out of his mind. Sounds clashing, rising, falling. Organised bedlam. I'd be scratching at the doors to get out.

Seven days later, Esther was discharged.

'The wheeze?' I asked.

'Voluntary,' replied the overworked doctor, a hint of exasperation in his tone. 'We've given her every test, scan and X-ray that exists. There's nothing unknown.'

'So it's deliberate,' I said.

'Yes,' he replied, 'voluntary.'

I settled Esther in the car. 'That wheeze. The doctors reckon it's fake,' I said, getting straight to the point, letting her know we were all on to her.

'I never play-act,' she snapped straight back. 'Tempts fate to deal you a backhander.'

'Yeah, right. But. Just so you know, it won't work with me. Ok?'

Three days later, the manager of assisted living called and suggested Esther should return to hospital.

'Why?' I asked through gritted teeth.

'Her wheeze is quite bad. She says they discharged her far too early.'

'They extended her stay for seven extra days and couldn't find anything wrong. The wheeze is voluntary.'

'Oh. I see.'

One day, when Esther was late for our lunch date, I chatted to the receptionist, who had the patience of Job. 'You're amazing,' I said, when the last internee had departed after making a series of complaints.

'Old people are cranky because they're in pain,' she replied. 'I would be, too.'

'Yeah. Maybe.' I wasn't convinced. *Not enough to do*, I thought. *Throwing their weight around to prove to themselves they are still alive and relevant.*

'Esther keeps talking about a rabbit,' I said, changing the subject. 'Is it real?'

'It is to her.'

One day, lured to her room by a long list of chores, I stood at the kitchen sink doing the dishes with my jaw hanging open. 'Your rabbit,' I said, with surprise, 'it's real!' A fat, fluffy, brown-and-white bunny with long whiskers and a twitchy nose was tapping at her garden door.

My mother gave me a smug look, put her thumb to the tip of her nose and wiggled it. 'Get him a biscuit. He's rather fond of Scotch Fingers,' she said.

I had planned to tell her about our new property, but in the end all I said was that Bob and I were going away for a few days. I didn't feel strong enough to handle any questions about our future plans when, in truth, I didn't know the answers myself. I knew, too, that she would worry and obsess about what might become of her.

'Have I ever abandoned you?' I once asked after Bob and I returned from an outback camping trip and her eyes filled with tears of relief at the sight of us.

'Your postcards. They stopped coming. I thought you were dead,' she said.

'Not many postboxes in Arnhem Land,' I replied. I sat beside her that day, put an arm around her shoulders, and asked again: 'Have I ever abandoned you?'

'No,' she said. 'But you might!'

13

IN THE SPECKLED SHADE OF A COPSE OF GUM TREES we sat in our camp chairs sipping spine-building billy tea. It was late afternoon at the beginning of a rampant summer. Four years had passed since that first phone call from Michael Baker, asking Bob if he could build a new kiln. As a child, four years had seemed a lifetime. As a woman on the verge of oldness, when the sameness of rituals – no matter how cherished – caused years, seasons, days to seep anonymously and politely into each other, it felt like a blink.

A fire hissed and murmured in the drum. Our clothes reeked of wood smoke. Staring into flames bleached by daylight, I thought of my mother confined to her small, white, boxy room with only diminishment to look forward to. Grateful I'd sidestepped the trap of complacency and committed to grabbing a potent future instead of being rolled over by it. With Bob, as always, the catalyst.

It was our second camp on the property and we'd been roughing it for three days straight. Despite thorough goings-over with a wet flannel and a bar of soap, the unruly aromas of the countryside seeped into hair, skin, even our bedding. To put it mildly, we stank. But we were past noticing or caring, seduced once again by the physical world. Blood-red sunrises over valleys carpeted with fog. Roaring, cloud-filled sunsets of gold and peach. Paddocks and hills of green and blue. Above them, a silver moon rising out of a shell-pink sky. Magpies sounding their melodious liquid notes at dawn. The pure, clear flute of bellbirds spooling through eucalypts in the late afternoon. Cattle grazing in the distance. It was primal and primal instincts felt reawakened. I knew this feeling well. It swelled and resonated with the first sight of red spinifex plains in the wide open spaces of the outback. Arose again, when I gazed at a setting sun through the spiny branches of a thorn tree in the vastness of the African veldt. Or wandered outside a tent high in the Andes to see a glacier shining electric blue in moonlight.

'What if it's the open spaces we love? Feeling part of the bush? At one with the land? What if building a house spoils the magic? What if we're coming at this from the wrong angle? What if we just need a bigger tent on a permanent platform? Same as those safari tents where we stayed in Botswana? The ones with king-size beds, soft pillows and large bathrooms?' Bob raised his eyebrows. I sighed. Escalating desires. A human affliction. 'Ok, ok, so where do you think we should site the house?'

We'd narrowed down the options to three: the easy-access but uninspiring Bottom Hill favoured by the real estate agents. The Great Hill, favoured by me. The Back Paddock Hill, a late entry into the field. Sheltered from cold southerlies and burning hot westerlies, it was a soft, practical option but also dull.

'The view from the Great Hill is magnificent. I'm sure I can see a thin blue line of ocean. That's got to be where we build,' I said, pushing my case and refusing to acknowledge the pitfalls – and expense (shades of my mother?) – of bulldozing a switchback track up a gut-busting slope to a house that would have to be erected on stilts to half-guarantee an even keel when you stood at the kitchen bench.

Bob's eyebrows tangoed. He took a quick series of shallow breaths. The silence spun out.

'So. You're having second thoughts about that location,' I said flatly.

'Won't be easy,' he said. I braced to argue. But after more than a decade together, my face, like his, reads as simply as the alphabet. He held up a hand. 'But it's worth a go.'

I pulled a hat lower over my eyes to hide the victory in them. A wedge-tailed eagle appeared high in the sky. Another followed. I scooped Chippy onto my lap. 'Majestic,' Bob said, watching their aeronautics through narrowed eyes. 'You needn't worry about the dog. She's too heavy for them.'

'No point in taking risks. God, they're elegant. Not like the noisy infestations of clumsy white cockatoos at Pittwater.' We watched the great raptors in silence for a while, neither of us tempted to stir although the sun had travelled and beat hotly on us now.

'Remember when we married? No one could decide where we should live – your house or mine.'

'Yeah,' Bob said, chucking the dregs of his tea on the fire. 'I heard it was the talk of the bays for about a minute.' He kicked the fire drum with a booted foot. Red-hot coals collapsed into a heap. Levered himself out of his saggy camp chair to get another log from a tidy pile he'd chainsawed earlier. Swinging the splitter with such accuracy I asked him where he'd learned the art.

'Every country kid of my generation chopped the wood,' he said, as though it was a no-brainer. He chucked on a gnarly lump, like an elbow joint, building the fire-bed to cook dinner. 'And those cockatoos, they're tantrum-throwers but they make you laugh. So,' he said, sinking back into his chair, 'what was the collective opinion about where we should live after tying the knot?'

'We should sell both houses and build one together. You could carry me over the threshold, they said. Mind you, I was much thinner then.'

'Ah.'

'Took us a while to get around to it but the community knows best, eh?'

'Well, the community always has an opinion whether you're after one or not. And I was thinner then, too. What's for dinner?' he asked.

'A slab of rump steak. Three inches thick. We'll carve it London broil style, have the leftovers in sandwiches for lunch tomorrow.' As I spoke, the forty-strong herd of agisted steers came into sight. They ambled towards us in a slow shuffle, making soft ripping noises as they cropped. 'Sorry boys, too much information. Close your ears,' I murmured.

I got up and put Chippy on the chair. She sighed without waking. I moved down the hill to shoo them off. Childhood memories kicked in: Never let a steer get you in a corner. Never spook a herd. Never turn your back on an animal. Never try to outrun it. Step aside if it charges you. 'Get back,' I shouted, waving my arms about. 'Get back.' The rear-guard obediently spun and headed off at a trot. The baldy held his ground. About a dozen others, emboldened now, backed him up. The bolters slowed and stopped. Turned to see what their mates were doing. Regrouped. The herd came towards me. I lost my nerve in an instant. Walked backwards. Where was Bob? The cattle lowered their heads and kept grazing, shuffling forwards at a surprising pace. My stomach lurched. Cattle are so bloody big. I ran the last few metres to the ute.

In a few more minutes, the herd would amble or crash through the middle of our campsite. I started the engine and kangaroo-jumped forward, my hand holding down the horn. 'Get back, you bastards,' I shouted out the window. The herd spooked and turned. Only the baldy, with his stupid, stubborn, blank white face, held his ground. I kept hiccupping down the slope until the bumper bar was within a couple of inches of his nose. Hit the horn in short sharp blasts. We were smack in the throes of a Mexican stand-off. I held the horn down. He gave me a long, cold look then raised his boofy head, threw back his shoulders, and galloped off. From behind, the gleaming muscles of his black flanks rippling, he looked magnificent. Where was Bob?

I chucked a U-turn and went back up the hill. Bob stood at the campsite with Chippy in his arms. 'Helluva racket,' he said. 'You woke the dog.'

'Bastards wouldn't ride to orders. And that baldy's trouble. Thanks for helping out.'

'Knew you'd manage. There's a country girl buried inside you. Always has been.'

Girl? I kissed him hard and we dragged our camp chairs into the shifting shade. Bob tossed another piece of wood on the fire, disturbing the ashes. The smell of charcoal, achy and ancient, mingled with a puff of white smoke. The eagles had flown off and the sky was turning deep pink. Hillsides were lurid green, red and gold in the evening light. Soon, the sun would sink behind distant blue and violet hills stacked up against the horizon like frozen waves.

———

Looking back, they were heady, splendid days filled with the fecund scents of a wet spring with hints of the summer heat to come. Rain fell steadily and regularly. Grass grazed our knees. Freedom from the pressure of responsibility for my mother's wellbeing was like being relieved of a great weight. There were many quiet hours by the fire drum when I thought about the serendipity of one choice versus another, and marvelled over and over at the string of small miracles that had led to a point in time

I understood fully was sublime. But the outdoors was the real magic. As soon as the fire was lit, the camp chairs put out, the tent secured, I felt nothing dreadful could touch us here.

'In a perfect world,' Bob said thoughtfully, 'what would you like in a house?'

'To bring the outside in,' I replied without having to think.

———

During one of our camps, the former owner of our land roared in on his trail bike, stockwhip twirled around one shoulder, boots heavy with mud, battered hat on his head. 'Bob around?' he asked. The two of them had spoken on the phone but never met.

'Over there.' I pointed a long way off. 'Your cattle,' I added accusingly, 'they don't ride too well to orders. Tried to turn them back the other day. One of them, the baldy, dug in. Thought he might get nasty.'

'Nah. They're a quiet mob. Cattle are curious. That's all. Got any idea what you're going to do with the land?' He leaned back on the bike, ankles crossed, arms folded across his chest. Not unfriendly, but distant. Like the jury was still out on Bob and me.

'Not a clue. We're both novices and haven't got the faintest idea what we're about.' A grimace crossed his face, like he'd been struck suddenly with a crippling pain in the gut. He said not one word. Swung his leg over the bike. Took off towards Bob with a roar. I stood there like a complete git.

Too late, I remembered interviewing a nuggety young bloke who from the age of nine had farmed sheep and wheat through droughts, floods, freezes and heatwaves alongside his soldier settler dad. 'There's blood in every corner of this land. Dad's blood and mine,' he'd said. I was almost certainly standing in a pool of blood, sweat and tears. All that work, he was probably thinking, for a couple of dilettante townies to build a house with a nice view and play at farming while weeds, bushfires, rodents and every other rural pestilence ran rampant. I cringed with shame.

When he rounded up his Red Polls and drove them along the dirt road to their new home a few kilometres closer to town, the baldy behaved impeccably and it was a peaceful swap-over. There was clearly an art and skill to handling cattle, although when I talked to cheery Don at the organic fruit and vegetable shop in Wingham, he told me he'd once been put up a tree by a wild beast.

'Bull, was he?' I asked, trying to sound knowledgeable.

'Nah. Steer. Rounded up out of the bush by men on horses with nipping dogs to persuade the most cunning draft dodgers to fall into line.' He must have seen the naked alarm on my face. Quickly added: 'Cattle are raised differently these days. Handled nice and easy from the start. Members of the family, some of 'em.'

'Yeah, right!'

———

After every farm stay, the tension between my mother and me abated for a short time then, in the brief span of a beachside picnic lunch or restaurant lunch, once more intensified to fierce levels. I no longer excused her cruelties as thoughtlessness or poor attempts at wit. Now when she aimed her knife at me, I turned it straight back on her. She immediately took shelter in a transparent lie. 'I was only joking,' she'd say, over and over. As a result, silences stretched out between us but less blood was spilled in the confined capsule of the car.

As her world kept narrowing, her anxieties about minor details, more to do with her convenience than her wellbeing, seemed to increase. 'We're very short-staffed,' she said. 'And even so, they're trying to cut back everyone's hours. I didn't get bathed until ten o'clock this morning.' A hint of outrage in her tone.

Bathed? As though it was a spa pampering instead of a quick hose while she sat in a plastic invalid chair.

'Never mind,' I said, refusing to be drawn in.

'It's all going to pot, you know. I told Stefan about it. He was terribly worried for me. He offered to buy back my old unit.' I sat up at this.

'I thought Stefan was terribly ill.'

'Oh, he's much better. We've been lunching again. His daughter is quite wonderful to him. Makes a difference, having a daughter like that.'

'I'm sure it does. But even so, I doubt he'd buy your old unit, Esther. You must have misunderstood. Anyway, I told you at the start, there's no going back.'

'I didn't misunderstand anything. He has a house in the mountains where I can stay until it's all sorted out.'

'Don't be silly. You can't even pull up a side zipper without help.'

She continued as if I hadn't spoken: 'I went up there the other day. To my old unit. It's a wreck. Rubbish chucked all over the place. Terrible, what's happened to it.'

'It's still empty, Esther, but it's fine. Just the way you left it.'

'I've seen it with my own eyes! It's been trashed. Vandals, probably.' She sounded adamant, but I knew absolutely that she was now physically incapable of the distance from assisted living to her old unit and that management would clean up a mess left by vandals in a flash. Messes and vandals were bad for business in retirement villages offering security, safety and lifestyle for the over fifty-fives. Except the over fifty-fives aged, and after a couple of decades lifestyle didn't mean much. Only life mattered.

'Did someone take you there?' I asked, trying to get to the bottom of it.

'Nobody had to. I walked up on my own.'

'You sure?'

She nodded, impatient with me. So losing her mind or a secret agenda, I wondered. We sat silently. I made a mental note to call the manager of assisted living. Esther's medication needed adjustment or she was suffering from a low-grade urinary tract infection. I knew by then that they were the two most likely triggers for the sudden onset of a woolly, scatty and even hallucinogenic mind in the aged.

'He wants to marry me, you know,' she continued. And now I was sure her brain was crisscrossing, that she was confusing dreams with reality until neither made any sense. 'Can you believe it?' she said. 'Imagine anyone thinking about marriage at his age.' I raised my eyebrows. Hastily, she added: 'Or my age.' She played with her rings for a while.

'Those rings are too tight, Esther. One day I'm going to call in and all your fingers will be lying in a pile on the floor, rings still attached.

'Fiddlesticks.'

'You need to be careful. Those pain patches deaden senses. You sure you need them?'

A baleful look. 'Wait until you're my age. Then cast the first stone.'

'We both know, Esther, that you've always had a . . . taste . . . for painkillers. I am not being judgemental. I am not being critical. At your age, you're perfectly entitled to do as you please. I am just trying to point out that if you use drugs unwisely, there's a serious downside. The day may come when you're in desperate pain, and you'll need a dose that would kill a horse to have any effect.'

She thrust out her chin. Stubborn. 'I was a nurse, remember.'

'Nurse's aide,' I muttered.

After a long time, she said, 'If something happens, let me go. I've had a good life. A great life in the early days.'

'Hope you don't expect another wake,' I joked.

'Bury me next to Wally.' Wally was her Rottweiler. Even though pets were permitted at the Village, the rule didn't extend to Rottweilers. He moved in with us, and when he died of old age we buried him at Tarrangaua, near the chook pen. 'Don't put me next to your father. They shifted him about thirty years ago and I've no idea where he is now,' she added. She'd mentioned this before, so I knew to let that one slide into the atmosphere without remark.

'So you want to be cremated,' I said.

'Good god, no. Don't believe in it. The soul has to leave your body and it can't if it's burnt.'

'There's a law against burying bodies in backyards,' I responded. 'You'll have to have another think about all this and let me know.'

Our tone was jocular but it was a sad conversation. *Fifty years of escalating disappointments*, I thought, *resulting in having someone wash your backside and being buried alongside your dog.* I was knocked flat by the waste. Vowed to avoid a similar scenario at any cost. Wind picked up sand, spinning and twirling it upwards in red clouds until it disappeared into nothing. Like us, when it was all over. And I suddenly grasped that if my mother died before me, despite the uneasiness and even quiet fury that hovered over us at every meeting like smoke from a fire, I would grieve. Be lost and, for a long time, anchorless. So I told her in fumbling, grudging encouragement: 'You can't die. You're the source of my best material.'

She replied in a snippy voice coupled with one of her sly looks: 'The longer I live, the better *your* genes stack up. That's the real reason you're barracking for me.'

'Yeah,' I said. 'It's all about me. Hang in anyway, will you?'

That day, I handed her an éclair on a china plate with a linen napkin I'd brought along to pretend for a moment we were dining in style. She barely noticed. I sipped my coffee. Passed her the cappuccino.

'Leave the lid on,' I reminded her, as I did every time. 'Sip through the slit.'

'The girls tell me you and Bob are leaving Pittwater.'

Ah, I thought, *so that's what prompted the death discussion.*

'Where would they get that from?' I asked, genuinely surprised.

'Some story about you in the paper. You were asked if you'd ever leave Lovett Bay. You said you might.'

'We're not leaving Pittwater, Esther.'

I told her, then, about the farm. 'We have bought some land; we plan to build a simple, sustainable house that we will visit when the weather gets cold. But we belong in Pittwater. Always will.' Then, in a cunning but inspired confabulation worthy of my mother, I added: 'You're getting too old for us to leave for too long, so we've given up overseas holidays. We'll never be far away anymore if you need us.'

She smiled, smug. The look on her face suggested she deserved all this and more. Then she asked for her handbag. She rummaged and eventually removed an envelope, handed it to me with a flourish. 'Electricity bill,' she explained. I opened it. Somehow, in a one-room apartment not much bigger than a ship's cabin, in one month she had racked up a debt of nine hundred and seventy-eight dollars.

'You've got to be warm,' I said, 'but it does seem high. I might get someone to check the meter.'

'I have the windows open all the time, of course. Fresh air is very healthy.'

Later, Bob said, 'I'll bet she doesn't know how to work the heating remote control so she boils and opens the windows to cool down.'

———

A few days later, the Village manager told me Esther had set off the fire alarm in her unit at 2.50 am. 'She was making toast,' the manager explained. 'Why would she be making toast in the small hours of the morning?' I could think of a million reasons but I shrugged silently, knowing I would have to remove the toaster because the fire brigade fee for every false alarm, we were both informed, was seven hundred and fifty dollars, and this was already her second offence (if that was the right word).

'I'll have to confiscate the toaster, you know,' I told her.

'Don't you dare!'

'No choice. Sorry.'

'I'll buy another one,' she said defiantly.

'I can't help you if you won't help yourself.' And she backed off without firing another shot. To soften the blow, I added: 'I will bring it back in a couple of weeks. We just need to show that we're doing our best.'

'Yes,' she said.

We both understood that the toaster was gone forever.

14

EACH TIME WE SET OFF FROM PITTWATER for the farm, there was a great sense of excitement. The property was a blank canvas waiting to be transformed. On the four-hour drive we tossed ideas back and forth, energised by the whole project and the sense that our dreams might be realised. After we were clear about our aims, Bob suggested a chat and a site visit with a couple of Wingham architects who'd helped Michael work through complicated council regulations for the installation of the new brick kiln. They'd lived in a small town long enough for any transgressions – small or large – to surface, and the general consensus was that they were bold, clever and practical, understood the meaning of budgets and listened to clients. It was a place to start.

Russell Austin and Carolyn McFarland, a husband and wife team, suggested we take their all-wheel drive to the property. It was a grey day. A wafty drizzle dampened the ground. Out of town, and beyond a forest of shedding paperbarks growing in low-lying swampy land, green paddocks rolled out like endless carpet. It was impossible to conceive the possibility of drought, of grass so dry underfoot it broke with a snap, the green turned to dull yellow. Dust kicking up in clouds thick enough to blind you. First impressions were believed to be the constant norm. Change a cruel trick.

The men, Bob with short grey hair, Russell with black hair pulled into a ponytail, sat companionably in the front seat, talking quietly. In the back, Carolyn and I chatted about her children, our Pittwater life, where to find great coffee or a decent sandwich. At one point, she suggested a visit to her home to better understand their style to be sure it suited us. That way, we would all have a clear idea of direction. 'For your own sake, let's make it a day after the cleaner's been,' she said, smiling.

After all the heavy rain, the floodway was deep and running strong, the dirt road past the decrepit dairy shed rough with rocks, potholes and stony outcrops where the gravel had washed away. At our front gate, Bob jumped out, swung it open. The Great Hill was hatted with cloud. The drizzle threatened to ramp up a notch. Bob directed Russell through a pretty grove of gum trees, pointed out the turning on to a mushy red clay cutting that divided the Great Hill into two layers, like the filling of a cake.

At a subtle dip, the car skidded in a single, sweeping fishtail, leaving the front wheel on the passenger side and both back wheels hovering over the sludgy edge of the cutting. We froze in stunned silence. A small nudge and we'd all be somersaulted to the dam way below.

'I'm outta here,' I said, feeling strangely calm. I opened the door very carefully. Almost slid to the ground on wet grass and clay.

'Me, too,' Carolyn said with what sounded like relief. We women stood together on level ground.

Bob and Russell remained immobile inside the vehicle. Finally, Bob said, 'Sorry mate, you're stuffed.' He climbed out. After a minute, Russell followed. Safely on firm ground, we all stood in a line, staring at the stricken car. Our damp woollen sweaters gave off a pungent, agricultural smell not unlike the wet cow dung around our feet.

Russell smiled with a touch of irony. 'Guess all-wheel drive isn't quite the same as four-wheel drive,' he said.

Bob pulled out his mobile phone and called the brickworks. 'We need a tow, mate. Russell has skidded off the track.'

Rural life, I thought. *Get used to it.*

While we waited for help, Carolyn and I trekked through fog and mist to the top of the Great Hill, carefully dodging steaming piles of cow shit. I bent often to pull out weeds. 'Every little bit helps,' I said. Soon, Carolyn joined in. A puny effort but it gave us both a chance to pause and catch our breath, to gaze at country blurred by a soft grey haze.

'Shit!' I dragged a boot through the grass trying to clean it. 'Prolific blokes, aren't they?' I pointed at another pile so Carolyn could avoid it.

When we reached the summit, Carolyn gazed in awe. 'Beautiful,' she said. 'I can see why you fell in love with the place.'

'Bob and I think this is a great site. Are we mad?' I asked her.

She hesitated a fraction too long. 'It could be spectacular,' she said finally. 'It won't be easy, but the result will make it worth it.'

'Yeah. It's all good.' After a while, in the distance, we could see Michael's dark-blue ute travelling along the road. Carolyn and I descended in silence. It was more slippery and harder on the muscles than the ascent.

Michael quickly decided two utes would be better than one. He called Norm, who drives the truck and excavator at the brickworks. 'In a bit of bother, mate, can you get out here?'

After a while, Norm arrived in a battered white ute. Circling the car, hands on hips, he bent to look under the chassis, humming and hahhing. 'Made a pretty good job of it, mate,' he said. 'You were bloody lucky, if you want my opinion.'

Chains were attached. Engines revved. Hands waved to direct the turn of the steering wheel. Tyres spun. The car was even more perilously perched. 'Saw a bloke working his paddock not far from here,' Michael said. 'I'll drive over and see if he can lend a hand with his tractor.'

Carolyn and I looked at each other: 'Would you be going back to town after that?'

'Yep, ladies, if you'd like a lift.'

'Would we!' We brushed droplets of drizzle from our shoulders, jumped into his ute, slammed the doors and abandoned our husbands without a second thought.

—

Over coffee, I gave Carolyn a list of features I'd like to see included in a design. 'At Pittwater, we spend most of our time on the verandah,' I said firmly, 'so we'd like to factor in an equivalent in the new house. I love texture,' I added, pulling a magazine out of my handbag to show her photographs of a late-nineteenth-century, high-country cottage near the Victorian ski fields. Brick floors, rough slab walls, whole tree trunks as supporting beams, handmade tiles. Undeterred by the shocked silence, I kept on: 'I prefer old stuff – you know, sofas, chairs, tables, odds and ends. So a design that works with old stuff, if you can. Oh, and I really love brass taps and concrete sinks.' She gave me a funny look, a mixture of a frown and a wobbly smile. And it dawned on me that I was way out on an antiquated limb all by my time-frozen self. But I continued: 'When I turn on a shower, I want water – preferably hot – to fall down. None of those fancy wall sprays or automatic temperature settings I've read about. Oh, and I want a clothesline and bookshelves marked clearly on the plans. Ok?'

'No problem,' Carolyn said after a while.

'And a place for a chair. Not swish. Just comfortable. Where there's plenty of natural light to read a book.'

'Goes without saying.'

Later, I was told the architects referred to Bob as *reason*. I was known as *chaos*.

That night, when we were tucked into our camp beds, Bob told me that he and Russell paced almost every inch of the property while they waited for the tractor. 'Russell said the Great Hill is the most spectacular and it can be done.'

'But?' I prompted, because the expression on Bob's face meant there was more.

'He said that, generally, the tops of hills were considered to be sacred. We might want to think about that.'

—

Full of doubts, we drove back to Pittwater. It was at its sparkling best. Translucent blue water, soft sea breezes, the whiff of star jasmine on the night air to stir the senses. The Point was crammed with sunburnt tourists hoeing into pizza and icy cold beers after sightseeing trips on the *L. Duck*.

The revered but ancient *Curlew*, with its memsahib rear deck and wonky red, white and blue paintwork, had been decommissioned. It caused such universal grief in the community that the artists staged an exhibition of '*Curlew*' memories and moments to mark the end of an era. The new spick-and-span ferry, named for the *Curlew*'s much-loved driver, Lenny Duck, lacked the heart, history and abiding romance of the *Curlew*, but it was an efficient vessel and we all knew in time we'd get used to it, until one day it wrote its own history.

—

When the first rough sketches from the architects arrived, Bob took a couple of deep, steadying breaths and laid them on the table. He pointed at a courtyard area: 'Big enough for a couple of pot plants, that's all. And the front of the house is great . . . if you're into abseiling.' Without another word, he rolled up the printouts, tucking them under his arm. Grabbed his tea, went to his office and closed the door. Came looking for me just before dinner.

'It's all possible but we'd need to shift a lot of dirt. A lot,' he repeated for emphasis. 'It's a folly, isn't it?' I poured him a glass of red wine. A white for me. 'Like I said, it can be done. But we'd have to make a lot of compromises to avoid spending a fortune.'

I was struggling with disappointment at the same time as wondering (for the umpteenth boringly repetitious time) if we were both being reckless at a stage of life when caution was far more appropriate. 'We'd end up changing the shape of the hilltop, wouldn't we?' Bob nodded. 'Hilltops are sacred, according to Russell.' Bob nodded. 'We'd hate ourselves forever if we let our egos get in the way of common sense.' Another nod.

He spelled out the major problems: a switchback track on such a steep slope would always be vulnerable to storms. Maintaining it could send us broke. Supporting infrastructure – solar panels, water tanks, gardens, orchards and the shed – would have to be located at the foot of the hill. A gut-busting trek to fix any glitches. A single lapse in concentration on a night drive could end in disaster. Large trucks would damage the road. Very few, anyway, could handle the steep grade.

When it comes to making decisions, people generally fall into three categories: ditherers, doers and risk-takers. There were two types of risk-takers: go-for-broke and calculated. While we were both dreamers, neither of us was naïve or stupid enough to believe wishful thinking coupled with go-for-broke would win the day.

'I wouldn't be thrilled with the Bottom Hill,' I said, returning to my stool at the kitchen bench. 'All those glorious views wasted. A bit ordinary, don't you think?'

'There's another option – one Carolyn was keen on but that I discounted because it was so close to the boundary of the adjoining property.'

'Where exactly?' I asked.

'Couple of hundred yards from our campsite. Not quite as spectacular. Still pretty good.'

'Let's head up tomorrow and take a look. And I've been researching a name. How about Benbulla? It means high, quiet hill. Tarrangaua is said to mean high, rough hill, so there's a sort of symmetry, don't you think?'

'Benbulla,' Bob said, rolling the word around in his mouth. 'Benbulla. Yeah, That'll do.'

———

After every camp, we dismantled the site. Returned to Pittwater with the ute overflowing: tent, tent poles, tables, camp chairs, pots, pans, plates, cutlery, camp stretchers, bedding and non-perishable supplies. Even a small Turkish kilim I insisted on hauling along to grace the tent floor, as though we were bona fide nomads. The packing and unpacking was hard physical work, and when it rained we arrived home with a load of sodden chattels stinking of wood smoke and ripe earth. Us too. Not that we cared until Toby stepped back from a warm 'welcome home' with a wrinkled nose and a look of disgust on his face. 'Jeez, you been sleepin' in a cattle yard, mate?'

Soon after, Bob arranged to leave the heaviest gear at the brickworks but we didn't want to wear out our welcome. 'We need a shed!' Bob declared.

'Of course we do,' I replied without missing a beat.

He bought a prefabricated, corrugated iron shed from the new big hardware store on the outskirts of Taree that was slowly killing all the small, family-run hardware shops. 'Bad for country towns such as Wingham. Local money leaving the district,' I lamented. And yet, on the flip side, every bored, retired handyman or back-buggered builder within commuting distance had enthusiastically reached for a green apron without hesitation. The shed kit weighed a tonne but, using a hastily invented pulley system, we managed to hoist it into the ute, tie it down and set off.

At the boggy spot on the Bottom Hill, the back wheels skidded. I braced against the big flip that would land us upside down. We came to a slow, slippery, safe standstill but I wanted to vomit. I wanted to get out of the car and walk back to Pittwater.

'How about a cuppa before we unload?' Bob said.

'How about a double brandy?' I replied.

He looked at me, puzzled. 'What's wrong?'

I sighed. 'Get the fire going. I'll fill the billy.'

Bob didn't have the right tools. There wasn't even a flat, square area to line up the corners. The weather was hot – sunstroke heat if you spent too long in it. He laid out the panels on the grass. Read the instructions. 'The engineering that's gone into this is amazing,' he said. 'It's a simple but tough little system. Impressive.' Humming off-key, he began to put it together.

After a while, there was a fair bit of swearing and cursing. 'Can I help?' I called out.

'I'll let you know when I need you.'

'Right.' I went back to my book, settled deeper into the camp chair under the shade of a gum tree. Chippy dozed peacefully beside me.

'You got a minute?' Bob called.

'On my way.'

'Need you to hold the panels straight while I get the screws in. Then we'll call it a day. Finish in an hour or two tomorrow.'

'Our own shed. How exciting,' I said, patting him on the back in congratulation.

'No flies around to make the job harder than it is, at least,' he said. 'Heat and cow shit. A dream mix for flies. Thought we'd be infested by now. Right,' he said, handing me a plastic bag of screws. 'Let's go.'

Late the following morning, the roof was on and the shed stood upright. It was a surprisingly handsome building but so light a moderate wind would shift it or a gale would dump it miles away in a stranger's paddock. Bob thought for a while. Walked off to the ute. Grabbed a fistful of leftover tent pegs and some fencing wire he'd bought to do a couple of repairs. Then he anchored the four corners to the ground in a feat of engineering that would withstand a cyclone. Our first structure on our new land. It exuded commitment and permanence.

With a shock I realised that, despite my passion for the project, I'd mentally engraved an escape clause somewhere deep in my psyche that went like this: 'If we can't cope with the folly/ experiment/lunacy/challenge before we've gone beyond the tent, we can always sell.' But we'd make a mark now. Not a subtle nail in a tree trunk to knot guy ropes or a scratch in the ground to mark the days gone by, but a statement loud and clear. A solid structure. A clean-lined, silver, corrugated shed sitting proudly on the Home Hill for all to see. In hindsight, it was an epic moment. There would be – could be – no going back. Here was the evidence. And all because of a throwaway line about Cooktown. *Be careful of what you wish for,* my father would have said. My mother, who'd always had a healthy fear of God, would have inserted *pray* instead of *wish*.

———

I told my mother stories about our progress at the farm, struggling to keep our lunch dates on a friendly footing. She listened for a minute or two, then turned the conversation back to her own world, as if nothing beyond her security door was real to her. The same themes recurred without fail. The staff (terrible shortages). The carer (more than a daughter to her). Her terrible double vision. And how much everyone loved her.

'Do you remember,' I said to my mother, trying to introduce a new vein, 'when you taught John and me to play word games on long trips? Listen to the sound of them, you instructed us, don't worry about the meaning, pick the most beautiful sounding words in the world.' I have returned to this story many times in our lives. I'm not sure why.

'Did I?'

'I immediately shouted out that "beautiful" was my word. Even as I said it, I understood it was ugly and clunky. No, no, I said quickly, not beautiful. "Lake". "Lake" is my word! I think that was the moment I fell in love with language. Way back then.'

'You were lucky. You had brains. I never did.'

'You're rat-cunning, though.' It was out before I had time to register that my mother had just paid me one of the few genuine compliments I could remember and that *rat-cunning,* meant as a simple fact, could be construed as cruel.

'Oh, yes,' she admitted, unoffended. 'Not that it's ever done me any good.'

Her focus shifted to Christmas: the food, the decorations, where she would sleep. 'It will all happen,' I told her. 'Have you ever been without a bed yet?'

'I don't want to be a bother.'

'You're no bother.'

'I wouldn't want to be one of those old ladies who expect too much.'

'Of course not.'

'I know when I'm well off.'

'Oh for god's sake, Esther. We go through this every year. Same script, same emotional rigmarole. I will pick you up on Christmas Eve at lunchtime. As usual. Bob will meet us at commuter dock in the big tinny. As usual. We'll take it slowly. As usual. Drive you up the hill in the truck. As usual. Bob's even made a set of steps so you can climb into the cab more easily. You will have the spare room. As usual. Ok?'

'How long will I be staying?'

'We always take you back to the Village the day after Boxing Day. Any problems?'

'I won't have to clean the silver, will I? I don't think I'm up to it anymore.'

I sighed. 'The silver's been cleaned. You're off the hook.'

'So I've been fired, have I?'

Cut her some slack, I thought. *She's old.* 'It wouldn't feel like Christmas if you weren't there, Esther. Everyone says so. It's the first question they ask when they're invited to lunch. "Will Esther be there? How is the old girl?"'

Esther harrumphed. 'Not sure I like the *old girl* bit.' She fiddled with her hair, added chirpily: 'I think I'm doing quite well. At least everyone at the Village tells me I am. Do I really do this every year?'

'Without fail.' I observed her closely. Did she not notice that her feet had taken on a sliding shuffle that made a noise like rustling paper? How fluid collected at her ankles until her flesh folded over her shoes? How the physical slide was gathering momentum daily? Perhaps, like me, she'd given up looking too closely in mirrors, the shock of a total stranger staring back too much to bear. And yet . . . she made an effort.

'Do I look alright?' she asked each time I collected her for an outing.

'Terrific,' I replied automatically. Even managing to get in first occasionally: 'You look fabulous today, Esther.' She'd fluff up, wiggle her hips. Attention and admiration. Her drugs of choice from the very beginning.

When she was a child, she told me once that her parents gave her a doll for Christmas when she'd asked for an axe. She was four years old and her twin sisters, June and Isabelle, had just been born. Esther threw a tantrum. 'I snapped off the doll's head. Then I went outside onto the street, which was a very, very busy thoroughfare, and danced for pennies. I wanted the money, but really, I think I liked the attention more. My parents were horrified but I didn't care. Actually, I did quite well until they carted me away.' She would always be the little toe-tapper on the pavement dancing for pennies. Keeping up appearances.

'Some of those old girls at the Village,' she said, 'they're a bit slack with their personal hygiene.'

'What do you mean?' I asked.

'Smelly. Don't change their underwear often enough.'

'That's cruel, Esther.'

'I'm only telling the truth,' she said airily.

'You've got a stain on your shirt,' I responded. Her eyes blackened, shooting daggers. 'You can dish it out, Esther, but you can't take it. For a start, those old girls are younger than you. Secondly, they don't smell. And thirdly, compassion never goes astray. Oh, and by the way, your hem is down at the back.'

She didn't miss a beat. 'The laundry service at the Village is terrible. Rough as guts. I'll have a word to the staff.' Her tone was regal. As though she personally footed the bill for the stream of people that kept people like my mother functioning. 'Where are we going for lunch?' she asked, quickly changing the subject.

'Picnic in the car,' I said. 'You wouldn't want to be seen with that stain on your shirt, would you?' And underlying the banter, the deep, dark fear that this was also my future. That no amount of wafty dreaming or dabbling in new pursuits would serve to resist the inevitability of decline.

In Mona Vale, I parked in the shadiest spot I could find and dashed around, picking up supplies. It was a stinking hot day. The kind that felt like a flaying and made you worry that removing food from the fridge for long enough to make a sandwich could end in food poisoning.

'Yo, Susan?' I spun around.

'Lisa!'

'How're you doing? All good?'

'Great.'

'Now, tell me what I can make to bring to Christmas dinner?'

And we chatted, the two of us, for a few minutes. Perhaps more. I lost track. Then suddenly, 'Oh, Jesus. I left Esther in the car. She'll be cooked by now.' I bolted.

'A cake,' Lisa called after me, 'I'll make a cake.' I raised an arm in agreement.

Esther's head was thrown back against the seat. Her eyes were closed. *Oh shit*, I thought, *I've killed her*. Sick with fear, I pulled open the door. She opened one eye. 'What took you so long?' she asked.

I let go of a breath I didn't know I'd been holding. 'Lisa.' She sat up, both eyes open, alert now and excited.

'Is she here? Is she with you?'

'Nope. She had to dash.'

'Oh.'

'Just you and me, I'm afraid. So I'll have to do.' She didn't respond.

We were silent while young kids played on the beach making sandcastles, and surfers hung a long way offshore, hoping for a swell. Way out on the horizon, two yachts glided under sail.

Esther spoke: 'You always thought I was disappointed in you because you weren't beautiful. But you always had such *character*.'

'Well, character lasts much longer than beauty.' The arrow missed her completely.

'People told me I was beautiful, of course, although I never thought so.'

I bit into my pie, licked tomato sauce from my fingers. *What does she want from me?* I thought. *An endless stream of compliments to keep her ego propped?* 'You look very good for your age,' I managed. 'Good hair, good skin. You're doing well.'

She lifted a hand to her head, patted her hair, pushing it around a little to bring out the curl. The rings on her fingers catching the light. 'One of the nurses comes into my room and flops into a chair. He sleeps for about ten minutes. He asked me yesterday if I thought he was handsome. Then took a handful of chocolates and left.'

'Is he? Handsome?'

'No. He's quite fat.'

'Does he bother you?'

'I'm not sure what he's after.'

Chocolates, of course. What else? I glanced at her sideways. 'I'll talk to the manager and ask her to have a word with him. He shouldn't be sleeping in your room. Might start a scandal.'

'At my age?' she said, but she looked pleased at the thought.

Oh god, she thinks he's infatuated with her. I was suddenly curious. 'Did you ever have any affairs when you were married to Dad?'

She shook her head then admitted with a sheepish expression. 'Well, one. On that trip to London. I fell hard. He was an actor. Very good-looking. Never told your father, but I think he guessed. Probably dead by now. He knew I was married. It didn't seem to bother him.'

It was on the tip of my tongue to point out that it didn't seem to bother her, either, but remembering my own track record I held back. My father, I thought, might not have said a lot, but even after he'd stared into the bottom of several beer bottles he didn't miss much. 'Why do you think Dad guessed?'

'There was no one to meet me at the airport when I got home. I waited and waited then caught a cab. He'd gone to the races with your brother. Said he wasn't sure I intended to return at all. I might not have, either, if he hadn't announced he wouldn't send any more money.' We were silent for a while. I gathered the rubbish from lunch and went to place it in the garbage cans near the public toilets. Scraps of memory hovered at the edge of my mind, leading to questions I knew would and could never be answered. I reminded myself that parents were human, too.

—

On Christmas Eve, I collected Esther, her huge suitcase, various carry bags, her walker, and checked she had her medications. She'd forgotten her pills one year but didn't tell us until, by day three, she was very wonky and forced to admit she'd left them behind.

'Got your keys?' I asked. She'd forgotten those once, too. For some reason I can't remember, she'd insisted on going back to the Village after lunch and two guests kindly agreed to drop her off. The entire Village was closed for the holiday. It took an hour to find a security guard to open her unit.

'Please, never ask me to do that again,' pleaded the guest, only a decade younger than Esther. Today, though, my mother nodded.

'Show me,' I said suspiciously. She pointed at her walker where they were tied on to the handlebars with a piece of Christmas tinsel. Put her thumb to her nose and wiggled her fingers at me. I phoned Bob to tell him we were on our way.

At commuter dock, the boat was tied tight so it didn't rock. Bob held Esther's left arm, I went to hold her right. 'Don't touch it!' she yelled. 'It's my bad arm.'

'We need to hold you steady,' I said. She batted me away. I rolled my eyes, thinking unhelpful thoughts such as, *If you drown or get squashed to death between the pontoon and the boat, it's your own fault.*

'Get her left arm,' Bob said, stepping into the tinny. 'Esther, take a step. Let yourself go. I'll catch you.' He opened his arms wide. *Oh Jesus*, I thought. *She'll knock him flat. They'll both be dead.*

'Ooh, it's a long time since I've fallen into a man's arms,' Esther cooed, batting her eyelashes, smiling coquettishly.

'Watch what you're doing,' Bob ordered, ignoring the flirt.

We crossed blue water at a royal barge pace. Smoothly, comfortably. For no reason any of us could fathom, Esther winced.

'Not far to go now,' Bob said reassuringly.

I added: 'If we go any slower, Esther, the tide will take us back the way we came.' She winced again. Louder this time. Followed up with a groan. 'If this is beyond you, you should have told us,' I said, unable, as always, to separate reality from theatrics.

She made an obvious effort, grimacing but stoic. 'I can do anything,' she said in a way that was meant to win fans but was completely unrealistic. We caught a bow wave from a passing tinny. Water sloshed at our feet. The walker rolled back and forth as if alive. We passed the shallow water marker and rounded Rocky Point. Home stretch. Everyone still breathing.

Bob took his phone out of his pocket and called Michael at the boatshed. Asked him to stand by. 'We might need a chair to lift her out,' he explained.

'I'm sorry,' Esther said in a small voice.

'It's all good,' I said, gritting my teeth.

'We're nearly there,' Bob said. Up ahead, the escarpment shone in the noonday heat. The shallow estuary that meets the fresh-waters that tumble from a creek called Salvation glowed gold.

Pleasure wafted across Esther's face, easing lines, erasing a decade. 'So beautiful,' she murmured. She loosened her grip on the boat. 'It's really Christmas now.' Added: 'I'm doing alright.'

'You're game,' I said, grudgingly, 'I'll give you that.'

Michael waved. Bob dropped into neutral and coasted along-side the pontoon. Michael tied us on tightly. No gaps. Death traps for the frail and unwary. I hefted the suitcase. The walker. We all turned to Esther, still glued to her seat.

'Right,' Bob said. 'Let's get you on the truck and up the hill. Think we could all do with a cup of tea.' Half-dragging, half-supporting, we three coaxed her upright.

'Not that arm, not that arm,' she ordered, although no one went near it. Torn muscle or ligament, a doctor had explained. At Esther's age, they rarely mended properly. Another boat slid past. Another bow wave. The pontoon rocked. Esther's walker rolled. Went over the side with a splash. Webster packs of pills, her handbag, make-up, hairbrush, floated out of reach in a nanosecond. A few pieces of paper. Bills, probably.

'Oy! Tristan. Larnce. Get the pills!' I yelled.

At the next jetty along, the boatshed boys dropped tools. Sussed the current, judged the drift. Kneeled in position, ready to scoop. 'Don't worry about anything else, just get the pills!' I pleaded. Blood pressure regulators, heart steadiers, painkillers, a chalky balm for a whisky-worn oesophagus so she could eat comfortably. 'And grab the walker before it sinks! Her keys are tied to it.'

We steered Esther up the jetty. Bob leading and gripping a wrist, me with a hand on each of her buttocks, pushing. Safely onshore, she came to life and gaily called across the water: 'Don't lose my handbag!' The boys, laughing, held up their trophies. She grinned. Gave a regal wave. They cheered. My mother gave a little bob. Loving every second.

When she was settled in a cane chair on the verandah, we handed her a recovery cuppa and flopped down next to her. 'I'm doing alright,' she said again. Her hand knocked the mug. Hot tea rolled along the table and into her lap.

'Oh, bugger,' I said, leaping to my feet. 'Are you burnt?'

'No.'

'Are you sure?'

'It doesn't hurt.'

———

On Christmas Day, Esther hit the whisky and scoffed the turkey skin. She paid a mortifying price. 'This will be my last Christmas here,' she said, embarrassed.

'You'll recover and be back next year,' I responded, helping her into bed.

'No. Never again. I'm quite happy in my own little box.'

'Let's see how you feel in a year, eh?'

'Oh, I know how I'll feel. You won't have to worry about me. Quite a few people stay in the Village for Christmas.'

'You'll feel better in the morning. Have you taken your pills? Good. What's that mark on your leg?'

'A burn.'

'The tea? It burned you? Why didn't you say something?'

'I didn't want to make a fuss.'

'Do you need some ointment?'

'You forget, I was a nurse once. I'm fine.'

'I'll get some antiseptic.'

'I don't need anything. It's fine.'

'Ok. It's up to you. And you were a nurse's aide.' I closed the door. Made for the kitchen where I poured a large glass of white wine. Thirty-six minutes till the dishwasher cycle ended. One more load and the detritus of fourteen festive people would be sparkling clean and packed away.

I joined Bob, his daughter Meg, her handsome border collie, Tali, and her partner, Alan, on the verandah. 'Esther's got a terrible burn from the tea. No wonder she hit the whisky.'

'I can clean up after her in future,' Meg said kindly. 'That sort of stuff doesn't bother me.'

'My mother. My duty. But thank you. God, it was a nasty burn. I would've screamed like a stuck pig if it had happened to me.'

'We always knew she was tough,' Bob said with a hint of admiration.

'It's so weird,' I said. 'She skates over the big stuff and gets bogged down by the inconsequential. No wonder I never know whether to call a psychiatrist or an ambulance.' It was the analgesic patches, though, that blunted the pain. But I didn't work that out for a long while.

The day after Boxing Day we returned Esther to the retirement village with a bag full of sliced ham, enough plum pudding to hold a party and a bottle of whisky for medicinal purposes only. Then we set off in sparkling sunshine to show Meg, Alan and the dog the new property.

15

Bob and I have the luxury of travelling in retired-person time – weekdays and non-school holidays. Nothing could have prepared us for the horror of the F3 – a horrendously claustrophobic crawl of caravans, trailers, fishing boats, motor homes and small cars packed to the rafters with doonas, pillows, loose clothing and swinging soft toys.

'Thought the big exodus happened on Boxing Day,' I muttered, tapping the steering wheel impatiently. In the back seat, Chippy picked up the vibe and, looking for reassurance, made umpteen attempts to jump into the front seat. 'No! In your bed. Now!' Hard words that only made her more restless. In the passenger seat, Bob settled the debate by letting her sit on his lap. 'Good doggie,' I said, by way of an apology.

We cranked up the air-conditioning to beat back the heat coming through the side windows and slid along in minuscule increments. The urge to throw a brick at something was almost irresistible. We even had the brick. It was deep purple with more blue than red in it. Bob was experimenting at the brick-works, trying to find a unique product that might kickstart a business struggling in the aftermath of the global financial meltdown.

At Newcastle the cavalcade came to a grinding halt. 'We're never doing this trip at this time of the year again. Agreed?'

'Ok, ok,' I muttered. 'Some things don't need to be spelled out.'

We'd long ago stopped trying to keep Meg and Alan's car in our sights. They were out there somewhere in the stop-start mass of red-faced, foaming-mouthed holiday-makers. Alan, a safe driver, was behind the wheel. We trusted him implicitly.

We finally crossed the bridge over the Hunter River, the official halfway mark. There was a slight pick-up in traffic speed. 'I could murder a cup of tea,' I mumbled. Bob, who made mental adjustments to current conditions and simply coped, didn't answer. Why think about tea if there wasn't a hope in hell? Soon we hit our top speed for the day. Sixty. It felt like we were flying.

About twenty-five kilometres south of Bulahdelah, a holiday destination where houseboats beaded pristine waterways and the fishing and birdlife were said to be extravagant, we slammed on the brakes. Ahead stretched a serpentine parking lot. 'Oh, lordy. Check out the portaloos lined up on the side of the road,' I said. 'Makes you wonder if we'll be here for the night.'

Just then, the mobile rang. 'We're ok,' Meg said straight off, her voice loud and clear through Bluetooth, sending us both into instant panic. 'Nobody's hurt,' she added. 'We're just going to be delayed a while.'

At barely a crawl, they'd rear-ended a car on the Sydney side of the Hunter River, near Newcastle, slightly dinging the bumper. 'We could've dealt with it all in five minutes,' Meg explained, 'but the woman is hysterical. She reckons we've broken her best Chrissie present and wants the cops to make a report for insurance. 'So it's going to take a while for them to get here unless they come by boat.'

I hoicked myself back from the kind of superstitious cesspit for which I condemned my mother and locked in the spin: nobody died. It's all good. We arranged to meet in the main street of Wingham. Then, as if there was a drum beating up obstacles, the sky ahead appeared heavy and grey.

'Nothing like camping in the rain to separate the men from the boys,' I said, trying to sound cheery. I glanced at Bob. He had that haunted look he gets when events are spiralling beyond control.

We slipped into a deserted Wingham just after closing time. Argued about whether one of us should head off to the property to erect at least one tent and light a campfire before the heavens opened. 'Let's stick to the plan,' Bob insisted. His standard rule.

A few years earlier, we'd landed at a chaotic Heathrow after a full-blown terrorist scare that had virtually shut down the airport. When we'd finally cleared passport control I murmured something about staying away from the Underground. 'Stick to the plan,' he'd said. He was right then – cabs were caught in gridlock for hours, the fare would've been a fortune and we arrived safely anyway – so I figured he was probably right now.

We settled down to wait. When it was almost dark, Meg and Alan pulled up alongside. 'We stopped to give Tali a walk and grabbed a hamburger,' Meg said. Bob glanced at Alan, who shrugged in a way that indicated he rode to orders for the sake of peace.

'We love our dogs,' I said, trying not to sound cranky.

———

The air smelled tinny. In the distance, black clouds were heaped on the horizon. Racing to beat the rain, we unpacked our tent from the shed, laid it flat, hammered in pegs, raised the tent pole, tied down guy ropes. A few minutes' work. We were well drilled by now. A short distance away, Alan was struggling with one of those fancy new camping systems that included separate living spaces. Meg pushed him out of the way. Took over. Bob built a fire in the drum. I hauled equipment from the shed to set up the kitchen – table, chopping boards, bowls, knives, enamel plates and cutlery on an oilskin cloth printed with grapes, eggplants and onions. Meg let out a scream. Stamped the ground angrily. 'Bull ant's nest,' Alan came over to report. She threw a flip-flop at him. He ducked expertly. She threaded a final rod and their tent was solid. Came over to hold her hands out to the fire. Her feet were a mass of red blotches. A gust of wind hit the tents with a noise like a whip cracking. A few random golf-ball-sized drops of rain dropped from the sky. Five minutes later, rain fell in thick ropes. We huddled under an inadequate awning, crammed up against each other, leaning inwards to escape the worst. It was awful. Not even the brief advent of a brilliant rainbow could dull our dismay.

'Funny how in retrospect we remember shocker experiences with clarity and even fondness,' I said at one point. 'Perfect holidays are forgotten in a flash.' I gave a funny, cackly sort of laugh I didn't recognise as my own.

We returned to staring into the fire drum where, under an umbrella, Bob continued cooking T-bones as if it were just another glorious day in paradise. Wet, frazzled and on the verge of becoming uncivilised, he handed each of us a plate.

'Hang on a sec,' he said, making a dash for the ute and diving into the back seat. Seconds later, he reappeared holding a bottle of wine. 'Great moments like these should be acknowledged with a suitable vintage.' And he held aloft a bottle of Penfolds Grange in dripping triumph. 'To the new house,' he said. 'And family.' Let the rain come down. Let the wind blow. Let wet dogs curl on our sleeping bags. Let the fire burn hot and long into a wet black night. 'Wouldn't be dead for quids, would you?' Bob said, grinning, his face slick with water, drops falling from the tip of his chin.

THE HOUSE ON THE HILL

The following day – and primarily to thumb my nose at another of my mother's superstitions – I cut my fingernails on a Friday. Then I wandered off into squelchy bush in search of privacy. An eye out for snakes and goannas. And meat ants that sneak up on you with a nip that sears like a jab from a white-hot poker. The scent of eucalypts clung to the humidity. Every breath felt like a spring clean.

Soon after, Meg told us she was pregnant with her first child.

—

The storms abated and the skies shone bright and blue the moment we broke camp and set off for Pittwater. A few days later, we said farewell to Meg, Alan and Tali and settled into familiar routines, waiting for new drawings from the architects without feeling impatient. The holiday season had slowed us. I spent soporific afternoons on the bed on the verandah with a good book. Falling asleep occasionally. Waking when Bob rounded the corner with a cup of tea and a slice of Lisa's Christmas cake.

Lisa is the baking queen of the bays. Each year she takes out first prize (there's no prize, of course, beyond recognition and a slap on the back) in a contest amongst a few passionate offshore cooks who gather to share recipes and tips. It's an excuse, really, to get together over a few glasses of champagne enhanced by delicious cake, which we're obliged to eat because we're all judges. By the end, we are loaded with sugar, fizzing with bubbles and feeling no pain.

It is worth noting, I think, that some people are gifted cake-makers. Lisa is one of them. If each of the fifteen cooks precisely followed her winning recipes, her cake would still taste different, better. I asked her the secret one year.

'A strong arm,' she said, grinning.

'Nah, there's a trick. There has to be.'

She laughed. 'Good ingredients, Susan. Only the best. Makes all the difference.' But that's one of the characteristics of people with unique skills – because it's easy for them, they think it must be just as easy for everyone else.

Towards the end of January, my mother's nagging about double vision finally wore me out. Even though I was certain it was an act, I took her to an eye specialist to end the debate once and for all. When her name was called, I stood up. 'I'm coming in with you,' I said. She gave me a warning look, which I ignored. 'If I don't understand what's going on, how can I help?' She put a thumb to her nose, in a way I was becoming very familiar with, and waggled her fingers.

The specialist, a slight man with a kind manner and gentle hands, tilted Esther's face one way and then the other. 'You're eyes are pretty good. The first signs of cataracts, but considering your age, that's remarkable.'

'Oh, yes,' Esther replied, 'I have wonderful sight and I've learned to live with double vision.'

He frowned. Went through the motions again. 'Double vision, you say?'

'Yes, it's quite bad.'

'Well, let's do all the tests, shall we?' he said, clearly bamboozled. 'Did you bring your glasses?'

Esther shook her head. 'I never wear them, so I didn't think there was much point.'

I rolled my eyes. 'I think I'll wait outside, if you don't mind.'

The specialist called me back when all the tests were done. I took a seat, crossed my legs and listened intently: day surgery to remove the cataracts. New lenses on both eyes, but done one at a time. It would solve the problem of her refusing to wear glasses. Is she on blood thinner medication? Yes, I said. Tell her to stop taking it a week before surgery. I turned to my mother: 'Tell the nurse at the Village to stop giving you blood thinners a week before surgery. Do you understand?' She nodded. I made a mental note to check she'd followed through. We all stood to go. He shook my hand, patted my mother's shoulder. We exited his austere office. The receptionist wrote out the upcoming appointments. Handed the card to my mother. I asked her to write another card for me. Then Esther latched on to her walker, and we took off for the basement car park.

'He treated me as though I wasn't there,' she said, sounding grumpy.

'Did you make a joke of all his questions?' I asked.

'Well, it was pretty boring stuff. I thought I might liven things up.'

'Right.'

'He didn't even want to know about seeing double. Never mentioned it.'

'Maybe it's because it's all in your mind.'

She stopped short like I'd slammed a door in her face. Closed her eyes as though she was in pain and heaved a deep sigh: 'I know what's real and not real. And you wouldn't have a clue.'

'Right.'

A week later I called her to say I'd been unable to get hold of the nurse to halt her blood thinners. Had she mentioned it? If not, could she please give the instructions when her morning pills were delivered. Otherwise, we'd have to delay surgery.

'I've already done it,' she snapped.

Right.

A week after that, the operation was complicated by excessive bleeding. 'We managed,' explained the surgeon, 'but it would have been a lot easier if she'd stopped taking her medication.'

'Pish tush,' Esther said.

'Do you have any idea how dangerous it is to ignore instructions?' I asked angrily.

'Rubbish. It all worked out.' Outside the building, she looked at a new world. 'The colours,' she said, 'are quite spectacular. And everything looks so sharp.'

'If you'd worn your glasses for the last ten years, it would have been just as good.'

'They didn't really suit me, you know. And when I put them on, I felt like my nose was being nibbled.'

'You get used to them. But not if you don't wear them.'

We finished the trip in silence. I took her back to her apartment, made her a cup of tea. Asked if she needed anything else.

'Go on. Off you go, I know you're busy,' she said in a tone full of blame.

'Right. I'll see you in two weeks for eye number two.' I left to find the nurse. No mistakes this time.

—

'The second operation wasn't as good as the first,' Esther said. 'The colours aren't as bright anymore. And I'm still seeing double.'

I debated arguing with her and then gave in. 'Well, you've managed perfectly well for years. All you have to do is go on in the same old way and you'll be fine.'

She grunted. 'At least you believe me now. I don't tell lies. They come back to bite you on the bottom.'

We were locked in the car, having lunch, and I could feel a loop about double vision building. To break it, I asked the first question that popped into my head: 'How did you meet Dad?'

'Why?'

'It's not an inquisition. I'm curious, that's all.' Outside, waves lapped at the shore. A yacht the size of a dinghy in the distance scudded along the horizon. Esther gave me a suspicious look. 'How are the oysters?' I asked.

'Pacifics are better than Sydney rocks.'

'Ok, I'll get them next time.'

'And only a dozen. I'm not young anymore. I can't eat like I used to.'

'I know the feeling.'

'You could afford to lose some weight. Quite a lot –'

'So tell me about you and Dad. What was he like when he was young?' I asked, because so many of my memories are riveted to the drink instead of the man.

'I married him on the rebound. A mistake, of course.'

'Cousin Jayne said he was a big softie and he adored you,' I said.

'Oh, he loved me alright. But he loved a drink even more, and I've never been good at sharing.'

'On the rebound, you say. Rebound from whom?'

She told me stories that I'd heard before but without much detail. She was eighteen years old and, along with eight thousand other young women, joined the Australian Army Medical Women's Service as a nurse's aide. 'When I was interviewed for the job, the matron told me I'd never be accepted because I was too attractive,' Esther recalled. 'I said, "Matron, I am not, and have never been, flirtatious." God forgive me. But I got in anyway.'

She arrived in Darwin six days after the Japanese dropped their bombs. She had a whale of a time. So good that when her twin sisters told her they were joining the army as well, Esther wrote to her mother that life was too rough for such young, impressionable girls. 'The twins never forgave me.' The real reason she wanted them out of the way was because she was involved in an affair.

Here, Esther adopted a light tone, as though what she was saying was of no real consequence. 'He was a major, not just an enlisted man.' *In other words, he had class.* 'He was also married.' She paused. Her voice dropped to a whisper. 'I became pregnant.' Silence, thick and heavy, swirled in the car. 'All those army doctors and not one of them would give me an abortion,' she said bitterly.

'What happened?' I asked.

'I told the matron who told the commander in charge. He asked me for the man's name. John Brown, I said. That's what I called him. Not his real name.'

'Did you know his real name?'

''Course I did. It was a game we played.'

Barely eighteen years old and suckered in, I thought, feeling a wave of sympathy. 'What happened next?' I asked.

'I was given personal leave. Mum arranged everything. I was petrified, of course. A couple of days after the abortion, I received a note. *This is going nowhere*, it said. The cruelty of the man. One line. Not even a signature.'

'What did you do?'

'I got on with it, of course. What else could I do?'

'Did you ever tell Dad?'

'Not about the abortion, but I told him he wasn't the first when he asked me to marry him. Didn't want him to throw it in my face afterwards. Men do that, you know.'

'What did Dad say?'

'Thanked me for telling him, and then said we could now put it behind us once and for all. He was a wonderful man, in many ways. I just never realised until it was too late.'

We were silent for a while. Both of us, I guessed, surprised by a rare closeness.

Without being aware of it, my voice softened. 'Why do you think Dad drank so much?'

'He was ashamed. He never served in battle. Felt he hadn't done his duty. People thought like that in those days. Bit different now.'

'So you met him on the rebound after the Darwin affair ended?'

My mother shifted in the car seat a little, settling deeper. Our coffees remained untouched on the dash. Growing cold.

'No. By then I was in love with someone else. His name was Noel and he was a slipper salesman in civilian life. Not good enough for me, of course, but he was incredibly handsome. One of the most beautiful men I'd ever laid eyes on. I was working night shift on the switchboard and spent my time writing long, romantic letters to him. Pinned his photo on the noticeboard. Your father, in full uniform, used to stride past the barracks, stick his head in the window and shout, "Hello, Blondie." After I agreed to go out with him, he ripped up that photo. Then, on our first date, he informed me he was going to marry me. I laughed. But he meant it. Your father was a captain. Well-educated. He loved me. He really, really loved me.' She sounded wistful, even sad.

'What happened to Noel?'

'He resigned from the army and I never saw him again.'

She continued to tell me that she and my father quickly married in 1945 in Albury, in a simple church ceremony with just two friends, Daphne and Mack Young, as witnesses. 'Your father's mother was a rabid Catholic. My mother was a raging Protestant. The battle for babies would have begun before we signed the register,' Esther said. 'That's why we didn't want any family at the ceremony. In the end, we told them we'd eloped because we didn't want a fuss.'

Daphne wanted Esther to wear her wedding dress, but Esther had her own ideas. 'I told her I might damage it, then I bought a very expensive, gorgeous fawn suit embroidered on the collar with flowers. A little flowery hat to match. I looked most attractive, even if I do say so myself. Hats have always suited me. I have the right face for them. Not everybody does, you know,' she said, raising an eyebrow at me pointedly. 'Your father borrowed a car from a friend – he didn't really want to lend it to us but he couldn't say no – and we went off driving along the coast. It was a pretty good honeymoon. I remember, in Canberra, a very handsome man knocked on the door of our room and asked if I'd like to go to a dance with him that night. "Hold on while I ask my husband," I said. It was thrilling. The word "husband". Then, two weeks later, I read in the newspaper that he'd murdered someone at the dance. Never did find out why.'

Esther's mother sent a tea set as a wedding gift. 'Inside there was a note: *Knowing you, you won't have one of these and you'll need one now you're married.* She was right,' Esther said. 'Mum was always right.'

My own memory of my father in those Bonegilla days was of a giant of a man who every weekend, and most evenings after work, took up his usual stance at the bar at the club, one foot resting on the guardrail, a pot of draught beer clutched in a huge fist like a man dying of thirst. Sometimes, when there was a group, he'd stand upright, rocking on his heels, head and shoulders taller than anyone else. Always with an iron grip on his chosen tipple. At weekends, he drank to oblivion. By Monday morning, his hands were so shaky it took him until late afternoon before he could write a coherent signature on an order form. My brother and I, if we were at the club with him, being fed Coca-Cola and Smith's crisps to keep us happy, were always nagging him to take us home so we could catch the next instalment of a radio serial, *No Holiday for Halliday.* Sometimes he skolled his beer and we left. But not often. Dad drove a red, sun-bleached ute. Those rides home could be terrifying.

In the car, I glanced at my mother, wondering if her mind was racing like mine, her memories a tangled mass and snagging every so often on opportunities lightly tossed away to be regretted much later. She looked grey and defeated. I went to touch her hand but reached instead for her coffee.

'Drink it through the slit, remember?'

She gave me a filthy look. I cleared the lunch mess.

A year later, when Bob and I visited the orchard to see Uncle Frank and Cousin Jayne, I made a remark about finding it difficult to separate fact from fantasy in my mother's stories. 'Did she tell you about the abortion?' Jayne asked.

'You knew?' I said, astonished because not a word had ever been breathed.

'Oh yes. Everyone knew. It was a scandal. Your mother coped by making up a mad story about rushing home to help June [one of my mother's twin sisters] recover from *her* abortion. When June heard, she wanted to rip out Esther's hair.' Jayne added: 'Your mother got away with murder most of the time. For the life of them, no one could understand why.'

Although it didn't occur to me at the time, later I wondered if Esther's flimsy regard for truth was born out of a desperate need to hide her shame from herself if she were to find the will to get out of bed.

—

After a moderate hiatus, ridiculous amounts of money began evaporating from my mother's bank account once more. Withdrawn in weekly slabs of cash from Woolworths. This time, I called the carer who did her shopping. A warm, kind, practical and incredibly generous woman, I'd trust her with my life.

'I have no idea what she does with it,' she told me, 'but when I suggested she might not need so much, she was furious. None of my business, I thought. So I do what she asks.'

'Where do you think it goes?'

'Oh god, I hope you don't think it's me.'

'Not in a million years. But I just can't figure it out.'

'Neither can I.'

'Still, it's her money. She can do what she likes. I've warned her I'm not picking up the pieces when it runs out.'

'There's a market once a month in the big sitting room near the dining room,' the carer said after a long pause. 'There's lots of jewellery, clothes, knick-knacks for sale.'

'Ah,' I said. 'Thank you.'

That week I decided to skip the car picnic, where I'd be within easy range of a swinging handbag, and chose the restaurant for our lunch. Esther had a horror of unseemly behaviour in public places. To her, it was the ultimate personal disgrace. So there'd be no scene when I mentioned money – I could guarantee it. I dressed carefully. Ironed shirt, pressed jeans, a scarf. Polished shoes. Asked Bob to take me across in the boat so I wouldn't have to tie the tinny at commuter dock. Dry knees, no stains. I'd arrive clean. I even wore lipstick.

She was waiting in the reception area, her feet raised and resting on her walker. Head flung back, mouth open. Asleep and snoring lightly.

'She's been here for an hour,' said the receptionist.

'Sorry. I'm not late. She probably just wanted company.'

'Ah. Well, we had a good chat. She's got a great sense of humour, you know. Very quick wit. Had us all laughing.'

The sound of our voices had woken my mother. She gave a snort. Sat up straight, left her feet inelegantly extended. 'You're late!' she snapped.

'You were asleep,' I responded.

'Certainly not. I heard every word you said.'

'Ok, let's get this show on the road.'

She struggled to a standing position. Held the walker like a lifeline. Safely upright, she cast a critical eye over me. *Hah*, I thought, *there is nothing to fault*.

'How do I look?' she said, wiggling her hips.

'Great.' There were food stains on her jacket lapel. More on her shirt. Her stocking socks ended well below her knees. 'You look terrific,' I added.

She gave a little royal wave, shuffled towards the car as though she was walking the red carpet at the Oscars. 'That lipstick's not your colour,' she said as she passed me. 'Less pink, more red for you.'

'I'll keep it in mind,' I said, refusing to be baited.

16

FINAL HOUSE PLANS ARRIVED at the end of February. We printed two sets and retired to our offices to study them. First impressions stay with you forever: sleek, sharp-edged, modern, glassy, and yet perched lightly on the top of our high, quiet hill. *A butterfly*, I thought. *The house looks like a butterfly poised to take flight.* Hunkered between two soaring juxtaposed skillion roofs and set back a little to soften extremes of light, wind and rain, nestled what would be my office one day. This bodily link between those extraordinary wings ensured there would be no sideways distractions. Just a forward, distant view of rippling hills, the Blue Dam and our pair of wedge-tailed eagles when they surfed currents swelling from the gullies. Huge north- and east-facing windows would frame mountains, hills, valleys and dark hollows. A farmhouse way below, another a white speck in the distance. One neat hill with a topknot of ordered trees, like a Tuscan landscape.

Despite the exotic roofline, the house was a basic L-shape. The longest part of the building boasted a single kitchen/dining area separated from a sitting room by an enclosed two-way fireplace. A generous central breezeway, like an open carriageway in a gentleman's Victorian residence, had another large, open fireplace. *Wonderful summer living,* I thought, *sheltered from the sun but perfectly situated to catch cool air.* Further along and accessed by doors opening to an outside walkway – in the style of motel rooms – was the laundry, the guestroom and a spacious cupboard to hang wet-weather gear and stow muddy boots. A double-car garage was hooked at the western end of the building. Back at the short arm of the L, a hallway led off the sitting room to my recessed office, the master bedroom (I've often wondered why not *mistress*), and a bathroom with a separate lavatory.

'So much light and air and space and drama,' I said, trying not to think about how we'd clean five-metre windows and erase cobwebs from an even higher ceiling.

'Clean lines. No clutter,' Bob responded, satisfied.

'Not exactly cosy, though.'

'Double glazing. You'll never have cold feet again. We'll install underfloor heating as well. I've been working on a design that runs off the fireplace. We'll use every ounce of free energy to the maximum.'

'And all I'll have to do is flip a switch to get it going, right?' He gave me a curious look. I read it as assent.

But I began to feel oddly disconnected from the project, overrun and bogged down by Bob's technological zeal and the architect's pursuit of design perfection. At some point, I can't recall the exact moment, I stared at the plans and wondered out loud: 'Where are the bricks?'

'What bricks,' Bob asked, barely listening.

'For the walls.'

'We're not using bricks.'

'We're not using bricks?' I repeated stupidly. 'Why?'

'Architects decided against them. Site's too difficult. Costs less, too.'

'But bricks set us off on this whole mad adventure. How can

we build a house without bricks?' I scrabbled for words to explain that to bypass bricks felt like a terrible breach of responsibility to the brickworks. 'Where's the . . . the . . . synchronicity if you design a brick kiln for someone and then don't buy his bricks?' I pounded the drawings with an index finger. 'What are these walls made from? Concrete? Steel? Slabs? Local materials, that's what we've insisted on all the way. And now we're not using Michael's bricks!' Bob capitulated so easily it made me wary and even deeply suspicious.

Later that night, I asked, 'You're happy about using bricks, aren't you? Wouldn't want to push you if you really loathed the idea.'

'Bricks are good. What do you think of black bricks?'

My head spun. Black bricks? I couldn't recall ever seeing a black brick unless it was painted black. 'Michael's bricks?' I asked.

'Yeah. We're working on developing a black brick. Trying to find new markets.'

'Ah,' I said, and the pieces fell into place.

———

Over the next few weeks at Pittwater, I called up the plans on the computer repeatedly. Every so often, though, I raised my eyes. Through the window, yachts under full sail tacked back and forth on the water. Speedboats trailed wakes like long white ribbons. Light played gently, picking up red, yellow, green and blue from who knows where, making rainbows on the sea. The air was thinner, crisper, as though a chemical change had taken place with the onset of March. There was a new physical serenity, too, that followed the overheated unruliness of summer. Quite magical. Like Benbulla. Only different. But the old nag persisted. Why did we want more? Even cloaked in the political correctness of sustainability, our project still boiled down to two houses for one couple.

SUSAN DUNCAN

'Is it rampant profligacy?' I asked Bob over dinner one night.

He took a while to answer. 'We'll go there for good on the day we decide Pittwater is beyond us.'

'Not frivolous then,' I said, thinking I should have known better.

Bob reached across the table for my hand. 'No,' he said seriously. 'It's the endgame.'

A simple fact. Everything that is born must die, but I felt a twist in my gut for a long, long time.

—

In an effort to learn more, I raided the architectural bookshelves of our local library and bookshop. Immersed myself in the glossy pages of some of the world's most extraordinary homes, trying to fathom what essentially boiled down to my own idea of comfort and taste. The choices were mind-boggling. Geometrically juxtaposed roof angles. Off-centre windows. Nothing orderly. The perfect symmetry of the Greeks, Romans and Georgians, scrunched up like newspaper and burned. Rigid, form-versus-function homes ruled by acres of white – tightly upholstered white modular sofas, sleek white kitchens and huge, white-tiled bathrooms. No bookshelves. Simple? Cosy? No. Sparse. Minimal. Cold. Clinical. Kitchen benches like autopsy tables. Where, I wondered, had they hidden the bloody clothesline?

But there were smatterings of allegedly eco-friendly exterior walls and roofs sprouting live lawns and garden plants. Or better known in many cultures as mud. Not so different from the primitive houses in Amassine, where a mixture of earth and stone was packed tightly onto poplar beams and, ironically, terracotta tiles were available to the rich only. In today's vernacular, though, the practice was referred to as *thermal insulation* instead of *mud roof*. So much grander. Rather like truckies referring to the business of long-haul deliveries as *logistics*. My father, who would have approved of this modern resurrection of traditional methods, always said that the old ways were often the best (as in *tried and true*), but I wasn't interested in hearing that when I was young. If it was new, it was exciting.

Designs boggled the mind, too. A series of wooden shelters that could be swung like a stage set and clicked together to form one room. Plywood panels used to make tables and chairs were recycled to create houses within houses, the cut-outs slotted together so rooms burst forth as *Alice in Wonderland* fantasies. There were pavilions, glass galleries, box homes, terraced homes, prefabricated constructions and transportable, single-room studios plonked in the middle of meadows – presumably so when you tired of one view you could drag your shelter to a new site.

Underlying all the new architecture, though, was a single theme: reducing the ecological impact of construction and lifestyle. The new catchwords: environmentally friendly, sustainable, energy efficient, carbon footprint, thermal inertia. All aimed at harnessing the fierce energy of sun, wind and rain with techniques that included solar panels, mini wind turbines and 'harvested' water.

So many ideas, concepts, choices, materials, philosophical perspectives and new building practices promising to lighten the weight of our steps on the worn-out soil beneath our feet. All bundled into a morass of fancy words that boiled down to constant and ancient themes: keep dry, warm and well-watered. It seemed to me, too, that what was eco-friendly one year could easily be an eco-nightmare the next.

I took to the bed on the verandah with a cup of tea and a slice of apple tart. Tried to analyse what felt like a home not a house. A structure was what you made of it. When you stepped in, did you feel safe and comfortable? Was the chair close enough to the fire for the warmth to reach you? Did an armchair embrace softly? Was the light right for reading? Did the kitchen revive and restore tired spirits?

Although I am instantly seduced by the vision of new light switches and fresh paintwork, beautiful rooms in exquisite taste have always made me afraid to sit down (for fear of leaving a dirty mark), afraid to say yes to a cup of tea (for fear of spilling a drop on a precious rug) and afraid to be myself (for fear of not measuring up to my surroundings). I found shiny newness intimidating. Doubted my ability to avoid chipping paint, denting surfaces, smearing instead of cleaning to sparkling effect. Ruining stylish perfection, in other words, by the very act of living.

How would two ordinary, pending-elderly people with deep laugh lines and long-gone waistlines fit with lean, sleek and dramatic? Would we appear as shabby as the treasured old pieces of furniture I planned to transport to the new house so there would be something of our past to flag who we were and where we'd come from? Was this the architectural equivalent, for us, of mutton dressed as lamb?

'What does it matter as long as everything opens and closes and turns on when you press the switch?' I asked Bob again and again as he obsessed over the finest details.

Finally, in frustration, he said, 'Hardware needs to be hidden. Gas bottles, hot-water tanks, solar batteries and panels. They should all be out of sight. Otherwise, it's like leaving your bras and knickers hanging out for everyone to stare at.'

'Bras and knickers?'

'You know what I mean.'

'It's the other extreme to Tarrangaua,' I observed. 'No one could ever call this a traditional farmhouse.'

'It's all about the future,' Bob said. 'We'll be completely self-sufficient when it comes to energy, except for bottled gas for the stovetop.' And then a swift change of direction: 'Where would you like the vegetable garden to go? And the fruit trees?'

This language, at least, I understood. No pointing fingers could accuse us of being slaves to design and technology over the construction of a simple vegetable garden and a few fruit trees. Of course I didn't know that Bob planned to build another shed, encased by tough netting this time, to keep out wallabies, bats and rabbits. He'd also install a solar-powered underground heating system to extend the growing season. All I'd asked for were a few raised beds to save my back and grow some herbs. I kept forgetting Bob was totally unlike my mechanically inept father and first husband. Every time I opened my mouth, I unleashed the dreamer, the inventor, the practical man. It was like owning a magic wand, wondrous and unnerving at the same time.

But there is no denying I felt a creeping paralysis, a desire to give in and give up before we added to an already over-burdened universe. Was I unwittingly falling into the undeserving mindset of the aging: I've had my go, and anything more is pure selfishness spiced with a slosh of ego? As though I had nothing left of any value to offer and was already taking up too much space and oxygen on earth.

Over dinner one night, when Bob again dismissed my desire for simple brass taps – one hot and one cold – I sarcastically asked whether he'd prefer a steel, chrome, glass, plastic, red, black, white, round, square, oval, linear, overhead or wall, shower head.

He looked at me as though I'd gone mad.

—

Plans were submitted to council for approval. While we waited, a strange euphoria enveloped us. It was like the unsettling but not unpleasant pre-holiday excitement you feel in the days before a risky trip into unknown territory. I put aside my impossible longing for the random and pleasing indentations of an old, well-loved and used home. 'They're a natural result of the passing time,' one of the Alans x 2, an architect, told me. 'You'll have to be patient.'

17

I DIDN'T REALISE IT FOR A LONG TIME, but the farm was forcing me to push physical and mental boundaries. It broke the unhealthy habit I'd fallen into – the same tendency for which I so quickly condemned my mother – of reducing them. As a result, my mindset was changing. I had stopped thinking of myself as a sixty-one-year-old woman with a limited future and, instead, focused on new projects. Where to plant fruit trees. A place for the vegetable garden. Ways to improve pasture. I investigated cattle breeds and even the possibility of breeding. Made plans for one season after another. Committed to creating new life. The future. Learning. Discovering. The mental spin helped to straighten my back, stiffen wobbly resolve. Forced me to dig deep to tap into courage and put a stop to inertia. Occasionally, I thought of my mother in her single room with her frog and her rabbit for company, and Stefan holding on to a single filament of life. Understood once again that I'd been privileged in all the ways that mattered, and that to fritter away opportunity for lack of effort or imagination was heresy.

So I became a completely different woman at the farm, like a foreigner anxious to fit in. My speech became slower, picking up the rhythm I heard around me. I adopted dry country humour, vivid country language. I was desperate to show we weren't dabblers who'd gobble local goodwill and generosity and then cut loose. Prove we were as basic and practical in our thinking as the next bloke. None of this was calculated. It was instinctive. And genuine.

But inwardly, there were days when I paddled hard as hell, unable to shake the awful feeling we were headed for calamity. And once the quicksilver shots of adrenalin ran out, we'd find ourselves overwhelmed, exhausted and beaten. Worst of all, without the warmth and unspoken support of the closely inter-twined offshore community to ease failure and disappointment, would we feel abandoned and alone? In the country, it was said you didn't become a local until you'd lived in the district for thirty, forty, fifty or more years. Bob and I didn't have that long.

One wet Monday we slid our feet into work boots and went searching for the cattle saleyards in Taree. Brickworks Michael had given Bob the name of a bloke who could help a couple of rank amateurs like us buy good, solid stock with the potential to fatten both their sleek rumps and our bank account.

The name was Foggy. He appeared out of the stink and slipper-iness of piss and shit in the cobbled alleyways between weathered timber post and rail pens. Impossibly clean in blue jeans, blue shirt over a white T-shirt, a sheepskin vest and an Akubra hat, he didn't say much. Just followed the bidding from one boggy pen crammed with bellowing cows, bleating calves, wild-eyed bulls and fractious steers to another. Every so often he'd point at a nervy group and say, 'Strong in the legs. A pleasing frame. Should fatten nicely.'

Apparently immune to the din, the auctioneer, who loomed high above the pens on what seemed to be a narrow, stage-like platform – but I couldn't really tell – spruiked with gusto. A gleam in his eyes. He picked up subtle gestures as easily as reading a poster. Tilted hat brim. Raised index finger. Nodded head.

A bloke with muscled legs, wearing KingGee navy work shorts, leapt in the pens, tapping rumps with a red rod, prodding livestock to show their best sides. He had to be quick on his feet. Cattle were volatile beasts. You could tell by their loose bladders and projectile bowels that had the range of a small shotgun.

'One sixty, one seventy, one ninety!' A slap of hands. The deal done. A penciller recorded the price, the number on an ear tag. The crowd moved along as orderly as soldier crabs, stepping over rivulets of urine channelled along the grooves in the cobbles. The stink was eye-watering.

'God,' I said, 'that's so cheap. How do farmers make a living?'

Foggy settled his blue eyes on me and explained matter-of-factly: 'We're talking per kilo here.' *Oh.*

'What's the average weight?' Bob asked, getting straight to the nitty-gritty.

'Around two hundred kilos.' *Oh.*

Foggy continued: 'It's a sellers' market right now. Prices are feisty. We've had a good season. Might be smart to hold off buying for a while.'

Bob and Foggy wandered off, following the crowd that followed the auctioneer.

I hung back, observing. Blue-checked, crisp cotton shirts, clean jeans, padded waterproof vests, polished riding boots, notebooks in back pockets: buyer's agents. Navy work shorts (despite the early morning damp and chill) and elastic-sided boots with tired socks spilling loosely over the top, cattle prod in hand: saleyard staff. Old fleeces over checked flannel shirts, trackie pants: battlers who'd buy a single beast and probably name it Rates or Energy or Car Rego. There were others I couldn't pinpoint: elderly women in conservative skirts and cardigans, polished lace-up shoes. Old, old men with faces gouged by skin cancers and watery, rheumy eyes, their clothes pilled with wear. A few kids who didn't appear to belong to anyone. I failed to pick up the scent of aftershave or strong soap that routinely clogged city elevators. I sniffed my own clothing. Wood smoke. Yesterday's sweat. The lingering aroma of last night's dinner. I'd still pick me as a townie in a flash. Something in the way I stepped around poo instead of through it. Hung back from cattle pens as though they were contagious.

I had a lot to learn.

Then I saw a black-and-white calf with gentle eyes, long lashes and a beautiful face lying serenely amongst skittish hoofs. The fenced-in, helpless sight of her broke my heart.

'Not sure I'm cut out for this business,' I told Bob on the way home.

'You eat steak, don't you?' he said.

'Not anymore.'

He whacked my thigh. 'You'll be right.'

But I wasn't so sure.

———

While we waited for council approval for the house, Bob called in Norm, who'd helped rescue Russell's car when it skidded off track, to build a rough road from the farm gate to the building site. In more or less the right week, he slow-hauled an excavator on a trailer behind a blunt-nosed truck, engine roaring under a canary-yellow bonnet. The truck, named Stormin' Norman, with a hissing chimney expelling black puffs, looked as though it had been born around the same time as Norm – about forty-five years ago.

Wearing trackie daks, a blue windcheater over a ragged polo shirt, and with a stained and battered cloth hat squashed on his head, Norm clambered out of the cabin, lowered himself into a camp chair like he'd been born and bred under a canvas awning with a billy on the boil nearby. It was time for smoko. He took his tea black, he said. In the bush, milk went off on a hot day quicker than you could snap your fingers and the stink in a lunch box gave you the heaves.

'Cake?'

'Well,' he responded, appearing to think through the question like a maths problem. 'I *am* on a diet. But considering the damage already done, one slice of . . .' He peered into the container. 'Chocolate brownie, is it? Well, one slice couldn't hurt much more, could it?'

He and Bob hauled their camp chairs closer to thrash out the finer details of hourly rates and road-building. I butted in: 'The track should wind gently. So much prettier in open paddocks, don't you think? Straight roads are . . . too disciplined.' I smiled brightly, sure they would get my point. 'Like highways,' I added, 'all about getting from A to B. No lovely, languid wandering.'

Bob frowned. 'But we need to follow the ridge,' he said.

'Yes, but it would be lovely to wind along the ridge.'

'But a ridge is a ridge,' Bob insisted, 'the top edge of a hill. It goes where it goes. You're stuck with it.'

'Yep. I get that. Nevertheless –'

'There's a reason for following the ridgeline. When it rains, water runs off both sides. There's less damage to the road.'

I felt my jaw tighten stubbornly. 'A couple of bends, for aesthetic reasons, surely won't make much difference.' And on we both went. Tit for tat. After a while, Norm politely cleared his throat. Bob and I turned to him in surprise. We'd forgotten he was there.

'Bob,' he said in his slow, lugubrious way, hands clasped and resting on the ridge of his generous girth, his eyes cast down to the toes of his muddy work boots stretched out in front. 'Do you want to be right?' He paused. 'Or do you want to be happy?

———

Gradually, Bob introduced luxuries to our bush camp. He scrounged an old kitchen sink from somewhere, built a frame with a draining board and a shelf underneath, and added a gleaming chrome tap with hot and cold water knobs. A promise of running water one day. The bench stood alone in the paddock like a relic from a long-gone house. Or modern art. He rigged a shower. Standing on a tarpaulin to keep our feet clean, we hosed each other down. Gave ourselves a vicious scrub and shampoo. Shed a smelly, scaly old skin. Rinsed off. Racing, laughing, to finish the job before the water – fed from a plastic container through a gas burner and stingingly, heavenly hot – ran out. In the open air, in full view of the wildlife, it felt hedonistic and daring, liberated but strangely vulnerable. Like swimming naked for the first time.

Most days I made vegetable or lamb shank soup for lunch and kept it on a slow simmer in a cast-iron pot over the heat from a bed of barely alive coals. Our old camping Furphy pot forgave, enhanced and enriched the simplest ingredients. After each use, I wiped, swizzled with water, oiled and then seasoned it again over low heat. Two crowd-sized cast-iron frying pans we'd hauled home from the US in our hand luggage in the early days of our marriage were treated with equal reverence.

Then, without warning, it rained like stink. All day, all night, all week. Puddles were so wide and deep that ducks took up residence in them. We huddled under the canvas awning – meant for shade from a hot sun – watching as our entire campsite sagged lower and, in odd spots, sank gently into the wet. Work on the road stopped. Chippy retreated to her bed in the tent, a bedraggled and accusing little doggie. *How could you do this to me?*

Bob rigged tarps. The wind spun. Water found new gaps to finger through. We bought more tarps, strung guy ropes from trees and fence posts until the site looked like a refugee camp. Still, the rain beat in. Across the hilltops and way into the blurry distance, black clouds kept rolling towards us like angry surf.

Every so often, Bob raised a fist and punched the awning while I stood with a plastic bowl to catch the water for the washing up. Damp seeped into our beds, clothing and food supplies. It was miserable. I bit back a plea to escape to Pittwater. To admit even a small defeat this early in the project was like letting failure get a toehold. Instead, I invoked a golden rule for offshorers: *don't let the weather hold you back.*

When skies finally cleared, we had a visit from a gangly Dutchman called Benny, with a thick accent and sharp blue eyes. 'I'm your neighbour,' he told us, holding out a gnarly hand to shake Bob's. Then he pointed at a large green building way down in a green valley.

'Ah,' we said, nodding. 'We wondered who lived there.'

'Thought we'd never see another house from our deck because nobody would be crazy enough to build up here.'

'Oh,' I said, feeling his disappointment at a pure view spoiled. 'Well, how about we plant a screen of trees along the fence line?'

'Ah, we'll get used to it.'

'No, I insist. Got to keep the neighbours happy,' I said. 'So, been farming long?'

'Retired four years ago. Funny, neh. I swore I'd never be a farmer like my father and brothers. Not even if someone offered me a million dollars. Then I retired from the roofing business. What was I going to do? Sit around all day? So my wife, Sini, and me, we bought this land. Funny, neh?'

As it happened, he had a few steers for sale. Was Bob interested? 'We'll take a look,' Bob said, as if we could already tell the difference between a beast that might bring top dollar and one you wouldn't waste time feeding.

We paddock-bashed our way in Benny's ute to where his cows and calves were grazing on a hilltop. They were a mixture of long-lashed, cud-chewing, toffee-and-black beasts, languid in leg movement – as though their joints were made of elastic – with pretty faces. The calves, already old enough to 'go to school', as Benny said, glowed sleekly in the sunlight. Limousin and Angus. French and Scottish. 'Molière. Flaubert. Camus. Sartre. MacDonald and MacDougal.' The names rolled off my tongue. The men looked at me blankly.

'Come for a drink on Friday night,' Benny said after a while. 'We can talk prices then. And maybe you shouldn't give them names.'

'You don't name your cows?' I asked, surprised. He seemed to have a close relationship with them.

'We had a Sirloin once. She was good eating, too.' His tone was ripe with approval. We banged our boots against the ute tread to shake off dirt and cow poo, and Benny dropped us back at our camp. 'See you on Friday. About four o'clock,' he said.

——

Two days later, in the rich afternoon light, we again cut across paddocks, this time in our own vehicle, opening and closing gates, dipping into and out of shallow waterways, grinding down steep inclines in first gear and climbing in second. Navigating by instinct when the house was out of sight.

In the paddock closest to Benny's house, we drove slowly past his bull. A huge, low-slung, golden beast that could've tipped over the car if he'd had a mind to. He gave us a cursory glance, as if we weren't worth much more, lowered a head that would look good stuffed and hung over a fireplace, and kept eating.

'My father always told me never to turn my back on a bull,' I said, dredging up the memory from what felt like prehistory. 'He said it didn't take much to set them off and they'd trample you rather than walk around you. Are you listening?'

Bob nodded: 'You worry too much. I don't take risks.'

'It's not about risks. It's about experience. And neither of us has had much of that.'

Bob pulled up at the last gate. I climbed out to open it. Shut it behind me with extra care. I seemed to remember the sight of bulls jumping fences. Men running. But I couldn't think whether it was a genuine childhood recollection or a conjured fantasy to suit the moment. It happened now, the worry I was mixing up imagination and facts.

Benny's wife, Sini, came out to greet us. At her heels, a mid-size, tail-wagging, tongue-lolling, fluffy black-and-brown dog greeted us like long-lost friends.

'Hello, new neighbours,' she said, wrapping her arms around me. The dog jumped up, yipping softly. 'Down! Get down!'

'You're Dutch, too,' I replied, picking up her slight accent.

'Yep. One of ten children. Benny's one of ten, too.'

'Lord,' I said, unable to think of anything else.

'What's the dog's name?'

'Sam.'

'He ok with other dogs? We've got Chippy in the car.'

'He's fine,' Sini said in a way that made you feel nothing ever bothered her. I opened the door and lifted Chippy to the ground. She and Sam did a quick olfactory tango, then Chippy took off, following scents known only to her.

'She doesn't go far anymore,' I told Sini. 'She's too old and arthritic. If there's any dog food lying around, though, we should probably put it out of reach. She's food obsessed. Hasn't always been that way. Only for the last year or so.'

'She might need worming,' Sini suggested.

'Nah. I'm always on top of all that. She's just old and her head's a bit funny these days.'

'Whose isn't?' Sini said with feeling.

Around a table on a deck that gave views along the valley floor and up towards our home site, Benny and Bob went head to head like rug traders, factoring the cost of agent's fees, trucking cattle to the saleyard and being at the whim of fluctuating market forces.

By the second beer, it was shoulder-slapping and hand-shaking all around.

It was after dark when we headed home. Somewhere, I'm not sure whether it was in our paddock or Benny's, we hit a neck-jarring bump. 'Lucky it wasn't a rock – the grass is too high to see them. Rocks roll utes.'

I swallowed. 'Yeah. Lucky.'

The following week, Benny and Sini walked four gleaming, toffee-coloured Limousins – Flaubert, Molière, Camus, Sartre – and the two Black Angus – MacDonald and MacDougal – through the paddocks. A sedate group. Even-tempered. Friendly. Calm. Like huge, boofy-faced pets. *Cattle farming. A cinch*, I thought with a mental click of my fingers.

Long after Benny and Sini had gone home, Bob and I sat around the campfire with a glass of wine, staring into the flames. Less than twenty metres away, the newest additions to our family cropped knee-high kikuyu. Rip. Grind. Moving every so often with a soft, swishing sound.

'It's rather peaceful watching them,' I said. 'Nurturing new life feels good. Even if they are destined to end up on someone's plate.'

'This property could carry seventy head,' Bob said.

'Well, we've made a start. Better to go slowly, don't you think? Until we know what we're doing.'

'Might give Foggy a call. Meet him at the saleyards on Monday.'

'Of course. Why not?'

———

Foggy was propped on the top rail of one of the pens, a smile on his face, hat tilted forward. Impossibly clean again, amongst the slush. He dropped to the ground, shook hands. 'Been watching you for a while. Wondered when you'd pick up on me.'

'All good with you, Foggy?' I asked.

'Yeah. All good.' We set off at a stroll, away from the auction-eer and the bidders. Checking out the pens of young animals. Limousins. Charolais. Herefords. Murray Greys. Angus. Brahmins. Plenty of crossbreeds.

'What do you reckon?' Bob asked.

'Prices haven't dropped,' Foggy replied. 'You'll be paying top dollar.'

'We've got the grass now,' Bob said. 'Might as well go for it.'

'Steers only. If you're not on site twenty-four seven, don't even think about heifers. And bulls are a full-time job, too. Anything that looks like dairy is a no-go.'

'Why?'

'Bred for milk not meat. All bones, child-bearing hips, teats and udders. How many you after?'

'Twenty?' Bob said.

'There go the new shoes,' I quipped.

Foggy grinned: 'Waste of money out here. You're better off with a good set of gumboots. Cost you thirty bucks. Last you a lifetime.'

The bidding was fierce. Through narrowed eyes, Foggy picked out a field of four buyers, oozing the kind of farmer charm that goes hand in hand with big acreage and five generations learning the tricks of the trade. The right outfits, too. Blue jeans. Riding boots. Checked shirts. Expensive wet-weather gear. No Rates and Energy here. Serious money only. A bloke with a short back and sides, and jeans that accordioned around his ankles, kept raising the ante. We were outbid pen after pen.

'He's starting to get boring, Foggy. What's he stocking? A whole farm?'

'That bloke? He's from Tamworth. He's got a truck out back and he's not going home without filling it.'

Just then, another fella who'd been a main player was knocked down as buyer of a pen of twelve. 'Wasn't bidding, mate,' he called to the auctioneer, 'they're not mine.'

The auctioneer didn't even blush. 'Two dollars thirty-five, all steers, you want 'em or not?'

'Just saying, I wasn't bidding right then.'

'So you'll take 'em?'

He shrugged and nodded. Moved on to the next pen.

'What was all that about?' I whispered.

'Auctioneer was running up another bloke and got caught out.'

'But –'

'It's an old trick. A nod there, a nod here, a finger pointed over there – we can't see if they're genuine bidders,' he said.

'It's dishonest.' I said, outraged. 'That man ended up with a pen of steers he doesn't want.'

'He's got the right to say he won't take 'em,' Foggy said, unperturbed.

'What happens then?'

'It all goes round again.'

'No ill feelings?'

'Nah. The bloke just wanted the auctioneer to understand he was on to him. You watch, the prices'll steady in the next pen.'

Just then, an antsy Brahmin bull kicked up a fuss. Snorting. Rearing. Pawing the ground. Blowing steam that looked like ropy smoke out of huge nostrils.

'What happens if he jumps the fence?' I asked nervously.

'Don't hang around to find out,' Foggy said. The words were hardly out of his mouth before a human stampede erupted. The bull was on the run. Just like Pamplona. Men vaulted fences to get out of the way.

'Jeez, Foggy, where's he going to end up?' I asked. We were pressed against rails in a laneway, far enough from the action to feel safe.

'On his way to Taree for a cappuccino, probably,' Foggy said, deadpan.

The excitement didn't bring the prices down, though. 'Get him,' I urged when the same bidder who'd trumped us at three pens looked like doing the same at a fourth. Bob gave me a weird look coupled with raised eyebrows. Who knew I had such a competitive streak? All it took was a minuscule drop of Foggy's good-looking chin and we parted with our hard-earned money for twenty-two steers on the back of a truckload of blind faith: that the rain would fall steadily and reliably for the two years it would take to fatten them for market, that the animals were strong, that prices would hold up, that the country wouldn't suddenly turn vegetarian.

'Riskier than putting a bet on the Melbourne Cup,' I grumbled. 'At least you know the odds before you back a horse.'

'You've got to love gambling to be a farmer,' Foggy said. 'Keep your nerve. Know what you're doing. Take the good seasons with the bad.'

'You got a home to go to, Foggy, or are you up for adoption?' I asked.

'I'll give you a hand, any time you need it. First off, those steers will need drenching. Show you how soon as you're ready.'

Bob headed off to sign the paperwork. I went back to the ute to give Chippy a quick walk. Landowners. Farmers. Road builders. When things move, they move fast.

———

Daylight had faded to a wintry dusk when we saw headlights, heard the truck rattling along the dirt road, the roar of cattle over the din. We jumped in the ute and headed down the track to the yards. This was our first ever cattle delivery. We wanted it to go well.

Foggy had given us our orders. Keep the steers locked in the pens for three days, hand-feeding them morning and night. Make sure they have plenty of water. By the end of the third day they'll come to you looking for food, quiet as lambs. Even the wildest steers, he said, gentled after a couple of days of tender loving care.

The truck backed up snugly against the race in the dark. The driver, waving a torch around, slid open the gate. The bawling sounded like throats were being cut. The driver cussed and prodded, yelled and pushed. One by one the cattle clattered into the yards. Then a blue steer, the last in the group, got the willies. He galloped down the race, screamed to a halt, turned around and took off back the way he'd come. Full pelt. At a stampede. Hitting his head against the sides, the back wall.

'Loony bastard, that bugger,' said the driver, unfazed. 'Make sure you tell Foggy this one's crazy. Reckon he's blind into the bargain. Hasn't got a fuckin' clue which way he's meant to be headed. Might ring Foggy meself. Bit of luck, I'll interrupt his tea.' He laughed, slapped his thigh. Kept at the steer with his prod, trying to get him in the pen before he killed himself. 'Watch that blue bastard. He's the kind of beast that'll kick you in the head soon as you turn your back.'

When it was all over, the driver turned down the offer of a cuppa. He was headed home for his dinner and an early night. He slammed the back of the truck shut, checked the lock, swung into the driver's seat. Ground into gear and headed out our gate. You could hear rattling and clanking over the whine of the engine all the way to the bitumen road.

We gave the steers a bale of lucerne. Wished them a peaceful night. Felt for our closest neighbours, who'd hear the relentless racket that weaners kick up when they've been taken from their mothers. As though there's been a death in the family, which must be what it felt like.

In the morning, the yard was empty. Cattle-farming lesson number one: check gates are securely latched. After that, we had a paddock full of ferals. Couple of fence-jumpers, too, if you spooked them. 'Two in my paddock this morning,' Benny told us. A few days later: 'Four in my paddock today. You'd better get their ear tags on soon, or they might never find their way home.'

———

While we played at being cattlemen, Norm sat like a smiling Buddha in the cabin of his excavator. A giant, clawed bucket suspended from a long metal arm scraped away a one-point-two-kilometre route from the front gate to the campsite. Wherever he could, he chucked in a bend. Norm was a master of compromise. 'Like every bloke who's been married a long time,' he said without a hint of rancour.

By the end of a few weeks, neat pyramids of black soil were strung out like a necklace alongside the track. Loaded with tough, strong kikuyu runners, eventually they would form the basis of a green lawn around our new house, a perfect firebreak if the day ever came when that was all that stood between us and devastation.

We also had a stroke of luck. We discovered a disused gravel pit in a crevasse between the front and back paddocks. It meant free, on-site material for the road base. A saving of thousands of dollars.

18

ESTHER LOVED HEARING ABOUT THE CATTLE SALES, even if her interest was brief. It sparked memories of her childhood on eleven-and-a-half acres in Stintons Road, Donvale, on the rural outskirts of Melbourne. Bush country. Hilly. Valleys where fog and mist nestled lazily in flat white sheets until late morning. The ground carpeted with spider orchids. Green hoods. Pink fingers. Butterfly orchids. Bearded orchids. Snail orchids. Bachelor buttons. And pink and white heath. Echoes of Benbulla but more wintry than tropical.

'Had a sort of purity in those days,' Esther said. 'All houses now, of course.' She sounded wistful, sad.

I had my own memories of Donvale. Before it was destroyed in bushfires in 1962, there was a rough wattle-and-daub home that never quite kept out the bitter winter winds, no matter how often a lethal brew of mud and god knows what else – cow dung, probably – was jammed into the crevasses. The kitchen, small, with a simple table and four chairs where we kids were given a glass of Marchant's lemonade on Friday evenings, had a rammed earth floor. Up a few steps there was a sitting room. At one end, a massive fireplace; at the other, a round formal dining table (lace tablecloth on Sundays) and chairs. A towering sideboard along one wall displayed the best crockery and cutlery. Inside it, Nan stored the treasured family Bible. It was a huge, heavy, gold-leafed tome, where she meticulously recorded births, deaths and marriages in the tradition of that era. A sword, souvenired from the war, hung on the wall alongside her husband Felix's service medals. I recounted these memories to my mother.

'Your grandfather was very proud of his war record, although the gas gave him asthma for the rest of his life. Mind you, he was still strong as an ox. Could lift a hay cart if he had to,' she said, as though it was still something to boast about.

A master bedroom the width of the house ran parallel to the living room. The bathroom had a deep, claw-footed tub. It never had more than a couple of inches of water heated by a wood chip burner that went cold very quickly. The dirtiest person leapt in last. When Nan's hips and knees wore out, Felix splurged on an inside flushing loo. Uncle Frank and Auntie Belle, who lived a short run past the dam and down the hill, had a drop loo a good distance from their house. It froze in winter. Stank in summer when you could hear the drone of flies long before you opened the rickety timber door. It was smart to watch for snakes, too. Red-bellied blacks curled in a corner, waiting for bush rats to make a move. No one ever understood why I steered clear of the fancy loo and took my chances with red-back spiders and snakes. There was a dog, Petey, a wily fox terrier. Dead before my time but a family legend. When the possums bred to infestations in the roof, Petey, was sent up a ladder to chase them out.

The house always smelled of kerosene lamps. The smell of char, too, from the fire that burned constantly in the kitchen stove, but mostly from the open fire in the sitting room. Especially pungent when the wind blew the wrong way. That black cast-iron stove, chipped and loose-hinged, so you had to lift the door a little to close it tightly, flickered through heatwaves, torrential downpours and gales straight from the South Pole. There was hell to pay if Nan went out for the day and someone let the fire go out. It took a good day or two to heat up again, and about the same time for her to stop rousing on anyone within hearing distance. Nan used to throw damp tea leaves on the dirt floors when she swept. The smell was lovely. Like a good cuppa.

Esther told me she and the twins shared a one-room shack called the Humpy, a short walk from the house. 'We had a canvas curtain to divide the room. Me on one side and, when they were old enough, the twins on the other. My bed was pretty grand, I'll have you know. Wrought iron and brass. Must have cost a fortune. We had horsehair mattresses, which sound awful, but they were warm and comfortable. Mind you, the roof always leaked. Mum put old enamel bowls in a corner. A couple of buckets for the big storms. They filled up quite fast if the rain really came down. You could hear the plops all night.'

'I really loved Auntie Belle,' I said for no reason except it was true, and she died far too young in a car crash, leaving Uncle Frank a widow for the rest of his life.

'When the twins came along, it was always two against one,' Esther said with a hint of wistfulness. 'If I sided with Belle or June in a stoush, they instantly formed ranks and I was back on the outer.' Once, she said, she leaned down and bit the hand of one of them as she lay in the pram. 'The baby screamed, of course, and Mum came running. But she was just so beautiful I wanted to eat her. Mum didn't say a word when I explained. What could she say?'

By the time my brother and I were born, the Humpy had been more or less abandoned except for family holidays or when stray guests showed up unannounced. Window panes were news-papered over and holey, cracked linoleum covered bare earth, the pattern faded and worn beyond recognition. It still leaked badly and smelled of damp soil and wet wool. Esther's bed was there,

SUSAN DUNCAN

gone to ruin, but Dad, Esther, John and me squeezed into it every time we visited. I remember it as a horrible, dark room, thick with dirt and shaded by a long, dark line of giant cypresses that groaned painfully through winters. Gloomy, sad trees with outspread arms. On stormy nights the Humpy filled with a keening sound. It scared me silly if I was out there on my own while the grown-ups and my older brother stayed up talking in front of the fire. I'd scream blue murder, too frightened to make a run for the house. In the end, Esther would send John to bed so I'd have company until I fell asleep. Mostly, I was terrified Felix would creep in silently while everyone was gathered and distracted in the house.

There was a rough stable near the Humpy with boxes of bran, oats and chaff, with heavy wooden lids to keep the rats out. Felix used to call me to help feed the horses. When I said no, my mother and Nan thought I was being lazy and sent me after him with a push: 'Go and help your grandfather.' The yeasty smell of bran. It still makes me feel nauseated.

Chooks roamed all over the place by day but roosted near the horses at night. Winters were cold and frosty. Or perhaps felt colder because there was only the open fire, and you were reprimanded firmly if you stood so close in front of it that you hogged all the heat.

To celebrate a birthday or Christmas, Felix would steady a log under a graceful old willow tree near the house, catch a chook by the throat and swing an axe to chop off its head. The bird, eyes staring sightlessly from the ground, ran in headless, frantic circles, blood spurting like a fountain, until it finally dropped dead. The smell of death and hot shit and the bird's squawking hysteria was awful. Felix would stand back and laugh, his barrel chest shaking with mirth.

To me – a kid already accustomed to electricity, running water, indoor flushing loos and houses that kept out the weather – it was a dirty, bare-bones life, underlaid with fear, shame and

214

helplessness. To this day, though, my greatest shame remains one that I instigated: Felix, who was a clever wood turner, built my cousin Jayne a very tiny chest of drawers where she could store the small treasures of childhood. Rings out of sweet packets, pressed wildflowers, shells, all kinds of worthless but valuable mementoes. On a visit, when I was about nine or ten years old, he held it in front of me like a bribe. 'I could build you one, too,' he said. He must have watched the fierce battle between greed and integrity play out plainly on my face. I shook my head for a long time, but in the end, I nodded.

All these years later, I cannot be sure of the look on his face when I succumbed, but I seem to remember a sheen of victory in his eyes, a grin of inviolable certainty that by accepting I'd given him temporary ownership of a thin sliver of myself. He gave it to me on our next visit. It was a shabby, ill-built little thing tainted indelibly with my own humiliation. I couldn't bear to look at it and hid it away until everyone had forgotten it existed and I could throw it out. I have mistrusted the motives behind gifts ever since and been immune to the bribes and occasional coercions that routinely cross a journalist's desk. I can, at least, thank my grandfather for that.

Uncle Frank, Auntie Belle and Cousin Jayne lived in their modern fibro house down the hill from the dam where we fished for yabbies to boil over a campfire on the bank.

Uncle Frank grew food for the table. Belle churned her own butter and washed Jayne's hair over the kitchen sink once a week. She also made the best apple pies I have eaten. Ever. Although I kept a wary eye out for the whole cloves she added to spice the fruit. Jayne was a dark-eyed, very pretty kid, at least a head-and-a-half shorter than me. Thanks to her mother, she knew her way around the bush like a scholar and yelled *watch out!* if I wasn't paying attention and was on the verge of trampling a delicate spider orchid.

My mother looked down on their working-class industrious-ness. Dad was an educated man in an era when not many kids stayed at school beyond the age of fourteen. We had a cleaner who came once, sometimes twice a week. One of the migrants, a gentle, woolly bear of a man called Nicky, worked the garden. Uncle Frank always said my father spoiled Esther rotten. I think Dad gave in to every demand to make up for the drink, but also for peace. My mother never took no for an answer.

One day, when I was talking to Esther about her childhood, interviewing her really, because by then I'd decided to write this book, I said, 'I remember the smell of kero.'

'Do you?' Esther said, surprised. 'But you were so little.'

'Oh, I remember. Smells like that get locked inside you. There's not much I've forgotten about those days.' My tone was grim but she smiled happily, the good times shining through more brightly than lesser ones. One of the greatest blessings of old age, I'm told, is the ability to reconfigure – or even entirely forget – dark days and even dark eras. But I'm not that old yet, and some memories can't be spun.

And so, after a long hiatus, a familiar chorus began thrumming in my head once more: *Did you know? Did you not know? Did you know? Did you not know?* A cant in the same vein as *he loves me, he loves me not.* Roiling with a confusing mish-mash of memories and a deeply held conviction that she must have known what was going on. The signs – surely as bright as neon lights – were all there. Does a child really end up with cystitis from spending too long on a seesaw? Does a child run away from her grandfather if she trusts him? Does a child beg to be allowed to stay home with Uncle Bob and Aunt Mary instead of holidaying with Nan and Pa? Does a child finger-paint only in black and white if she is not carrying a secret so dark and damaging it is the only way she can express it?

But then I'd glance at Esther's face, pale with an underlying tinge of grey. Increasing numbers of five-cent-sized brown blobs on her cheeks, ever deeper channels in her forehead. The outline of her mouth faded into the skin of her face. And I couldn't bring myself to utter a word.

Sometimes, on a sleepless night, I imagined the way a conversation between us might unfold.

Me: 'Did you ever wonder why I was such a strange kid?'

Esther: 'Well, you weren't beautiful but you always had character.'

Me: 'Weren't you ever curious about the reason I hated holidays at Donvale?'

Her: 'You never got over the chook's head being cut off.'

Me: 'There was a much bigger reason.'

Esther: 'Don't tell me this is about which of you three kids was given the last drop of lemonade out of the bottle?'

Me: 'No. This is much bigger.'

Esther: 'What do you mean?'

And that's where it ends. Even in my internal dialogues I could not conceive of going any further. I would ask myself then if closure really mattered at this end of a life that had played out with so much for which to be grateful? But it was the not knowing that ate away and hung between us like a malevolent force. Twisted my relationship with her in dreadful ways. At a time when she needed and deserved compassion, I used the past as an excuse to deal out grudging, high-handed duty as if it was all she had a right to expect. I was not proud of this, but it was beyond me to do any better.

———

I've spent many years trying to block all memory of Esther's father but never succeeded. Everyone who knew him said he was painfully good-looking, which may explain my mother's lifelong obsession with physical beauty. I recall the smell of him. Musky. With overtones of what I now know was rum. The way he sucked his teeth. A sound that, half a century later, still makes my blood freeze and, along with the word *Pa,* triggers an instinct to bolt. As I sat in my office writing this, I said it out loud. *Pa.* It was still there. The instant nausea invoked by a two-letter word.

Outside my window, as always, light played on water. Clean and sparkling. *Let it go,* I told myself for the umpteenth time. Instead, I called up his army records online and found a blurry sepia photograph of him as a very young man. I stared and stared, enlarged and reduced it, but still I wouldn't have recognised the man who'd been the axis on which my life had pivoted if he'd been standing right beside me.

I went on to read that Felix Hampton Parker joined the artillery in World War I and served in Palestine, France (where he was gassed) and Belgium. I remembered stories he told about rubbing shoulders with royalty when he picked up the handkerchief of the King of Belgium (who happened to be passing by).

According to Esther, her mother, Henrietta Esther Nicol, never quite forgave herself for losing her virginity on the eve of Felix's departure to fight overseas. In her mind, it meant she was promised to him forever, even if he was killed on the battlefield. She told a young Esther: 'Marry a man who finds out on your wedding night that you're not a virgin, and he'll throw it in your face for the rest of your life.' Esther repeated those words throughout my youth, building prison walls around my already dreadfully compromised sexuality until it seemed that even to kiss a boy was to destroy what she always referred to as *reputation.* I realise now that she was terribly afraid that I'd end up pregnant and unmarried, disgraced and ruined. But even more, I suspect she didn't want me to be forced to carry the lifelong guilt, sadness and regret of abortion. Like her.

Felix and Henrietta (Pete and Hettie) began their married life running a grocery in Abbotsford. According to Esther, her father was clever and mathematically gifted. 'That's where your brother got it from,' she said. One of her clearest memories of the shop, she confessed, was finding Myrtle, who helped out, on her father's lap at the back of the fruit shop once or twice. She'd thought it was odd, even though she was too young to understand what it meant. 'Even odder that she was waiting for us at the new place in Donvale,' Esther said. 'Sitting on a log with a silly grin on her face. Never saw her after that, though. Don't know what happened to her.'

Esther's parents were professionally scammed and forced out of the fruit shop in the desperate days of the Great Depression. Felix, a man's man, by all accounts, charmed his way into a job in Jones Bond Store and remained there until his retirement. 'He rose quite high in the ranks,' Esther said, as though it mattered nearly half a century after his death.

'Did you like Felix?' Even as I asked, my breath got short, my gut clenched.

'I loved Mum. She was a wonderful woman. Always had time to make a batch of scones for the swaggies who turned up at the gate. Sewed new dresses for the twins and me, too, for every Saturday dance. Dad always wanted a son. I tried to be as good as a son for years after the twins were born. But I was always a girl to him.'

Felix routinely returned home with jars of whisky, rum and gin. 'He acquired them legally.' Esther paused, smiled ruefully. 'Sort of. Said they were *gifts* from Customs and Excise. Mum didn't approve of alcohol before lunch unless it was a special occasion, so he stashed the grog in a hidey-hole in a big gum tree in the bottom paddock. On weekends, as soon as the men announced they were off to chop firewood, I knew they were headed for Dad's Bar. That's what we kids called it. The men returned for Sunday lunch with a sheen in their eyes, sloppy smiles, and the wives were cranky right up to bedtime. There wasn't much wood chopped, either.'

Out of the blue one day, my mother confessed she'd always dreamed of travelling the world. 'Not sure where that ambition came from. The King family, perhaps, who were neighbours. They were from . . .' She paused, struggling to remember. 'Lobatse! In South Africa. That was it. Not a bad memory for an old duck, eh, kid? I used to listen to their stories until I was dragged away. I always meant to write a book about them. I was on a train in Africa, when I went to visit you. Remember? The train stopped in the night and, just by chance, I looked out the window. And there it was. Lobatse. Strange, don't you think?'

'Write a book, eh?'

'Don't laugh. You're not the only writer in the family. I wrote three books.' Her words brought a quick end to lunch. We'd been down this route many times. When I'd quizzed her for details, she went all wafty and vague. A few scribbles on a page, perhaps, but never any books. I was sure of it. It was a cocktail of fact and fantasy.

Even as young children, my brother and I guessed she led a life of lies, half-lies and forgotten lies. Once, when Aunty Belle visited us at Bonegilla, she was shocked to hear everyone calling Esther *Sister Duncan*. Cousin Jayne said, 'Your mother reinvented herself after the war when there wasn't anyone left who knew the truth.' But Esther's confabulations were always combined with a truly funny, quick-witted bravado that hauled her out of whatever new pit she'd dug for herself. She'd give an airy, dismissive wave if someone pulled her up on a fact: 'Oh, I can't remember the details.' And to be honest, sometimes it suited us to go along with the fantasies. They were so much brighter and cheerier than the reality.

'I wrote a story for *New Idea*,' Esther added, realising I hadn't fallen for the three-book claim. 'About trying to make a sponge cake in the tropics. It was published, too. And not bad, even if I do say so myself. I was paid quite well for it.' She gave a nod. *So there!*

19

WHEN THE BENBULLA LANDSCAPE was swathed in a golden, autumnal luminosity and the evening sky filled with clouds the colour of strawberries, temperatures regularly dropped under ten degrees after dark. I'd topped our sleeping bags with feather doonas, insisted on saving enough billy water for a hot water bottle every night and taken control of a leopard-print dressing gown I'd originally bought for Esther. Although it was thick fleece and extremely warm, it wasn't very practical for a little old woman. She'd caught the wide sleeves on the electric jug and narrowly escaped serious burns. She'd tripped over the hem and narrowly escaped a broken wrist. She'd caught the belt in the washing machine and narrowly escaped being flung around at eight hundred spins per minute. An exaggeration worthy of my mother, but you get the picture. In the end, even though she loved the lurid garment passionately, I removed it before it killed her.

So in the chill and vibrant light of late afternoon, I slipped it over my clothes like a coat and strolled around the campsite until bedtime like a large wild animal on the loose. The only benefit beyond feeling very toasty – and admittedly difficult to prove – was the disappearance of rampaging packs of wild dogs, whose bloodcurdling yowls by the light of the moon made the hairs on the back of my neck stand up. To this day, even though I know an extensive baiting program was under way, I believe Esther's dressing gown scared them off. The best little doggie in the whole wide world, with her grey snout, arthritic knees, deafness and increasing blindness, was safe. But she, too, was feeling the cold.

One day she nudged so close to the fire drum that Norm looked up from his tuna and dry biscuit lunch (another diet) and said, 'If you don't want your little doggie to burst into flames, you might want to move her.' I looked down. Her fur was singed brown and smoking. I snatched her away.

'She didn't even wake up,' I said to Bob later. 'She didn't realise she was almost on fire.'

Despite awesome crystal nights, my excursions, faithful fold-up dunny in hand, were becoming increasingly challenging. The ground was wet with dew. The cold bit through my pyjamas. I found myself setting up the mobile ensuite closer and closer to camp, but I still crawled back into bed with dew-soaked pyjama legs and chattering teeth. In the morning, instead of sliding my feet into the cosy, lamb's wool luxury of Ugg boots, they were sticky with dampness. The tent, too, smelled dank, and every night thick rivulets of moisture trickled onto the ground sheet where they formed small pools. 'It's just condensation,' Bob said, as though it was a minor issue. But damp is damp. It tainted everything it touched. Bob chopped wood and got the fire roaring while I hunkered down, waiting like royalty for my first steaming cuppa of the day and a plate of hot buttered toast. Both smelled of smoke and tasted, ever so slightly, of charcoal. I waited until the sun burned off the long white ribbons of fog that knotted the valleys before finally throwing back the covers and bracing for the morning chores. Cleaning the tent, shaking out our bedding, hanging it in the sun on ropes strung between gum trees to dry out, rinsing dirty clothes and wiping down chopping boards and the plastic cloths on the kitchen tables. Easy, mundane stuff compared to the hard physical and mental yakka Bob put in from dawn till dusk.

One particularly cold, starry night, despite layers of clothing, the leopard dressing gown and a roaring campfire, my back felt frozen.

'I'm going to bed,' I said. 'It's just too bloody cold to stay up.' Bob nodded without saying a word. He hit the button to illuminate his watch face. It was not quite eight o'clock. I unzipped the tent door, peeled off the layers and, in a shivering rush, pulled on a pair of thick flannel pyjamas. Then I climbed under a feather doona and an arctic-weight sleeping bag. I added a mohair blanket across my feet and pulled the pillows tight under my neck to hold back draughts. A few minutes later, Bob came in and handed me a hot water bottle. Chippy gave her fluffy bed a short go, then opted for the feathery warmth in the crook of my knees.

'We'd better get a proper shed built,' Bob said. 'Or I don't think I'll be seeing much of you here over winter.'

'Sorry. Cold makes me miserable.'

'You've got to dress for it,' he said, standing there in four layers, including a heavy woollen jacket, collar raised, with thermals under his jeans and his feet snugly encased in sheepskin boots.

I pointed at the pile of clothing thrown down at the foot of the bed. 'Couldn't move if I added any more,' I said, hoping I didn't sound as whingy as I felt. 'What kind of a shed?' I added, sparking up a bit.

'Big enough for a tractor and a workshop, as well as my office, with a bathroom and a flushing loo.' I was so smitten by the gloriously decadent idea of an interior flushing loo instead of my current al fresco dunny stool, the word *tractor* bypassed me completely.

'Will it cost a fortune?' I asked.

'Nah, it's all part of the infrastructure.'

Infrastructure, as it turned out, was a big word that encompassed a massive amount of mind-bending detail and the skills of a clairvoyant. Look at an open spread of landscape, reshape it, fill it and make sure it worked on a human and practical scale. For us, it meant moving fences, building new fences, erecting new gates, shifting old gates, building new cattle grids, choosing the perfect spot for the septic, the water tanks, the solar panels and, ultimately, the exact location and angle of the new house. Measurements were critical. There were rules for every kind of construction – from the distance between star pickets in a fence to the length and depth of the transpiration pit for the septic. A whole new vocabulary emerged. Purlins. Girts. Bar chairs (nothing to do with cocktails). Joists. Columns. Fly bracing (nothing to do with insects with bad backs). Wind bracing. Tek screws. Holding down bolts. Screeds (nothing to do with writing). Helicopters (nothing to do with flight). Top hats (nothing to do with fashion). C sections (nothing to do with surgery). Portal base joints. Base plates. Trusses (nothing to do with roasting chickens). Mullions. It was like a boys-only foreign language. Bob, who shied at even attempting one or two words of French, Spanish or German when we travelled, spoke it fluently.

I retreated to the tent with the dog. I knew I was not up to coping in what was essentially an alien environment. Some days I dozed despite the roar of Norm's machinery. Some days I just sat in my camp chair. Still. Content. Engaged in country. Some days, even though I was about as competent in a building environment as a bandicoot with a hammer, I felt an irrational resentment at being excluded from so much of the decision-making process. Some days I felt as though we'd been attacked by a mind-altering virus that manifested in dangerous recklessness. Some days I felt furious about the whole project and wanted to scream out loud:

'Let's quit now before it's too late!' Some days – quite a few – I felt too old to begin again. But there were just enough days when I felt what we were doing was brilliant. And so we strode on.

———

While we waited for council approval on the house plans, we discussed the fine details with Russell and Carolyn in their shop-front office: blinds open to the street, bare floorboards, doors lying flat on trellises for desktops, chairs on wheels, sleek Apple computers with cordless mouses (mice?). A wall lined with plywood bookshelves slotted together in a complicated but clever series of notches and locks. Not a nail in sight. Some architectural books but mostly product listings in large folders. Tiles. Paints. Wood oils. Fittings. Many more. Out the back, a slapdash kitchen with a state-of-the-art coffee machine. All very casual and utilitarian. But with a cutting-edge style, too.

I came to understand that when I veered off on a personal mission (brick floors in the kitchen please, showers without screens please, an outside fireplace please), the conversation immediately shifted to tedious infrastructure details: Stainless steel versus copper nails. New wood or recycled. Industrial ply or marine ply. Mixer taps or one hot and one cold tap. Aluminium window frames. Or timber.

I drifted off, although occasionally, as though waking from a dream, I made a comment out of the blue: 'I don't want a bar of retro. You probably weren't even born when I lived through those burnt orange and mission brown years. Orange still gives me a headache. While we're on the subject of colour, I'm not fond of pink, either. And bright red makes me feel cross.' Once, during one of my drift-offs, Chippy went missing. After calling ourselves hoarse –Pittwater dogs have no idea about roads and traffic – Bob found her next door, at the rear of a fast-food shop, with her snout buried deep in a pile of old fat. She looked triumphant.

Bob picked her up and carried her back inside. She stank like stale chips.

Seeing my distress, Carolyn kindly suggested a coffee and guided me down the street to a café where the cake was very good. Being wonderfully diplomatic, she gently tried to dispel my quibbles about colour at least: 'Strong colours are fine but they're best used as accents instead of features. We're thinking shades of grey for the house. Or maybe green. Colours that blend with the landscape.'

'Grey is good,' I said quickly. 'Green can look a bit mouldy in the wrong light.'

Carolyn looked at me askance: 'We would never, ever, suggest a mouldy green, Susan. Trust me. Never.'

I smiled openly, as though we were sisters under the skin instead of two women separated by the great cultural divide of age. I couldn't help wondering if I'd been as sure of myself in my early thirties. I was living in New York City then, writing primarily for the *Australian Women's Weekly* and riddled by gnawing doubts and dread that one day someone would see straight through the bravado and discover the shallow, insecure, hard scrabbler I knew myself to be. If I'd had any chutzpah at all, it came from the knowledge that I was somehow functioning successfully in arguably the toughest city in the world.

While I was searching for signs of hesitation in the firm-voiced, confident young woman opposite, it occurred to me that I was being ridiculous. But houses are inextricably tied with powerful emotions. From the moment the front door is opened they shout who we are and the kind of forces that formed us from childhood. While I have long stopped worrying about what people think of me or my (ratty) clothes, I found myself getting absurdly twitchy about some details.

'Floorboards should run at opposite angles to mark the separa-tion of rooms,' I said. 'Bricks are better laid two-by-two or even three-by-three, but definitely not one-by-one . . .' And on and on I babbled. Every so often, I would remind myself I was a woman who'd looked down a long dark corridor of diminishing possibilities when a doctor explained the pea-sized lump in my right breast might be a killer. I knew better about what mattered and what seemed to be important for a brief moment in time. But a sort of silent hysteria gets a grip of your psyche. It's to do with expense, I think, and the fear that you're putting yourself at risk for a project you may well end up loathing. In the mix, too, was the worry that I would be judged by some indefinable standard my mother would refer to as *breeding* and found lacking in every department.

A while later, Carolyn called to say she'd arranged a meeting with a local builder. 'He's a perfectionist,' Carolyn said. 'He sweats over every detail. He built our house five years ago. One of the tradies hammered a single nail out of alignment on the deck. Still drives him mad. We've become quite fond of that nail, though.'

I thought of Amassine and handwoven rugs strewn on the ground in that magical bowl of a valley where purple orchids and midnight-blue hyacinths grew wild. They'd been transported on the backs of donkeys, along with two large tureens of saffron soup and tough flat bread for our lunch, so we could better appreciate the way the natural dyes, textures and designs breathed in harmony with the landscape. Although there were some rugs that roared and splattered like a Jackson Pollock painting. Who knew what was going through a weaver's mind as she painstakingly tied one small, tight knot after another and created an artwork that fiercely bucked tradition? In the end, I understood it was the subtle changes in dye lots, the momentary waver in a knot or design – the lack of perfection, even that single much-loved nail out of alignment – that humanised a task and was integral to the beauty.

'Only God is perfect,' said the head of the weaver's co-operative, a tall, gentle man with a talent for business.

So I told Carolyn: 'Perfection can be cold-hearted.'

'Not in buildings,' she responded quickly, firmly. 'You want the doors to close properly, don't you? The windows to shut tightly? The corners to be square? The floorboards to keep out draughts?' I must have looked sad, because she added: 'Every piece of timber has a personality. So does every brick. But trust me, it all has to fit together perfectly.'

After a while, I realised that every time I raised even a small quibble, Bob addressed the problem immediately. *Happy wife, happy life*, as Norm would say. But it was much more than that. We were a team. We did the big things together. Underlying the partnership was unfailing support. Like a piece of music, when the left hand grew weak, the right grew strong. When the right became exhausted, the left picked up the tune and carried on. 'We complement each other,' Bob had said in the very early days of our relationship. I liked the premise even though I had no idea, then, how deeply that creed could and would run.

There was one blindingly shattering wake-up call when I stood stock-still in the hallway at Tarrangaua and stared closely at the Bahtiyari rugs. Red and orange. I rushed around the house, throwing open doors, looking at details I'd long stopped seeing. Red and orange jumped out from every corner.

20

'WHAT'S YOUR FAVOURITE COLOUR?' I asked my mother when we next met.

'Red!' she said without hesitation. I thought about her room: red leather chairs, red afghans on the bed, red feather boa, red dresses in the wardrobe.

'Yeah. Well, there are many shades of red, of course. Bright red just doesn't do it for me,' I said.

'I'd stay away from most reds if I were you. Not your colour at all.'

A memory popped into my mind: in the early weeks of my first job I'd blown a two weeks' pay cheque on a very expensive new red pants suit and my father reacted badly. My mother took me aside and explained: 'Your father thinks only women with loose morals wear red.'

The following day, I exchanged the suit for a white one. He nodded when I showed it to him, but he didn't say a word. At the time I thought he'd objected only to the colour, but now I think he'd seen stirrings of my mother's extravagant personality emerging in me and it rattled him badly.

Across the restaurant table I could see my mother was feeling angry and unsettled. 'I should never have let you sell the Wallacia house from under me,' she said. 'I was happy there.'

I pounced quickly: 'Firstly, I didn't sell it from under you, as you well know. Secondly, you'd had two falls and broken both wrists. Thirdly, it was only a matter of time before you had another fall that would have killed you. And if another fall didn't kill you, one day you'd reverse down that Everest of a driveway and end up in the Nepean River. Drowned.'

Esther refused to listen. 'It was a beautiful house. I had friends there. That new young couple who'd moved in next door were wonderful to me. I had Pat and Ilmar, too. And a beautiful garden.'

'The garden was a weed-infested wilderness. And Pat and Ilmar were nearly as old as you. If you'd stayed there, you would have been dead years ago.'

'I'd have been happily dead, though.'

There was nowhere to go with that, so I shut up.

After a while, she spoke again. 'At least I don't have to worry about you anymore.'

'What do you mean?' I asked, puzzled.

'Well, you've got Bob now. You're in good hands.'

'You've never worried about me. It's always been about you, not me,' I said, stung into biting back.

'Hah! You'll never know,' she said, fiddling with her rings.

I realised with a shock that since her heart attack I'd routinely gouged into my worst memories. A trick to divert my attention from the increasingly frail, fearful, desperate version of a woman before me who was still my mother? A way to avoid acknowledging her awful vulnerabilities, because to do so would break my heart and I might never again be able to step over her threshold? Yes. But deep down, too, I clung righteously to the irrefutable fact that she'd failed to protect me.

'The only times I've ever known you to be generous were when there was something in it for you,' I said. I expected her to rise in fury.

'Maybe,' was all she had to say with a tired shrug. The fight gone out of her. To me, in the mood I was in that day, her response was as good as a confession, an affirmation of the selfish character I believed her to be. I held on to it like a prize.

It wasn't until much later that I thought about what my mother must have seen when she looked at me after my first husband and brother died and before Bob brought order to my life: a scatty, erratic woman who drank too much, made disastrous choices romantically and was headed for self-destruction. Who once, very drunk, shook loose a handful of pills before climbing into a tinny with the intent of roaring off into oblivion forever. A friend saved me. A friend and the fact that I was too drunk to untie the boat. No wonder my mother worried.

And yet, when my father died I'd expected her to march on bravely, competently, independently. This, a woman who didn't even know how to pay the electricity bill. No wonder her life was a toxic blend of a vivid imagination, play-acting and outright fantasy fuelled by pills and booze and endless disappointments. I was painfully aware there was a very strong chance I could easily have gone the same way. She must have seen signposts and the danger as clearly as a white flag waving from a battle zone. But by now I had the red means.

'I get it. If I died, who would look after you?' I said. She gave me a look that once reduced my brother and me to quivering messes. I smiled sweetly so she'd realise she'd wasted the effort.

'Oh, think what you like,' she snapped. 'But understand this: a mother worries about her children from the day they're conceived. You'd know that, if you'd given me grandchildren.'

Bile rose in my throat. I swallowed it down.

'I'm only joking. I never wanted grandchildren,' she added quickly, trying to gain back neutral ground.

'Yeah. I remember. What was it you always said? You're on your own. Don't expect me to look after any kids.' I'd never been so close to revealing the past. *It is only a matter of time now,* I thought.

———

'Tell me about your schooldays,' I said one day when the silence between us went on for far too long.

'Why?' she asked suspiciously, smelling a trap where there wasn't one.

'If you died tomorrow, I'd know very little about you before I was born. I'd regret that.' I grinned, added: 'I think.'

She took the bait. 'We kids walked to school at South Warrandyte. Five miles.' I raised my eyebrows. 'Alright. Maybe four and a bit. Country tracks. Hardly saw a soul.'

'Did you excel?'

She wiggled her head, jiggled her shoulders in a coy and self-deprecating way. 'Essays were my favourite subject. I used to write one a week and they'd always be read out in class.' She preened a little.

'Topics?' I asked, to keep her going and off the subject of staff shortages at the Village.

'Oh, anything. Once I wrote a whole story around a flower. It was quite good, as I recall.' She went on to say the teacher, Mr Hamilton, told her she was smart enough to get a scholarship to Fintona, an exclusive girls' school. His daughter was Esther's best friend and already booked in the following year. Esther wanted to try for that scholarship more than anything else in her life. 'But Dad said we couldn't afford the books, let alone the uniform, so I stayed where I was.'

Stuck in a twelve-student school that didn't teach beyond grade eight. Like everyone else, she left at the age of fourteen. A wound that never healed.

'Mr Hamilton's wife taught sewing on Friday afternoons. The twins were great sewers. I preferred reading. Anything I could get my hands on. I'd grab a book, climb one of the cypresses and read until dark.'

There were two old cars under the trees. Falling apart. Rusted. Full of spiders and probably a snake or two. One was a 1921 Ford called Chrissie. The other a Chevy. When we spent holidays there, my mother would point at them and say they'd be John's property when he turned eighteen. He could restore and sell them. It would give him a financial start. My brother, who skedaddled at the first hint of anything mechanical, didn't shed a tear when they were reduced to rubble in the bushfires.

'I remember you telling me about Mr Brooksbank,' I said.

'Oh, he was a lovely man.'

'He taught you for a while, didn't he?' Her eyes filled with confusion. 'Your tutor,' I added, trying to jog her memory.

'No, no. He was the local priest. A good friend of Dad's. They enjoyed a drink together. I wore a bright-red cardigan one day that I thought was pretty special. He took me aside. Said a beautiful, well-dressed woman turned heads when she entered a room, but no one should be able to remember what she was wearing. Never forgot that.' I waited patiently for more, but she'd run out of puff or become lost in her memories. (Later, I checked Mr Brooksbank's details with my cousin Jayne. He was a friend and neighbour, nothing more).

I drove her back to the Village. Retrieved her walker, helped her to her feet and stayed at the entrance while she disappeared into the main lounge. She looked frail and terribly old. For a brief moment I thought of going after her. Looked down at my feet until the impulse went away. I had no idea what to say. Then I noticed a food stain on the front of my shirt and couldn't decide whether to laugh or weep.

The following week I collected her earlier than usual. Bob and I were leaving for Benbulla and I wanted to get Tarrangaua cleaned and organised before we left. 'A quick lunch, if you don't mind,' I said.

'I know you're busy,' she retorted.

'I'm here, Esther. I could've gone without seeing you at all.'

'Don't think I'm not grateful.'

'Well, an occasional thank you wouldn't go astray.'

'How many times have you thanked me in your life?' I drove in silence to pick up picnic supplies. Tried to remember if I was a thankless child.

I was born with a birthmark down one side of my face, a turned eye, developed great blotches of freckles from the moment the sun first hit my face, had a nose like a beak and copper-coloured hair. Years later, Esther added that I'd also been covered in a furry down at birth: *like a little wolf.* She'd despaired, of course. To be born beautiful in her generation was like winning the lottery. Handled with care, wisdom and a whiff of animal cunning, it was valuable currency and a passport to glory. Or, at the very least, a dizzying step up the social ladder.

From day one I needed to be pointed in different directions to most girls. Even though the doctor told her to be patient, the marks on my face were caused by pressure and would disappear in time, Esther insisted on radiation treatment. No one knew then that radiation caused long-term cell damage. She attacked my turned eye problem with equal gusto. For weeks, in the wintry predawn light, my father drove us twenty kilometres along rough country and narrow bitumen roads – although they were called highways then – to the Albury train station for the journey to an eye specialist in Melbourne.

My mother dressed in her best gear, her face smelling of face powder, her lips bright red, eyebrows coloured with a little brush she moistened with saliva and then dipped in a brown cream. She always wore a hat. I was consistently dressed in an itchy green tweed, knee-length skirt and matching jacket with a green velvet collar. Black court shoes polished to a mirror shine, white socks. (I still have a portrait wearing that suit, titled *Susie 1958*, which hangs on my office wall.)

I was admitted to a Melbourne hospital for surgery to weaken the muscle in my left eye. The specialist, Dr Box, told my mother I would have to wear glasses one day, but the scar under my eye would disappear. All these years later, if I am tired, stressed or angry, my eyes go wonky and, for a while, I look vaguely demented.

After surgery, I crawled into bed with my mother every morning to do a series of eye exercises – following her finger left and right, forwards until she touched the tip of my nose, then backwards as far as her arm would stretch. But we both tired of that boring routine very quickly, so she taught me sewing instead. Hem stitch. Back stitch. Blanket stitch. Embroidery stitch. I'd forgotten about the sewing lessons until, when I was packing her belongings, I found a badly embroidered pink galah on a yellow linen doily. I value it alongside my father's writing desk and the watercolour of the Murray River. It proved love. Tenderness. Care. None of it born out of the self-interest that conjoined with our adult relationship.

'I've thanked you repeatedly for making sure I had a good education,' I said. 'Thanks for making sure my wonky eye was fixed, too. The radiation is a black mark, though. I reckon it had a lot to do with all the skin cancers on my face . . .'

'Rubbish. You refused to wear a hat when you were a kid. Threw it off the second I put it on your head. Went off stark-naked a lot of the time, too. I remember the migrants bringing you back time after time. *Mrs Duncan, here is your daughter but we don't know where her clothes are . . .*'

'Well, consider yourself thanked, ok? I won't see you next week. We'll be at the farm. The new shed is being built.'

'How many sheds does one man need?' she grumbled.

—

At Benbulla, Bob measured and staked out the shed footprint. A few days later, Norm cut lightly into the ground with his excavator to establish the base. With a pencil, notebook and an old-fashioned dumpy level instead of a high-tech laser level, Bob and Norm worked to scrape a plot as level as possible.

'Every little bit of effort saves using extra concrete,' he said. 'When the slab is poured, it can't be more than five to ten milli-metres out or it makes it that much harder to erect the frame and walls. Harder means it takes longer. Longer means it costs more. It all has a knock-on effect.'

It's like making a cake, I thought, *all the ingredients should be balanced to avoid a sinkhole in the middle.* I held the pole for Bob to make his calculations, but mostly I contented myself with making blueberry pikelets (recipe on side of buttermilk container) for smoko and keeping the tent in a pristine condition. Who knew a little white doggie could shed so much hair? Chippy did have one great skill – she'd sussed food times with absolute accuracy. Breakfast, smoko, lunch were routine. But sometimes, if I was in danger of napping through knock-off time, she yapped in my face. Beer o'clock – the easy, wind-down period after the hard slog and before the tradies went home – included cheese and bikkies and a cold beer while chores for the following morning were debated. A ritual that took the edge off the day's grind. Chippy lived for the cheese and biscuit titbits that no one had the heart to deny her.

'Her obsession with food is getting worse,' I told Bob one day, worried. He didn't say a word but I heard every thought. 'Ok, so maybe we're genetically related. Seriously, though, do you think there's something wrong?'

'Worry if she doesn't eat. Not before.' But there was a new, almost demented look of concentration in her eyes around food that was increasingly disturbing. As though she'd lost her reason for a while.

The slab for the shed was poured on a bright, sunny day. The few dads and sons we knew in Wingham turned up just after dawn to lend a hand. Sunny-humoured country boys. Unafraid of grabbing a shovel and doing backbreaking dirty work. Three massive concrete mixer trucks wheezed up the hill. Tanks on their backs like turtles, they lined up to spew grey sludge down mobile channels until the framework was filled. The day grew warmer.

The builder had a ritzy new high-tech laser level, so we put the old dumpy level away. Gradually the dance floor – as I thought of it – was covered. In knee-high gumboots, the men and boys ploughed through the ooze, raking and shovelling, spreading and patting. Those young backs bending with the ease of sappy green timber until the air bubbles disappeared. Gradually, the foundation for the shed – Bob's shed – took shape. But the day grew too warm.

'We don't want the concrete to go off too soon,' Bob said.

'Why?' I asked. Wasn't the whole point of concrete to set hard?

'You've got to be able to work it to a perfect level before it dries. It has to cure properly. Otherwise it's weak. Vulnerable. Concrete gains strength over a month until it's bulletproof. You need toughness when you're driving a tractor in and out.'

'What tractor?'

'Every farm needs a tractor,' Bob said, giving me a slap on the backside and walking off with a bounce in his step. But water was our Achilles heel.

—

At last the slab was done. 'Write your name and date in the concrete,' Bob said, happy. 'This is a big moment.'

I wrote both our names: Bob and Susan. And the date: March 31, 2012. I gazed at our nearby campsite nestled under the gum trees. It already looked flimsy and insignificant. As though a slight breeze could carry the canvas away, like Dorothy's house in Kansas. It was silly, really, because it had withstood torrential rain and strong winds, and for so long had been a safe haven on a high quiet hill.

At the end of the day, when everyone had gone, we jumped in the ute with a couple of beers, some cheese and salami, and drove to the top of the Great Hill. I spread a kilim on the grass and we sat cross-legged, gazing at the slab way below. Sixteen metres long and nine metres wide, it looked like a foreshortened tennis court. We twisted the tops off our beers and clinked our bottles to toast the new shed. 'To Benbulla,' we chorused. I tried not to think of it as a new scar on a pristine landscape.

The next day, Bob checked the levels – they were almost a hundred millimetres out. The batteries in the flash, infallible, high-tech laser had been dodgy. 'A disaster,' Bob said. 'Everything just got so much harder. I should've checked and double-checked. Standard procedure and I didn't follow it.'

A long time later, he looked up from the fire where he was cooking dinner: 'He who trusts, busts. That was the kind of blue an old bloke would make.' He looked beaten and vulnerable in a way I'd never seen before. Above the campfire, in a pale-blue sky, Venus shone brightly.

'This is only the beginning,' I said. 'We're still not in too deep to quit if it's all too hard.'

Bob turned a horrified face towards me: 'Quit? Why would I do that?'

The next day we went out and bought a diesel-driven generator with enough power to run the big tools needed to cut, trim and grind steel to build the shed. The amount of unsustainable matter required to reach a state of sustainability was mounting at a rapid pace. *Hmm.*

—

Pears, Gazza, Tom and Tim joined Bob, Norm and me in the circle around the campfire. A ragged collection of blokes with deep and gentle souls. Off-site, Gazza was a long-haired, bearded, part-time poet, part-time plumber who grew grapes and made wine. Tom, a young bloke home from the UK on a holiday to see his mother, was a quiet, steady worker with tickets to rock concerts nearly every other weekend. Pears loved a chat, loved his two little daughters, loved his work. Mostly. Tim, a tough ex-rodeo star who'd once ridden bulls and had the scars to prove it, shifted fencing to keep cattle off the Home Hill. He worked his old blue tractor on our steep hillsides with the same skill and intuition you needed to ride a skittish young horse. No more wading through cow poo from now on. A pleasing thought.

Their hats matched their personalities. Young Tom in a trendy baseball cap. Pears in a spotless white terry-towelling hat. Tim in an Akubra with a rakish upturned brim. Norm in his uniform, slightly grubby, battered cloth hat. Gazza didn't bother with one. Not that I can recall, anyway.

'Was Gazza wearing his work boots on site?' Brick-works Michael asked when we told him the project was going gangbusters.

'Work boots?'

'Yeah. Flip-flops. In winter he adds a pair of socks.'

There were many, many decisions to make every day. Some were as simple as the right nut and bolt for truss lintels compared to portal base joints. But two had ramifications that would go on for as long as the shed remained standing: Should we increase the angle of the skillion roof by ten degrees, as the architects suggested, so it would reflect the same angles on the house? Should the corrugated iron sheets run vertically or horizontally?

'It's just a shed, for god's sake,' I muttered. 'What does it matter?' In the end, after a long and intense debate, aesthetics were tossed aside to accommodate costs and practicality. Turns out it's cheaper to lay corrugated iron sheets vertically than horizontally. And a costly extra ten per cent angle on the roof meant more space for swallows and willie wagtails to move in and raise their families. The dreaded tractor would fit nicely under the doorway without raising the roof, anyway.

———

I did not want a tractor. Tractors were dangerous. Tractors were especially dangerous on steep slopes. The bloke who helped haul Russell's car off the track edge once rolled his machine – and his land was comparatively undulating. Our terrain was the Swiss Alps in comparison.

'If you kill yourself on that bloody tractor, who will chop the wood?' I asked.

'Don't worry about it,' Bob replied in a casual way that made me worry even more.

'I thought we'd said we would hire contractors when there was tractor work. Thought we'd decided we wouldn't use a tractor often enough to justify the investment. Thought we'd agreed: no tractor!'

'When?' Bob asked.

'Now!'

He took my hand: 'Let's go and have a look at what's available. Might help us decide whether it's pointless. Or not.'

A week later, a brand-spanking bright orange tractor with a rooftop, bucket and slasher was delivered by the salesman, a denim-clad, Akubra-hatted, leather-belted (with silver and turquoise buckle) bloke who looked like his jeans had been tailor-made. He gave Bob a technical run-through, then climbed into his dashing, chrome-encrusted ute and waved goodbye. He was so good at his job that a few weeks later we returned to buy a lawnmower and came home with a small tractor that, with the right accessories, could do all sorts of tricky small-area jobs (hoe, level, dig) as well as cut grass in a five-foot wide swathe.

'That's your personal tractor,' Bob said, grinning.

'You mean I'm the designated mower of lawns from now on.'

'Always said you were a smart woman.'

'Huh!' After that, I saw the infinite potential of new technology to eliminate the grind and sweat of land care. As long as we could foot the bill for the machinery and the fuel to run it, dilettantes like us might survive, and even thrive. I riffled through farm machinery catalogues obsessively. Told Bob we'd probably need another shed. No wonder they called me chaos.

At the end of a day of test runs, Bob parked Big Red, as the tractor became known, on a slope. Bucket raised. It was beer o'clock. I handed him a frigidly cold beer.

'Seems to go alright,' I said.

'Yeah . . . Oh shit.' The tractor was gently rolling down the hill towards the dam way below. He sprinted off, caught up, leapt on board, found the brake and sorted himself out. Back at the shed, he took up his beer once more.

'Might be a good idea to drop the bucket when you park in future,' I said.

'Yeah,' he agreed.

Later, I heard that farmers who try to catch runaway tractors frequently get caught between those head-high, rolling black tyres and squashed to death into the ground they're trying to tame. Bob had been lucky. I threw the machinery catalogues into the campfire.

21

By the beginning of winter, as kangaroo grass turned rosy pink along the roadsides and grey gums shed the last of their bark, the framework for the shed was in place. The new fencing to isolate the home paddock from the cattle paddocks was also completed. A trench the length of a cricket pitch had been dug by Norm and his excavator for the transpiration pit, and Brickworks Michael had supplied a truckload of broken bricks to go on top of a gravel base. Eventually, moisture would drain into a dense and diverse plantation of nearby gum trees: iron bark, blackbutt, spotted gum, scribbly gum, red mahogany, grey gums, cadaghi and bloodwood. A magnificent tallowwood, too. Near the edge of this forest, the bony arms of a dead gum stretched high with a mighty black bulb near the top. A white ant nest, Norm explained when I asked him what it was, but not the same species that turned timber houses to dust. Although there were plenty of those around, too.

In happy anticipation of the flushing loo to come, Gazza had thoughtfully rocked up with a real porcelain dunny on a large styrofoam slab that he'd removed from another job. The plan was to set it somewhere in the bush, but I couldn't quite get my head around how it might work without water and stuck with the fold-up dunny chair.

As it turned out, the local council was in the process of changing rules about septic systems. Aspiration pits were now banned and, in a sweeping, across-the-board dictum that failed to take in individual sites and conditions, had been replaced by tertiary effluent treatment systems. Essentially, this meant two tanks, an electric pump and recycling water through a treatment system. Trouble was: we didn't have any power source and, even when it was installed, solar was limited by overcast days. Trouble was: we'd already dug the pit. Trouble was: we didn't have the luxury of town water. Negotiations with the council began.

A month or so later, the final approvals for the house plans arrived and we met the builder for the first time. He didn't say much. Nor did he remove his hat – an incongruous straw pork-pie affair positioned at a jaunty angle. Tanned, compact, with eyes that kept you at a distance. I had no idea what to make of him.

Afterwards, I said to Bob, 'His name's Cross. Same as Norm's. Do you reckon they're related?'

'You wouldn't get long odds on it,' he said.

'He didn't put in much of a pitch for the job,' I said.

'He knows it's in the bag. I've met him before. He built the brick kiln. Thought he was an arrogant prick at first. But he's not afraid of work and he does things right. No cutting corners. Kind of bloke you trust.' He paused: 'The engineers in Taree? The ones we're using for the steelwork? They're his first cousins.'

I wriggled my nose: 'Better not offend anyone then. Insults could go right down the line and we'd end up a bit lonely on site.

'Yeah,' Bob said.

Meanwhile, the framework for a raised timber floor for Bob's shed office – which would be our cosy winter abode – was set out. As usual, it looked too small to me, but Bob said it was more than adequate. He wouldn't be doing much engineering work in future anyway.

—

The day arrived when the shed was watertight. Bob moved our increasingly shabby but stalwart tent into the south-west corner, bolting it into the concrete so it became a permanent fixture. One less job every time we arrived on site. We lost the soft give of the earth under our feet but we gained shelter from rain and wind, although it was still draughty as hell. There was an unsuspected downside. The sun couldn't finger its way into the corner to burn off the chill and damp. Then a family of swallows set up house in the rafters above. Poo rained down, slid along canvas in chalky white trails. The knock-on effect, again. Bob discouraged the swallows with a large broom while I scrubbed away the poo.

Norm, who felt like a member of our family by now, scraped out a site for a water tank behind the shed. A truck arrived with clean, soft sand to lay the base. A couple of days later, two self-contained and efficient blokes installed a one-hundred-and-fifteen-thousand-litre steel tank, panel by panel, lining it with a plastic sheath before plonking a slightly curved corrugated lid on top. The tank men politely declined a campfire cuppa, pointing at their iceboxes, and departed to complete another installation on a distant farm.

Bob and Gazza connected a PVC pipe to the shed guttering to feed run-off water into the tank. It was completed in less than a day. Bob pulled out a calculator to work out how much water we would collect from an area of one hundred and fifty square metres. One hundred and fifty litres for every millimetre of rain that fell. We had our own catchment area at last. Which meant independence from the kindness of the brickworks, where we'd been filling our jerry cans from the beginning. Late in the afternoon, a truck delivered ten thousand litres of water at a cost of a hundred and eighty dollars.

'Flattens the plastic and holds the tank down,' Bob explained. 'Otherwise we could lose the lot in a high wind.'

'Shouldn't we get a second delivery?' I asked, feeling anxious. The tank water level had reached a single bar. It didn't seem like much.

'Nah. It'll rain.'

But it didn't. Suddenly, after weeks and months of water falling from the sky so regularly we thought it was part of a reliable pattern, each day dawned in sunny yellow dryness. It was as though the gods were determined to make us understand who was the real boss. Got a fancy tank and think you're set for life? Won't do you any good without rain. Got a flushing dunny and think you've hit the comfort zone? Won't make any difference until you have water. Think you control the elements? Think again. Everything, as my father would have said, was in the lap of those pesky, nameless gods.

All the basic necessities we not only took for granted but considered a democratic right were no longer available at the flick of a switch, the turn of a tap. Sustainable living, even with the mod cons of roofs, walls, plumbing and heating, is not for sissies. After too many dry weeks to count, it was all I could do to nod and grin with rictus insincerity when anyone applauded the sunny weather.

Then the winds came. Dust, the inevitable legacy of construction, kicked up and took ownership of every new nook and cranny. Once or twice, willy-willies erupted furiously out of nowhere and then collapsed into nothing. Despite the long dry, I planted grevilleas to hide the septic tank. Bob and I carted every drop of used and spare water in a plastic bowl, determined to keep the young trees alive.

Sometimes, by the time we returned to Pittwater for a week of respite, I felt hammered.

By mid-winter, Bob's office was close to completion. Only the plywood walls were missing. Pears, who'd been stoic about even the smallest, seemingly inconsequential details, finally cracked when he learned Bob wanted a black stripe in the half-inch gap between each panel of plywood. 'I hate painting,' Pears moaned. 'I bloody hate painting.'

'It's just a thin black line. It doesn't have to be perfect. The timber will hide the edges,' I said, trying to placate him.

He groaned. 'Mate, when you hate painting, you bloody hate painting.'

Gazza arrived each day wearing genuine work boots. 'Wait till I tell Brickworks Michael you've been corrupted. Your reputation's shot,' I joked.

'Trench work in winter,' he responded. 'Flip-flops and socks just aren't up to it.'

Then suddenly the shed was completed. Bob's office, with a raised chipboard floor, boasted a squat little wood-fired heater that sat on a bed of bricks. A bathroom (tiled floor) with a flushing loo, shower and an adequate basin, was conveniently located two steps outside the office area. Towels were stacked on a shelf like the old-fashioned luggage racks on trains. The same gas water-heater we'd used for our alfresco bathing was hooked on an outside wall and plumbed into the bathroom. The sink that once stood alone in the middle of the paddock was now installed with hot and cold running water. I washed and folded the mobile dunny seat, putting it away with a hint of regret. As cold and damp as those night-time forays undoubtedly were, there was also a raw magic in them.

Power came from two solar panels on the roof. Long after the sun dropped below the horizon and the valley was cloaked in darkness, lights burned brightly in our cosy nook and computers fired up at the touch of a button. We could also boast that great game-changer of the twentieth century: a fridge. It meant the end of melting ice, soggy foodstuff and the worry of meat going off overnight. We transferred our camp chairs indoors in front of the pot-bellied stove, bought a queen-size bed and laid a Gabbeh rug on the floor. A new bright-white radio took up residence on the windowsill.

Each morning after the news bulletin at 6.30, we tuned into Kim Honan on ABC Mid North Coast Radio for the rural report. The countryside, with its stories of bees and bananas, of tea, turf and tapioca, became part of our new neighbourhood. Some mornings we rejoiced in victories – a bumper year for blueberries, a dairy deal that favoured farmers instead of super-markets. Some mornings we wiped away tears – a lifetime's hard labour destroyed in a freak storm; a child lost in an awful farm machinery accident. We listened to weather reports as though our lives were at stake.

In a separate, large area that would be Bob's workshop, we set up the kitchen and dining area with a large gas ring with three settings. No more cooking over a fire in the rain. Hooks, made from bending leftover fence wire, were lined up along a steel brace. Billies, frying pans, colanders and kettles hung within easy reach on what I now knew were called top-hat sections. I lined up sugar, flour and tea in second-hand enamel canisters. Black plastic containers stored enamel plates, cutlery and supplies, keeping stuff safe from mice, rats and antechinus. Although I would happily have brought down a shovel on the head of a rat, I had a soft spot for antechinus, the cheeky-faced marsupials that moved with lightning speed and seemed to grin and wave as they scampered off.

To house a growing library, Bob built a couple of small tables out of scrap timber in what seemed like minutes. They were rough and utilitarian, and I treasured them above all else because he'd made the effort when he was busy elsewhere.

It was simple, small-scale and manageable. Wake in the morning, make the bed, sweep the floor, shake the rug, dust three window ledges. Wash up, sweep the kitchen floor, wash tea towels, wipe plastic tablecloths. Quite quickly we bought a washing machine. No more hauling laundry back to Pittwater but, even more significantly, we kept a permanent set of clothes on site.

We transplanted a television from Tarrangaua and followed the advice of a salesman in Taree who suggested a twenty-five-dollar pair of rabbit ears before committing a few hundred dollars to a full-size antenna. The ears worked perfectly. Every saving helped. But something changed with the introduction of television into our rural lives. We invited in the bigger, more brutal world. The effect was to leave us – well, me; it didn't have the same impact on Bob – jangly, when not so long ago I'd been soothed and stroked by stars and the night air. Even when it rained and blew, there was a deeply satisfying elemental, visceral connection to the physical world. Those lazy chats gazing into the campfire ceased, struck dumb by the roar of current affairs illustrated with grisly pictures to hammer home the horrors. Wars. Plagues. Floods. Droughts. Economic meltdowns. Political mud-slinging. Death. Destruction. Evil. Freak events that made me wonder over and over: how is it that one person survives and one doesn't.

—

It was a momentous day when the survey pegs were pounded into the ground to mark the home site. Soon after, Bluey, a hard-working, practical man of few words, arrived with an exca-vator to scrape a level pitch for the slab. Bob looked worried when he should have been elated.

'What's up?' I asked.

He walked me over to a rock in the ground. 'Not sure whether this is a floater or part of a deep outcrop. Should've dug around, checked it out. Basic research and I didn't do it. If it's an outcrop, we're in strife.'

'What kind of strife?'

'Money strife.'

It is a terrible truth that building a home from the ground up is like riding the stock market. Every decision has a possible downside and, even if you're a blue-chip-planner instead of a risk-taker, curveballs scream out of nowhere. Weather impinges on each step – seasoning timber for the floor or outdoor cladding, curing a slab until it's tough enough to withstand a stampeding herd of cattle without a chip, even deliveries of material. Tradies are resilient, but when torrential rain turns the building site into a clay pit, when gale-force winds spin planks like a whirligig, when heat sucks the last pinprick of oxygen out of the air, tools are packed into aluminium trunks with (mostly) the kind of care and order a surgeon uses for his instruments. They're loaded onto the tray backs of utes and the men take off. Every day is a dollar. Every week eats into the schedule. Every delay is like standing over a toilet and flushing money down the drain. Even the most sanguine, cashed-up owners, I am certain, cannot be immune to the stress of a vanishing bank balance – and we were neither.

We had a budget, and while we'd blithely proceeded on the basis that at our age saving for my father's oft-quoted rainy day was pointless, nevertheless, if we hit a rocky outcrop on day one, it signalled the beginning of what already felt like an almost witch-like evaporation of funds. And, yes, we hit a rocky outcrop. Our single, barely visible, comparatively small brown protrusion from a thicket of bladey grass turned out to be part of a large metamorphic knoll thoughtlessly and inconsiderately pushed up by volcanic action in a past millennium. At least that's how Bob explained it later.

Meanwhile, Bluey stood over the offending boulder. 'The brown stuff. This,' he said, reaching down to prise loose a fragment of rock the colour of burnt toffee, 'breaks up easy.

No problem. But see this?' He kicked at some mean-looking, blue-grey material. 'Tough stuff. Bloody hard as . . . a bastard.' The two men, Bob and Bluey, stood alongside each other, staring at the ground.

'Any way to guess what you'll find?' Bob asked.

'Not till I get in there,' Bluey said. 'I'll be back tomorrow with the rock breaker. See how we go.'

We'd budgeted one man, one machine, for half a day. In the end, Bluey spent three days being shaken by a large hydraulic jackhammer in a way that you felt must rearrange his vital organs and leave him senseless. He took short meal breaks and only once crabbed with ill temper when his eager young grandson fired up the excavator during the sacrosanct peace of smoko.

'What do we want to listen to that noise for right now?' he yelled. The kid, a capable boy less than ten years old who knew his way around the equipment like an adult, killed the engine instantly. But you could see he itched to have a real go.

Quickly, I learned to differentiate the low-throated growl of brittle brown rock from the ear-splitting, high-pitched rage of stubborn blue rock. Rage beat growl by a wide margin and meant that, before we'd even hammered a single nail, the original house plan needed adjustment. 'Knock-on effect' was fraught with new meaning. Bluey had to drill so deep we now had a cellar-like space under what would one day be the sitting room, a space that also drifted under what would be my office. Two new underground rooms. More bricks. More concrete. More work. More costs.

Bob is a deeply practical man. Not long after he'd made one of the first cups of tea I shared with his late wife, Barbara, he confessed that he'd done a cost analysis of tea bags versus tea made in a pot with tea leaves.

'Why?' I asked, dumbfounded that anyone would bother.

'I was curious, that's all,' he replied.

'And what was the upshot?'

'Tea leaves are half the price of tea bags.'

My face must have registered disbelief. 'To keep it in perspective, a tea bag might cost two cents. A proper cuppa costs one cent.'

Many years later, when he recalled that story, I said, 'You failed to factor in the value of flavour.'

'Ah,' he replied, smiling. 'That's unquantifiable.'

So Bob pored over the plans, trying to find ways – like governments who inherit budget deficits – to cut and paste to make up the shortfall. But every compromise felt like a sacrifice to the overall concept, a betrayal of the architect's commitment to give us something wonderful. Again, I felt a pang for Kevin McCloud's dreamers at the same time as wondering what strange little quirk in the human brain makes us able to ignore unpleasant facts and focus, instead, on the fantasy. I shoved the money issue into a neat little compartment and locked the lid. Shades of my mother. Never too far from the surface. But there were days when all I wanted to do was run for cover. Bob just dug in deeper, thought outside the square, made adjustments and kept up the pressure to find solutions to each new challenge. I might have been wilting, but he was thriving.

Although the rock outcrop created a problem, he told me one night, there were also positives. Instead of erecting tank stands in the open, the water tanks – including the hot-water tank – could now be protected in the large area under the house. The large bank of batteries to store energy from the solar panels would have a spacious home instead of being crammed into a specially designed holding pen.

There was room for a wine cellar, too, in a deep, dark area that remained at a constant, cool temperature. Like the champagne caves in France. Well, not quite, but the thought was there. It would also be shelter if – god forbid – we ever needed to escape from a firestorm.

22

IT BECAME HARDER AND HARDER to wrench ourselves away from Benbulla, especially when the rain came down and ended the long, gut-wrenching dry as winter drifted into spring. It fell softly at first. The ground greedily sucked in the wet. Then it bucketed in torrents so thick and heavy the shed felt like a stage with a curtain drawn tight around it. It was too much too quickly, but the dams filled and, in what felt like no more than an exhalation of breath, whiffs of green appeared on the roadside, the slope leading to the shed, the paddocks.

'How quickly the country recovers,' I said, warm and dry, looking out the window.

'Want to drive down to check on the floodway level?' Bob asked. I reached for my boots.

Our track was slick and slippery all the way to the front gate. From there, the bumpy council road held fast, with rough-cut, rocky gutters carrying off the overrun.

'If this rain keeps up, we could get locked in. Want to hit the supermarket for extra supplies?' I suggested.

Bob nodded. Turned up the speed on the windscreen wipers. He muttered something, which I didn't catch.

'What?'

He dropped down a gear to take a sharp bend. Mud kicked up from the tyres, flicked loudly against the side of the car. 'Might have left our run too late,' he said, pointing ahead. The floodway was deep and wide and running fast. On both sides, strong grasses were bent double. Fence posts lay drunkenly, tethered by wires. The high-water mark showed a depth of almost two metres.

'How about the other way?' I said. 'Towards Mt George?'

Bob slid into reverse, engaged four-wheel drive. Backed into a gateway and turned. Water sped down the windscreen. Wipers slapped it away furiously but couldn't keep up.

About two kilometres further along and heading west from our front gate, we found a raging river where once there'd been a trickling watercourse. We got out of the car to take a closer look. Broken fences. Logs. Branches. Unidentifiable detritus. All spinning and speeding in deep, muddy water to end who knows where.

'A no-go,' Bob said, a tinge of awe in his voice.

Back in a car that stank routinely of wet wool, wet plastic, wet leather and underlying all of that, the persistent aroma of cattle shit, we headed home.

In the shed, we settled in for the duration, content to watch clean blue water gush into the tank from the rooftop until the gauge crept out of the red zone, signalling near-empty, and into the black zone. We cheered when it hit the full mark. Then water fed through the overflow pipe and torrents spilled out to flow down the hill. Losing it felt like blasphemy. But in front of our eyes, that first, fragile, patchy film of green pushing through dusty yellow soil transformed into a thick, emerald-green pelt.

It was a fact, an old-timer told me later, that farmers are like women who have just given birth. Within minutes they forget the pain − of droughts and barren paddocks, of crows growing fat and sleek on carrion while the stock did it hard, of standing helpless while the wind carried off precious topsoil to another State. When a season came good in a rush, that was more miracle than luck, he said, and all around, new life wiped the slate clean of hopelessness – it was like being reborn. Farming was lifeblood, he continued. Why else would anyone keep busting their guts with the odds stacked against them? But it could break people, too, he added, nodding his head as if agreeing with himself. He'd seen more than one good man brought to his knees in his time.

The rain pounded harder during the night, hammering the tin roof so we had to shout to be heard. A little before dawn, sudden silence and a deep, dark stillness woke us. Quite quickly, across a sodden landscape and way in the distance, a rising sun managed a few weak yellow shafts through the last storm clouds. The shimmering bush suddenly came alive. On fence wires, fire finches, willie wagtails and jacky winters, fluffed feathers. Magpies sang from the tops of the old gum trees in front of the shed. Down in the gullies, a new web of waterways fed into overflowing dams. The sky filled with lemon, orange and red, then bled into a heady turquoise colour. Leaves suddenly lifted from their sad droop; light glistened and bounced from wet treetops. Sparkly and energetic. Exhaustion and anxiety lifted from land, trees, grass, cattle and us, the apprentice custodians of all the above. Bob and I went outside in our pyjamas. The fresh, green smell was touchable.

We scoffed pancakes slathered with butter and jam, gulped strong tea. Pulled on our gumboots and drove off to check the floodway.

On the other side of the cattle grid, Bob told me to slow down. 'We're not going anywhere,' he said, pointing ahead where a waist-high, oozing mountain of red clay blocked the track. One of the hundreds, perhaps thousands, of underground springs, loaded beyond capacity, had quietly collapsed and slid down the hill. 'Reverse back along the track. Don't even try to do a U-turn.

The edges will be soft as putty and you'll slip over the side,' Bob said.

'You drive,' I replied, unbuckling my seatbelt.

Bob gave me a hard look. 'Just take it slowly and carefully. You'll be fine.' With a sheer drop on one side and a deep clay bog on the other, I wanted to squib. I gave up reversing when I started wearing multifocals. What looked a long way through one part of the lens was up close and personal through another, making it impossible to judge distances accurately. 'Slowly,' Bob repeated, leaving no way out.

I shifted gears and set off. Jerking. Braking. Stopping. Craning to see better. Feeling shooting pains in my neck. Going forward to improve an angle. Back again. Forward again. It seemed to take forever to reach the gateway to the Home Hill, where there was space to turn. Finally, facing safely forwards, I slumped over the steering wheel.

Bob slapped my knee in congratulation. 'Good work,' he said. But I understood the subtext: if there's a crisis, you have to cope because by the time help arrives we could all be dead.

Back in the shed, Bob called a neighbour who did excavating work to boost farm income. Turned out he had the cattle tray on his truck to take a few head to the local abattoir. He told Bob he'd try to deliver the cattle early so he could switch trays and help out as soon as possible. The level of the floodway, he said, had dropped back. He'd have no trouble crossing. Two hundred millimetres of rain, he told us, in just forty-eight hours. After the long dry we needed it badly, eh?

Richard, rock solid in shorts, a polo shirt and gumboots, arrived as a grey drizzle drifted in and light was beginning to fade. He shook Bob's hand, nodded at me. Inspected the red clay slush spewed across the track with a toupee of determined kikuyu clinging raggedly. Then eyed the gaping hillside where it once resided.

'Yeah,' he said in a slow drawl, 'it'll take a while.' He got to work. Lower the bucket. Scoop. Fill the bucket. Lift the bucket. Dump the contents over the edge of the track. Start again. Wearing it away. Going so close to the edge once that we thought he and his machine were doomed. But he dug the bucket in hard, using it as an anchor, and reversed back onto solid ground. Levelled the machine. Safe again. Heart in my mouth, I waved farewell and walked back to the shed, unable to watch.

Bob returned just after dark, hunched inside wet-weather gear, his rubber boots gluey with red clay. He yanked them off at the shed door and came inside in his socks. 'Wouldn't take any money. Said we were neighbours – one day he'd be in strife and would have to call on us.'

The following day we dropped a slab of beer at his front door. Not nearly enough to repay his kindness but we weren't sure of country protocols. Later, we were told it took him a while to discover it. Country people mostly used the back door.

—

The building of the house followed a similar format to the shed: concrete trucks shrieked up the hill in hourly instalments. Men wielding rakes, boards and shovels scraped, smoothed, filled and pummelled the gritty grey slop that spewed out. Terry Cross checked the laser levels. Bob, bitten once by dodgy batteries, dragged out his old dumpy level to do a double-check. But Terry, pedantic almost to bullying point, set perfection as a base requirement: 'No room for mistakes on a building site. Problems go down the line and you end up in a mess.'

The weather had turned dry again. It was ideal but the brickies were running behind schedule on another job.

'What about another crew,' Bob suggested.

'This is the last mob standing in the area,' Terry said. 'Most of the old blokes are either retired or their hands are bent with arthritis and their backs are buggered. And young blokes aren't interested in a dying trade.' It wasn't the kind of news that boded well for Brickworks Michael. Fashions changed – there's nothing more certain – but if nobody knew how to lay walls that didn't topple in a stiff breeze, then what difference would it make?

After a long line of tests and experiments, the inconsistencies and cost of making black bricks was pronounced unviable. We settled for blood-red, veering towards blue and purple, in a smaller, slim style. Handmade at the brickworks and fired in the kiln that Bob had designed in what felt like another era, they were elegant little things. The brickies hated them on sight.

'It's going to take longer to lay them,' Terry explained. 'And they're surly bastards anyway. Seems to go with being a brickie.'

It was undeviating, repetitive but specialised work, and the men were experts. Long straight lines rose up from the ground, layer by layer until a tall, straight wall emerged and the house became a solid reality instead of a fuzzy concept. Finally, we could see the shape and dimensions. How it would sit on the land. Then settle.

'It's huge,' I said, surprised.

Terry gave me an odd look. 'First impression for most people and they're shocked it's so small.'

Once the brickies – who turned out to be quite cheery blokes – finished their job, a new routine fell into place. At 6.30 am, Terry's white van rattled up the driveway, bounced past the shed and pulled up at the house site. A string of white utes followed twenty-five minutes later. The drivers emerged dressed in hi-vis orange-and-black shirts with Terry's logo emblazoned on the back. Navy shorts and wide-brimmed cloth hats. Except for Kane, the youngest – he pitched up in a boggling array of psychedelic board shorts and T-shirts. Standing out like a red Indian amongst the cavalry. Tools were downed at 9.30 for smoko. Cool boxes appeared. Dry biscuits with Vegemite. Ham and cheese sandwiches. No cake or sweet biscuits. Tea bags, instant coffee, hot water from a thermos. Never any milk. The men refused to join us at the campfire and sat on makeshift seats – a few bricks, a couple of boards, a cool box – at great distances from each other. As though they were dodging a raging flu.

Chippy, her legs stiff with arthritis, trotted the distance between the shed and the house site on the dot of smoko and lunch. Neither rain nor hail would have held her back. Every so often she scored royally.

'Couldn't resist her,' John said, apologetically.

—

The big trucks kept coming. More bricks for the breezeway fireplace. Steel beams. Rainwater tanks. Timber. Scaffolding. Cranes to swing tanks into place or raise and then lower steel supporting beams. Men straddled the beams, one by one, inching along like monkeys to reach the corner posts. Slipping nuts and bolts into steel plates. Tightening with a wrench until they held firm. Each piece built for a particular function. The scaffolding went up.

'The detail is amazing,' I told Bob over dinner one night. 'Everything has to be so precise. Who designed this part of the construction? Russell and Carolyn or Terry?'

'I did,' Bob said. I looked at him with new eyes.

'It's going well, don't you think? Everyone seems to be operating at a run,' I said.

'The rush is always on to get the roof finished. Once it's secure, work can go on even in a cyclone.' Not quite a cyclone, as it turned out. A couple of days later, two beams short of completing the frame, a dirty, dry wind rocketed in out of a still day like a raging virago, kicking up a long, narrow ribbon of thick brown dust, bending men double, buffeting the vehicles so it looked as though they'd roll over. Tools were locked away, ladders laid flat, tarps dragged over supplies and anchored with bricks. The site shut down and emptied out. All in a few minutes.

We watched from the shelter of the shed as the workmen drove off, turning dust-caked faces towards us with a nod and a wry half-salute. Even our mob of resident wallabies, lovely grey creatures with creamy chests and pelts as shiny sleek as mink, took off to wait out the wind in the shelter of the gullies. Weather, I thought, is like a corrupt dictatorship. It overrides logic on a whim.

The next day, as the last crossbeam slid into place a moment before knock-off time, Bob confessed: 'Made a blue. One steel plate facing the wrong way.'

'How many steel plates altogether?'

'Couple of hundred, maybe.'

'And one slipped through. Better than average, I would've said.'

'The boss makes a mistake and everyone notices. Hurts a man's pride.'

'It's beer o'clock,' I said. But you could see it in eyes clouded with uncertainty: was it age or carelessness, or the carelessness that comes with age?

I handed him a beer and patted his back. 'If you were thirty years old you'd shrug it off in a second.'

'Yeah,' he said. But he didn't look consoled or convinced.

A few days later I left for Western Australia for a writers' festival. A man on the plane was nuts. Off his face on drugs and deadset scary. Stripping off his shirt. Leaving the door of the loo open and splashing himself with water. Talking to himself in a loud, weird gibberish. The crew kept him under control, but I was spooked. Already paranoid about flying, I seriously considered catching the train back to Sydney. If there was a crisis, I wanted both my feet planted firmly on the ground. My fear of flying was turning into a phobia. I felt powerless to stop it.

While I was away, Bob rang every day after knock-off time to give me a rundown of the day's work. 'By the way, there's a brown snake in the woodpile.'

'Oh, god,' I said, 'keep a close eye on Chippy.'

He called the next day: 'The brown snake, you remember?'

'Yeah. Chippy –'

'She's fine, and you don't have to worry anymore. Concrete trucks don't swerve for brown snakes.'

'Oh. But keep Chippy away. If she chewed the head, the poison . . .'

He rang back ten minutes later: 'The brown snake? All good. A goanna is eating it.'

———

Installing the solar panels was a top priority. Builders needed power for big tools. A single generator would slow progress. The frame was erected facing true north and tilted at a forty-five-degree angle for maximum efficiency. Twenty-one panels fed energy into a bank of batteries weighing two tonnes, stored in one of the unscheduled man-made caves under the house. If Bob had done the maths correctly, we would effectively live as comfortably off-grid as on. Although the initial monetary outlay looked steep, it was a fraction of the cost of paying for nearly two kilometres of powerlines. We would also be kissing goodbye to quarterly energy bills, which were beginning to bite deep at Pittwater. But our primary goal was to make a contribution to the planet. Anyone who's driven past the blasphemy of an open-cut mine in the heart of fertile grazing land, or seen oil spills suffocate seas and leave greasy black blemishes on golden coastlines, or gas bubbling up in once pure rivers from botched fracking, or who's cried for the people of Fukushima after a tsunami breached the security of nuclear power plants and killed off life as it had been sustained for generations, had to feel some remorse and, if possible, embrace clean energy. Ours were baby steps, but they must add up eventually or where is the hope?

———

On my return from Western Australia, I spent two days at Pitt-water to fit in the obligatory mother visit. I called her to set the day and time.

'Where have you been?' she asked accusingly.

'At a writers' festival,' I replied, knowing she'd approve and it would cut off any complaints.

'How did it go?'

'Yeah, good. The organisers took us to see a fisherman's settlement on the Abrolhos Islands. Spent a night there. Amazing. It's a coral reef. It was like stepping onto an Anzac biscuit. You could see the sea moving under your feet. Very strange feeling. As though you could slip under and never be found again.'

'Well, while you've been away, everything's fallen to pieces here. If they cut any more staff, I'll be making my own bed.'

'I'm sure it's not that bad but tell me all about it at lunch. Picnic or restaurant?'

'Picnic. That way, I'll have you to myself.'

Trapped in the car, I allowed her a five-minute harangue. Then I steered her into talking about her past. I had ulterior motives, of course. My new book was taking shape in my head. I craved information.

Once again, she became suspicious: 'You were never inter-ested in my stories. I tried to tell you all this stuff years ago. You said it was boring.'

'You never supplied enough detail for me,' I replied.

'You mean you thought I made things up,' she said.

'Didn't you?'

She slid her finger under a milky grey Pacific oyster, big enough to cut in two. Tugged at the muscle.

'Sometimes . . . well, alright, I embroidered a little. But only to make it more exciting.' She slid the oyster into her mouth. Bit down. Swallowed. I handed her a paper napkin to wipe her fingers. 'There was a murder in the family, the only murder we've ever had. Only one we're sure about, anyway. I know some of us felt like cutting someone's throat occasionally.'

'Who?'

'Auntie Annie Wiseman. She and her niece, Phyllis. Both murdered. She was a sweet girl, Phyllis. Auntie Annie was devoted to her. She never liked me much. Probably why I never got a mention in the will.'

'Whoa, back up. What happened to Auntie Annie and Phyllis?'

'They were murdered.'

'Yes. And . . .' I urged her on, hoping she'd think back. Give me a story that went beyond a once-over-lightly.

'They caught the man. It was a famous case. In all the papers. I told you about it when you were a teenager. You sniffed and said it was boring.'

'I don't remember any of this, and I think I would. A double murder – you don't forget that in a hurry.'

'Auntie Annie put a pound in the collection plate every Sunday without fail. Lot of money in those days, but she was very religious.'

'When was this?'

'A long time ago. Anyway, he hanged. I remember that. And the fact that he killed two women for a pound. The money for the collection plate. Why don't you write a book about it?'

'I'll look it up on the net.'

'More interesting than most of your stories.'

'Right. You finished? Time to go.'

I did some research. The year was 1938. Annie, aged sixty-three – a couple of years older than me – was referred to as an *elderly* church-going woman. Phyllis, a typist, was just seventeen years old. Newspapers referred to the case as the Glenroy Horror. George Green, thirty-eight, a chimney sweep, broke into the house either late on Saturday night or early Sunday morning. He strangled Annie then raped Phyllis before ramming her head against her iron bed, killing her. Green maintained his innocence right up to the scaffold, but the case was heralded as the birth of forensic science.

'Did you look it up?' Esther asked the following day when I called her to say I was leaving for Benbulla.

'Yep. Shocking case. Phyllis was so young.'

'Annie loved that girl. She really loved her.' She let loose a long sigh.

'What did you say to her that got you written out of the will?' I asked.

'She was very proud of the family tree. Had every birth, death and marriage charted on the wall. We were all listed. She boasted we were a fine family, well bred – words to that effect – and descended from Lord Nelson. *On the wrong side of the blanket, no doubt.* That's what I said. She gave me a fierce look and shook her finger at me. *You'll regret those words, young lady.* My mouth got me into a lot of trouble in those days. I thought I was being smart but not everyone agreed.'

'There's a difference between being witty and being mean-spirited.'

'Have a go at me, why don't you?'

'Stating a fact, that's all. Did your sisters get a mention in the will?' I asked.

'None of us did. At least no one mentioned any windfalls. But they wouldn't have, would they? The twins, they thought I was spoiled rotten. There was a terrible fight when Dad died. He left me the house. Less land than the twins were given, but it was the prime spot. At the top of the hill. Magical views. Do you remember?'

'Yeah.'

'Belle thought it should've gone to her. She'd looked after Mum and Dad all her life.'

'So that's why the two of you fell out for such a long time.'

'Didn't you know?'

'Not really.'

'No. Of course you didn't. You weren't a kid who hung around during confrontations. You'd leave the room when talk turned nasty.'

'Did I?' It was a revelation to me. But one that rang true. We talked a little longer before saying cheerio. Later, I thought about researching the Lord Nelson angle.

Did it matter? No. Whatever Felix's lineage, I fiercely hated the man.

23

BACK AT BENBULLA, Bob announced it was time to drench and tag the cattle. But while Benny's Boys were gentle, good-humoured beasts that followed a bucket of grain like a holy chalice, our saleyard cattle were wild crossbreeds that bolted as soon as you fired up the ute. Bob organised a round-up: Fletch and his friend on motorbikes, Brickworks Michael and Bob in utes. The rest of us – a couple of extra blokes and wives – on foot.

We waded through dew-heavy grass, arms spread wide (a device to trick cattle into thinking you are bigger than them), the damp seeping all the way to our thighs. The herd took one look at us and, with an impressive speed that belied their heavy frames, scattered like birdshot into dense rainforest gullies where they stayed hidden until we gave up the chase in frustration and returned to the shed for a well-earned smoko. Blueberry pikelets, freshly cooked in a frying pan over the gas jet. Covered in sweet blueberry jam and thick cream. Slung along the table on enamel plates with the speed of frisbees and scoffed just as fast while we plucked inch-long, skinny black seed heads with a nasty little hook at one end from our clothing.

'Sticky beaks,' Michael explained. 'Also known as Farmer's Friends or Cobbler's Pegs. Won't even let go in the washing machine.'

'How do you get rid of them?' I asked, thinking there must be a quick trick.

'You pull 'em out one by one,' he replied, grinning with wicked glee.

Right. I walked over to Foggy. 'So. How do you know if you're looking at a weed or a precious plant?' I asked, anxious to learn.

'If cattle won't eat it, it's a weed,' he said flatly, leaving no room for argument.

A couple of days later, Bob came up with a new strategy to get the steers under control. He opened a pen in the cattle yard, nestled a salt lick in a corner. Cattle, we'd been told, were drawn to the heady mix of minerals like an alcoholic to booze. Each day, we looked out from our hilltop to see whether they'd fallen for the con. They remained aloof or obtuse. Or just plain canny and distrustful. I couldn't decide.

Then suddenly, six days later, I drove down the hill on the way to Wingham to pick up supplies. There they were, all twenty-eight of them, crowded into a single pen and jockeying with rough headbutting and violent hip-thrusting to have a go at the lick. I pulled up, took my time and, at an angle instead of directly – cattle spook if you walk straight at them – crept towards the main gate. 'Aha! Gotcha!' Slammed the lock shut. Double-checked. I drove off, slapping the steering wheel. Victory is sweet.

As soon as my mobile came into range, I called Bob. 'They're in the yard,' I shouted in the way my father once shouted on a landline, as if it might make his voice carry better over a distance of one hundred miles. 'Quiet as lambs. Sort of. Gate's shut good and tight. There's nowhere for them to go. You're a genius!'

The following day, Saturday, the utes turned into our drive, ready for battle. Brickworks Michael, Fletch, Foggy and his daughter, Sarah, who was studying animal science. Blue-eyed like her father, with silken-corn blonde hair and a face like an angel, she expertly swung a leg over the fence and jumped in with the steers.

'You're fearless!' I shouted, full of admiration.

She walked through the cattle as though they were baby lambs, slapping a rump, pushing a head out of the way, leaned on a steel rail: 'Dad doesn't have time for wimps.'

'So you breed 'em tough in the country, Foggy,' I said, lining up beside him with a clipboard, ready to note ear tag numbers and any relevant details for each steer.

Foggy, mostly quick-witted, funny and irreverent, looked up from filling an injection the size of a small missile with a vaccine called 5-in-1. 'You don't do kids any favours by spoiling them,' he said.

'Of course not. Goes without saying. So,' I said, grabbing the empty vaccine box, 'what's this stuff do?' . . . *for the prevention of pulpy kidney disease, tetanus, black disease, malignant oedema (blackleg-like disease) and blackleg in cattle and sheep, including swelled head in rams.* Swelled head in rams? Blackleg? Pulpy kidney? Bob and me, we were babes in the woods. I fought off a strong instinct to turn and run. Crossing dark waters on wild, stormy nights in a small tinny suddenly seemed like a doddle. I knew, though, that we were in too deep, committed to a new way of life that would make or break. It was up to us. *Rise to the challenge,* my mother used to say if I was feeling lily-livered about a chore. I grabbed the clipboard and tried to stand straighter.

'C'mon, c'mon.' Bob, Sarah, Michael and Fletch began to coax the cattle from the pen into the race — a narrow lane meant to force cattle, single file, into the crush. The crush is a small pen with a rear gate that locks an animal from behind and a front gate that slams shut against the neck, leaving the head trapped. Timing is critical. The steer can bolt straight through without being

SUSAN DUNCAN

drenched, vaccinated and tagged, and you have to start again. If cattle are familiar with people, it's a simple enough procedure. But ours were delinquents. Maybe Foggy was right – there's a price to pay when there's no early childhood discipline.

In a split second, they switched from quiet salt-lickers into bolshie bastards intent on havoc. Snot flew left and right, along with spit and green bits. Bolters climbed on the backs of the steer in front. Everyone started shouting, prodding, shoving. Just as one steer moved forward, another reversed. Pandemonium. I lost track in the melee.

'Muscle up,' Foggy ordered. I took a deep breath. Looked at Sarah and Fletch in the pens and found a skerrick of courage. *But cattle are so bloody big*, I thought.

A strikingly good-looking black steer with four white socks, a white tassel on the tip of his tail and black eye patches on a white face, like a mask, had a suspicious-looking sac hanging between his legs.

'Stag,' Foggy said. 'Someone didn't quite finish the job when his balls were cut.' He dug into his jeans pocket and pulled out a pocketknife. Made a quick, decisive slash. Blood spurted. High as a fountain. Everyone ducked and scrammed. I looked away. Fought off nausea. 'Not a nut, then,' he said, more to himself than anyone else. 'A blood vessel gone bad. Sarah! Twine from the ute!' She vaulted the rails, ran off. Returned seconds later. Handed him some frayed bits and pieces that looked like they'd been saved in the same way women save ribbon – because it might come in handy one day.

Foggy bound the wound, tied it off. Slapped the steer on the rump. Opened the crush and let it out. With a careful gait, like a woman who'd just given birth, the steer tiptoed into the pen.

'If the wound opens, do I call the vet?' Bob asked.

'Nah. He'll bleed out in a few minutes. By the time the vet got here, he'd be dead.'

268

'What do you call that?' Bob said, meaning the sac.

Foggy grinned: 'An unexpected loss, mate.'

The team went back to work. Bob took over my job. I'd been so distracted by the blood I'd lost track of the numbering. Failed at my first real attempt at farming cattle. Not a good start. *Muscle up*, I thought, hearing Foggy's words echo in my head, but the noise was like a rock concert gone feral. Clanging. Bellowing. Crashing. Shouting. All performance, as it turned out. The moment the cattle were released into a paddock where clover waited like a doggie treat for good behaviour, they trotted about twenty yards, slowed to a stroll, dropped their heads to the ground. Ripping. Munching. And, yes, shitting and pissing. In one end and out the other. As consistent as daybreak.

Jobless and redundant, I went off to get smoko organised.

'You're good with cattle,' I told Sarah at smoko. She shrugged, as if it was nothing.

'My sister and me, we've worked with them all our lives. A steer trampled me once. I was about five years old and Mum was away. We were helping Dad in the yards. Only time I've ever seen Dad go white. Mind you, he waited till the bruises came up before he chucked me in the car and called in on the local chemist – who happened to be his sister – for advice. She took one look and yelled at him to get me to hospital. Then the doctor locked Dad out of the consulting room. Said I could tell him if Dad was beating me up. He'd make sure I got professional help; there was no way telling the truth would get me into any trouble. "I got snotted by a cow," I said.' She laughed. 'It's one of the famous family stories now.'

'Would've put me off for life,' I said.

'Mum was furious. Dad made me get back in the yard soon as the bruising faded.'

The steer with the twine bandage walked carefully for a few days. He survived, though. Grew a new sac, too. He ended up with a beautifully rounded rump that brought a good but not top price when we sent him to the abattoir. Abnormalities, we discovered, bring down the price per kilo. It was a strange, new, hard-hearted way of thinking for soft-souled city people like us, who have never had to deal with the realities of birth, death and farm economics. But it was amazing how quickly we adjusted.

—

It was a long, wet summer. Strong plaits of kikuyu runners smothered weeds and pasted a deep emerald-green lushness across the land. The earth gave off a chocolate-scented fecundity. Eager young gum trees put on growth spurts of a metre, sometimes more. Spindly wattles rose up on hillsides like banners. Labyrinthine springs erupted in puzzling patterns, running like blood vessels under the ground. Why here on a slope? Why not here, in a gully? Mapped over millennia, no doubt, and for very particular reasons. Norm's track, though, held firm as one humid, sweat-soaked day followed another.

One morning, the ABC's Kim Honen reported a Three-day Sickness epidemic. Cattle were dropping, even dying. Bob and I looked at each other blankly. Bob dialled Foggy.

'Most cattle get over it without any problems, but if a steer goes down, get it back on its feet as quickly as you can,' he advised. 'Their lungs can fill with fluid and they'll drown.' Bovine Ephemeral Fever, we learned, was carried by midges and mosquitoes. Animals stopped eating and drinking, drooled badly, developed a nasal discharge and watery eyes, became stiff in the joints and even lame. They also ran high temperatures and suffered from depression. Steers? Depressed? We crossed our fingers. Hoped our elevation might work to our advantage. Tried not to think about Foggy's 'unexpected losses' column.

At daybreak, Bob drove around checking the herd. At sunset, he checked again. It wasn't until about two weeks into the epidemic that our first steers started to get crook. Heads drooping, sweaty flanks, shaky bodies – looking very, very sad and sorry. And, yes, depressed. Still standing, though. Just when we thought we might escape the worst, Bob noticed a big black steer lying under a spindly old gum with a crown of dead branches. He hadn't moved for a day. Not chewing the cud, then. Just crook, his hooves facing uphill. He'd need to be rolled over or he'd die.

It was Friday, just before lunchbreak on the building site. Bob walked over from the shed and asked Terry if he could step outside his official job description and help out with a sick animal. Terry nodded, slammed his straw hat on his head and, without a word, the two men set off down a track sludgy with the rain and springs seeping out of the hillside. The humidity was thick enough to chew.

When they reached the steer, one man stood on either side, looking down at the beast shaking with fever. Terry cleared a few fallen branches.

'Get his back legs,' Bob said. 'I'll grab his head.'

'Watch his legs,' Terry said. Bob didn't take much notice. He was standing behind the head. Out of range, he thought. But cattle are double-jointed. A hoof flew towards Bob's face. He ducked. Fell backwards on a broken piece of log.

'Barely got me,' he told Terry. There'd be a bruise at worst. They tried again. Pushing, pulling. Trying to roll it into a safer position. Miraculously, the steer staggered to his feet. Took a shaky step or two. Moved off with a slow, elongated, slightly stiff gait. He'd live.

Late that afternoon, curly-haired Lisa and her husband, Roy, arrived for the weekend. 'How's it going?' they asked. 'What a view, eh?' Lisa hauled iceboxes filled with treats. Cheeses, pâté, herbs to plant. A cake.

'You're in the spare room,' I explained. 'Also known as the honeymoon tent. Bunk beds. Hope you can manage.'

'We're New Zealanders, Susan. We can handle anything.'

'Proper bed linen, though, and doonas if you need them. Feather pillows and a milk crate for a bedside table.'

'Not too shabby, then,' Lisa said, grinning.

'Got to look after your mates,' I replied, linking my arm through hers.

We ate dinner at a picnic table under the gum trees while the landscape changed colour. Green. Purple. Mauve. Pale grey. Pink lines of light etching the contours of distant hills. A silver moon rising. Talked about Pittwater. Fire-brigade dinners. Who would cook? Mandatory life jackets – a good or terrible idea? Weed days. Would the bush regenners ever get on top of lantana? Beth's stroke. At almost eighty-five, would she come good again? Booming Mona Vale. Parking was horrendous, wasn't it?

The tug of another world. Still so strong but changing fast. One new rule after another – revenue raisers introduced under the guise of safety (or that's how it felt to me) – was deadening our once larrikin spirits. Not long before midnight, when our talk slowed and we'd caught up on all the Pittwater news, we said sleepy goodnights.

In the shed, I turned to Bob: 'Do you miss Pittwater when we're here?'

He unbuttoned his shirt. Folded it over the back of a camp chair. 'Nope.'

'Do you miss the farm when we're at Pittwater?' I sat on the end of the bed, removed my boots.

'Nope.'

The ease with which men compartmentalise, I thought, crawling into bed. Half an hour later, Bob tried to turn over and let out a yell.

'You ok?' I asked, sitting up in fright.

'Nope.' He tried to move again. Groaned. Tried to get out of bed. Fell back.

'What can I do? What do you need?'

'Hospital.'

I dressed in a rush, helped Bob with his clothes. His face was white. He'd aged a thousand years in a few hours. I begged those unseen forces my mother firmly believed in. Please, nothing life-threatening.

He struggled into the ute, refusing to let me touch or help him. I scurried through the shed in the pitch dark to Lisa and Roy's tent: 'Lisa, you awake?'

'Unngh.'

'Just taking Bob to hospital. No dramas. Stay where you are.'

'Unngh.'

Saturday night emergency at Manning Hospital, on this particular night, was like a CWA meeting. Home-baked muffins. Coffee. Tea. Lots of chat. A great sense of calm. Bob was gently eased onto a bed. One by one, doctors came by, pressing his body and asking where it hurt. Nurses checked his blood pressure, heart rate. He was taken off for a scan.

'We're worried about internal bleeding,' a doctor told me. 'His kidneys have taken a hit. We'll know more tomorrow.' At four in the morning, when there was nothing else to be done, I headed back to Benbulla. Fell into bed. Lay awake staring at the ceiling. A thousand familiar emotions writhed like snakes. We were putting ourselves at risk . . . for what? To prove we could deny aging its dues? We'd made a shocking mistake. Yes, we were a long way into the project, but life was more important than worrying about the financial fallout. Face it. We were mugs. Delusional idiots who were too old to take on a career that real farmers – worn out by hard slog, dodgy weather, fluctuating interest rates and strong boofy beasts that could be felled by a tiny little midge bite, for god's sake – retired from at the first opportunity.

Back in Taree a few hours later, I bought Bob a pair of pyjamas (he doesn't own any), a new toothbrush and shaving kit, a takeaway flat white, and returned to the hospital. Walking along the corridor to his room, I overheard a group of doctors: 'Bed twelve. Kicked by a cow. It's always a cow, isn't it?'

I pulled up. 'Are you talking about my husband? Bob?'

'That's the one,' said a woman with red hair, wearing a white coat.

'Is he ok?' I asked anxiously.

'We're going to run a few more tests,' she said.

Bloody cattle, I thought, torn between rage and fear.

They gave Bob every possible scan, test and examination, and ultimately concluded his kidneys were bruised but not damaged. On Sunday morning we drove back to Benbulla.

'Fit as a Mallee bull,' Bob said cheerily. 'That's me. Won't need a check-up this year. I've had one.' I was beginning to realise farming would always be an emotional seesaw; I would have to adjust or withdraw. Time to have a cup of concrete and harden up, as a woman once told me when we met on a camping trip.

At the farm, Lisa and Roy had a fresh cuppa made, cake laid out. Bob said, 'Roughest ride to town I've ever had. Susan found every bump and went for it.' I walked away and swallowed a sob.

After Roy and Lisa returned to Pittwater, Bob and I discussed the mounting workload.

'You need help with farm work,' I said. 'Just until the building is finished. Otherwise you'll be wrecked.' He nodded, still in pain, and called Benny to ask if he knew anyone who was looking for casual work. Benny recommended Eric.

Eric – stocky, wiry-haired, wearing patched jeans, a green T-shirt and heavy-soled work boots – pitched up in a black ute at 7.30 am the following week.

Bob asked: 'Can you drive a tractor?'

'Yep.'

'Do you mind hills?'

'Hills are ok. Most of 'em. But not the ones that are going to make me dead.'

'Fair enough.'

At smoko, he told us that the day before, along the dirt road and closer to town, Paul had rolled his tractor in a gully. He'd died twice in the helicopter on the way to John Hunter Hospital, but now it looked like he was going to pull through.

'Needed a whole roll of wire to stitch his busted bones back in a line,' Eric said. 'One thing I know for sure, when you come to the end of a steep cut and reckon you could do just a bit more, it's time to go home. It's the *bit more* that kills you.'

'What did you do before farm work?' Bob asked.

'Owned the local butcher shop.'

'Know much about cattle?'

'Oh yeah, a bit.'

'Live ones?'

'Yeah, them too.'

'Our bunch is pretty wild.'

'Takes a while, but they'll come to your call if you treat 'em right.'

'Let's get started, shall we?' They walked off together, heads bent, hands in pockets, like old mates.

At lunch, which he brought in a cool bag complete with cutlery, Eric told us his passion was working with scrap metal. Some people called it art. He called it fun. 'Best time is early evening, a beer in your hand, wandering around the garden thinking about what you're going to do the next day,' he said.

'So no more butchering?' I asked.

'Here and there when there's work around.'

A tiny bird landed on fence wire. 'What bird is that?' I asked.

Eric squinted. 'Pardalote.'

Bob and I looked at each other. Eric reached down to the grass near his feet and plucked at the clover. 'Four leaves. Meant to be lucky.' He held it out to me.

'Thank you,' I said.

'Ah, it's nothin'. There's plenty more.' He picked another one.
'Well, a little luck never hurts. You keep it this time,' I said.
'Nah. It's yours.'

At the end of the day I asked Bob what he thought of Eric. 'He's genuinely curious. Asks questions. Seems to be able to do anything. What did you do with the four-leaf clover?'

'Pressed it in one of the heavy architectural books. You've got to hang on to luck if you can.'

A couple of years later, I asked Eric what he'd thought of Bob when they'd first met. 'Oh yeah, he was ok. Took a while to work out how to talk to him on the phone, though. Those long silences. Kept thinkin' the line had dropped out.'

24

WE TRANSPORTED AN OLD TEAK TABLE and twelve folding chairs from Pittwater to the farm. At the end of every day, Bob and Terry plonked themselves on opposite sides and argued the finer, head-busting details of construction in a way that would send a married couple into therapy or divorce. Going head to head like two bulls until one or the other compromised. I waited for a big blow-up that would result in slapping on their hats and storming off in different directions. But after every confrontation, Bob took out his notebook, grabbed a pencil, scribbled sketches and calculations. Occasionally, he built small models or set out bricks in concrete to win his case. It took me a few weeks to understand the battles fired them up, got their adrenalin racing, set the bar for competition.

One day, Terry told us about a new litter of kittens. Rabbits, not cats. His wife was allergic to red meat and he bred them for the table. Turned out he was passionate about growing vegetables, too, and at the end of a day's work on site, he went home to relax by pulling weeds, turning soil, planting new seed. When it was too dark to see what he was doing, he went inside, pulled up a chair at the dining room table and mapped out a schedule for the following day. 'It's your money,' he said, bluntly. 'Reckon you don't want me wasting it.'

Now we, too, had a dining room. To celebrate, we invited everyone we knew to dinner. Pea, zucchini and feta fritters served as a nibble, followed by coq au vin with a twist: chicken pieces seared and then simmered with bacon, French shallots, mushrooms, red wine and ultimately flamed with brandy in the big cast-iron frying pan. One-dish cooking. Easy. A salad. Tiramisu for dessert. Utterly decadent with a kick of coffee. No cooking, made ahead and left in the fridge. Strawberries macerated in Kahlúa on the side. Strawberries – no booze – for the kids.

Brickworks Michael and his wife, Adele, and son, Fletcher, arrived in a plume of dust, followed by cattleman Foggy, his wife, Jenny, and their daughter, Sarah, who was home on holidays from university. The architects, Russell and Carolyn, their two young daughters, Anna and Sarah. The builder, Terry, and his wife, Ali.

Candles, enamel plates, wine served in water glasses. Salad served out of a pan that doubled as a wok. Bread sticks scattered down the table to be broken and dipped in the sauce from the chicken. There were no expectations from our rough dinners. I suspect guests understood the bare bones of shed living – it's how most new landowners started out – and that took all the pressure off.

'There's no such thing as a free lunch,' I said at one point. 'Everyone must perform. A song. A poem. A story. A joke. Whatever you like. We'll make our own entertainment.'

There were embarrassed murmurings, a few negative head shakes. Then Bob started off with a joke – he tells terrible jokes. This one, something about a genie granting three wishes, was no exception. After his dismal performance, everyone relaxed and had a go, except the architects. They proposed their two daughters as stand-ins, and the girls sang a duet with some skill and plenty of giggling. As it turned out, Sarah of the silken hair and angel face, who was once snotted by a cow and lived to tell the story, could sing like a dream. The shed fell silent from her first note. Clear and pure, unfaltering on the high or very low notes, she was spellbinding. After the applause died down, Sarah's mother turned to me and said, wistfully, 'I always thought she could've been a singer. But her father introduced her to cattle and they've been her first love ever since. Pity.'

Terry broke into a rich, deep baritone, strong enough to shatter terracotta drainpipes. He faded after a few notes – confident on a building site but overwhelmed by shyness at the table. Hidden talents everywhere.

It was as though the shed was sung into life that night. For a long while after, I managed to put aside the emotional seesawing and outright fear that we'd begun a project that might end in disaster. *Bitten off more than we could chew*, as my mother would say. Then Chippy died. I blamed the farm.

———

It was late evening on a Sunday night, Chippy shook violently from head to toe, as though possessed by an evil spirit. I picked her up and held her on my lap until she quietened. When I put her down she walked off sideways, legs crossing like a horse doing dressage. I picked her up again. Held her hard against my chest to reassure her in a way I could never have done for my mother. Whispered gently in her ear: 'Who's the best little doggie in the whole wide world? You are. You are, little doggie.' I'd seen these symptoms before. A neurological *event*, the vet said. Nothing could be done. She'd recover in her own time. In my childhood no one took a sick dog or cat to the vet. If an animal made it through the night, there was a good chance it would survive. Otherwise, grab the spade and start digging a hole. Chippy made it through the night. I waited for her to bounce back as she had in the past, but by nine o'clock in the morning I knew she was in trouble.

'We'll run some blood tests,' the vet said, easing her out of my arms. Promised he'd call as soon as he had any information, probably by late afternoon. I walked away. Fretting. Called him an hour later: 'I can't leave her there alone. She'll think I've abandoned her.'

'Come and get her then,' he said kindly. 'She's just resting until we get the results anyway.'

I carried her to the ute, placed her gently on the passenger seat. Back at Benbulla, I settled her on the bed and the two of us spent the afternoon there. Mostly she slept, groaning every so often without opening her eyes. She hurt all over. Anyone could see that. When I carried her outside to pee, she could barely stand up. Her piddle was the colour of claret. 'Who's the best little doggie in the whole wide world?' I murmured, stroking her ears. We'd been together for thirteen years, through good and tough times. The thought of losing her was awful.

The vet called to say she'd had a stroke and her vital organs were failing. He could keep her alive for a while longer, make sure she wasn't in any pain, but her days were numbered. And, by the way, did I know she had Cushing's disease? That crumbly texture on her nose was a sign. It often caused a fixation on food. It ruined kidneys, too. Hence the purple pee.

No. I didn't know.

There were dreadful, emotional decisions to make. Life for a few extra days? No matter what the cost to the animal? Or muscle up and do the right thing by an old dog that had never done anything but her best?

'You promised me twenty years, little doggie,' I whispered. 'How come you're not keeping your end of the bargain?' I stroked her old body, the grey fur around her snout. Memories rushed back. A husband lying on a mattress on the floor where he'd fallen in the hospice. A second mattress beside him for me to lie close. My brother, so thin and white and ephemeral he barely existed. One eye closed, already half-dead. The loss of both within three days. A blow so hard and heavy I thought I'd never recover. 'She's a dog, for god's sake,' I told myself. 'Just a dog. Get over it.' Not just a dog, though. My companion for almost as long as I'd lived with my parents.

Bob and I, we took Chippy back to the vet. I held her on my lap as the green needle went into her leg. Stroking her. Speaking softly. Goodbye, old doggie. Goodbye, best little doggie in the whole wide world. And then she was still. Bob drove back to the farm. Dug a deep hole in earth so hard he needed a crowbar to chip it away. We wrapped her in a blanket and laid her down. I stayed until the last sod was heeled in.

Those old undercurrents – helplessness, inadequacy, grief – which you think you've beaten and buried so they can never bring you undone again, flooded in. Just as raw. And I realised they'd always be there, lying in wait to unravel my heart, my head, until nothing made sense anymore, and suddenly the only clear solution to the pain was to blow up my current existence.

'I want a divorce,' I told Bob as we walked back to the shed. 'The farm, the house, the bloody cattle, all this. It's crazy. I want out.' He said not a word. I cooked dinner. I said hurtful things.

'If you want an argument, Susan, you're looking in the wrong place,' he said at last.

'I'm leaving. Right now.' He shrugged. Turned on the television.

I stomped outside into a moonlit night. Considered driving off in the ute forever and then realised I'd be leaving Bob without a car. I started walking. At the gate to the Home Hill, I waved my arms. Shouted. Let loose a riff of great, heaving sobs. Kept walking. Bawling. But where was I going, late at night and fourteen kilometres from the nearest town, which went into lockdown at five o'clock every afternoon anyway? I turned back. Crept into the shed like a thief. Bob was fast asleep. I lay on the bed beside him. Placed my hand lightly on his shoulder. How did I get so lucky? He turned over and gathered me in his arms. How did I get so lucky?

In the morning, he suggested three flowering gums to mark Chippy's grave. 'Yes,' I whispered.

Terry came over at smoko: 'Sorry to hear about Chippy.'

'Everything's got to die some time,' I responded, as if I was handling it well.

He nodded. 'That's the sad truth.'

I wandered over to the building site at lunchtime to give myself something to do. 'Sorry about Chippy,' said the tradies.

'Yeah.' Then as an afterthought: 'She had Cushing's disease, you know, so it wasn't her fault she was greedy. Not her fault at all. She was ill.'

'She was a good little dog,' said John, the others at a loss for words.

'Yeah.' But my heart felt like it was breaking. *Fill the gap quickly*, I thought. *Fill it now. Anything to seal off the void.*

'I want another dog,' I told Bob a week later.

'Wait a while,' he said.

'No.'

I trawled the net searching for Jack Russell puppies. Found a woman in our area (who turned out to be related to Brickworks Dave) with a litter that would be available in two weeks. She had three girls to choose from. One boy. We set off in the late afternoon. 'I know a shortcut,' I said. An hour later, after finding ourselves lost on muddy dirt tracks in dense State forests, we somehow ended up back where we'd started. Bob didn't say a word. He knew I was half-crazy.

'We're not putting this off,' I said vehemently. 'We'll go the long way this time.'

Well after dark, we arrived at a home that smelled of red wine, mushrooms and slow-cooking beef, a fire burning warmly, and the puppies tussling on the floor. The boy had one blue and one brown eye, and a coat like singed wool. He played rough. Then fell in a heap. The girls were all stayers.

'It's impossible to choose,' I said, preparing to leave, understanding for the first time that all I wanted was my old dog back. That finding room in my heart for another was impossible. Then I noticed a dog in a child's cot in a corner. She leaned, unbalanced and unable to straighten. She looked just like Chippy after her stroke.

'What about this one?' I said, reaching to pick her up.

'No, no,' said the breeder, taking her from me. 'She has cerebral palsy and she's our special dog. Sleeps on the bed, lives inside with us, not in the kennels. We adore her.'

'Yes, of course. Sorry. Look, your puppies are lovely, but I'm not up to choosing right now. I hope you understand.' I fought back tears.

The breeder just smiled: 'Don't worry, dogs choose you.'

As if on cue, one of the girls, a white fluff ball with soft brown eyes and three spots on her back, pounced on my shoe. I scooped her up. She licked my cheek, gave me a sweet, flirty look. And I was gone. 'We'll call her Spot,' I whispered.

Three days later, she found the rat poison and ate it. A week later, we realised she was a born car-chaser and no amount of scolding or punishment was going to cure her. A week after that, she got stuck in one of Bob's boots and we thought she was lost forever. If we left the ute door open, she jumped in when no one was looking. If we weren't careful, we could shut her in on a stinking hot day and kill her.

At Pittwater, she took off into the bush after dark, got lost and Bob, Boatshed Michael and I searched with torches until Michael found her sitting on a rock way beyond the house. She didn't even have the brains to whine. He scrambled up a sheer face and lifted her down. She was covered in blood. A big fat leech was attached to her backside.

She had an unerring nose for disaster, but she was also sunny-tempered and joyful with a knack for spreading happiness. 'Oh look,' she'd say (well, that's what I understood her to say), 'a leaf. Isn't it perfect?' And her eyes would peer up at me with such wonder that I, too, would stare at the leaf until I saw the magic in it. A little further on, she would halt once more: 'Oh look, a twig. Have you ever seen a more beautiful twig?' And I would stop again.

On each return to Pittwater she charmed Michael and Marybeth, the boatshed boys, and anyone passing. She also fell in love with a newborn, fluffy brown-spotted seagull rescued from a yacht hauled in for an anti-foul. Every morning, straight after breakfast, she raced down the steps and the two of them would sit and gaze at each other for hours. One day, Michael told me, Spot crept closer than usual and the chick hopped backwards in fright. Then the chick, recovering its hubris, hopped forwards. Spot instantly sprang back. Soon after, Michael said, the chick flapped its wings and lifted off the ground for the first time. Spot got such a shock, she barked. The chick squawked. The noise got quite bad. Sometimes, Michael said apologetically, he had to order Spot home.

The relationship between Spot and the seagull continued over several weeks, rekindling effortlessly after farm stays. Around the time the chick began to turn more grey and white than dirty brown, Michael said, 'You should've seen it, mate. We all cracked up. The chick suddenly realised it could fly. It raced down the wharf and took off over the water. Spot tore after her, was airborne for a split second. And sank.' He wiped tears of laughter from his eyes. 'Your puppy, she's never been near the chick since.'

But Spot loved the boatshed. Made a beeline for it the moment we opened the gate. Hanging out with the boatshed dogs: Jessie, a blue cattle dog. Link, a black dog. Banjo, a red kelpie, and manic Nutmeg, another red kelpie from the other side of the bay. Nutmeg was harmless, though, so no one minded. Safer than the farm, we thought, where there were a thousand stories about dogs dying from snakebite, going under tractors or taking baits. But Spot had an infallible instinct for trouble, and I often shook off a shiver, a fear that she would never make old bones. Bob and I, but especially Bob, watched her like a hawk through puppyhood.

2 5

EVERY EVENING AFTER THE BUILDERS WENT HOME, Bob and I wandered the shell of our new house trying to get a sense of the space and how we'd live in it. While we waited for the doors and windows to be manufactured in a town called Bago, about an hour north of Wingham, we debated the kitchen bench. Four-and-a-half metres long and a metre wide, if we agreed with the architects.

'A single piece of timber, how good would that be?' Bob said enthusiastically.

'Something that size would completely dominate the house,' I muttered.

And there we were again, embroiled, *pitted*, in non-life-threatening decisions as though a millimetre here or there – even a half metre – might tilt the balance between pleasure and pain for the rest of our lives. It was like a virus, incurable for the duration of construction and possibly beyond. The core issue, anyway, was unresolvable. I wanted to see finished pieces before committing. Bob wanted to create from scratch. We were at loggerheads. But while I trekked around city stores determined to have my way,

Bob called Jarrod, entrusted with building our blackbutt door and window frames, to find out where he might locate a single, huge slab of timber.

Later, Bob said, 'There's a man in a place called Rollands Plains. Buys trees from all over the country. Mills them on site. It's not far from the factory and Jarrod said he'd take us there.'

A week later I gritted my teeth and we set off.

—

We drove along a tree-shrouded dirt track in what felt like *Deliverance* country. Came to a stop at an open wire gate. Ahead of us, cattle, not long weaned, wandered amongst hundreds of stacks of timber, some covered by black plastic, some left out in the open. There wasn't a soul in sight.

A junkyard, I thought, full of rotting timber and snakes lurking under every plank. 'They're not open,' I said, hoping it was true. Bob ignored me and we kept going along a rutted clay track. Pulled up somewhere in the middle of the paddock and got out of the car. Bob and Jarrod wandered off. I stepped around steaming piles of cow poo and found – like cakes in a bakery display window – more piles of poo on what might end up as our kitchen bench. To say I was cranky and horrified was an understatement. Then, away in the distance, a man in shorts, T-shirt and a faded baseball cap was hopping into a battered farm vehicle and heading our way. Behind him, a young fella drove a forklift. His son, it turned out.

'Name's Malcolm,' he said, holding out a leathery hand. Without messing around too much with a ream of the standard country manners I'd become adjusted to, Jarrod – young and wiry with an easy smile and quick mind – moved on to explain what we were looking for. Malcolm rubbed his stubbly chin thoughtfully and, head bowed, set off. He wore rubber flip-flops as though he was headed for the beach. *One strike from a brown snake*, I thought, *and he'd be history.* I rolled my eyes ineffectually and followed the men from one anonymous pile of timber to another.

'This is cedar. See!' He spat on the wood, rubbed the wet spot with his hand. 'This is blackbutt. Over there, that's Queensland maple. Red gum next to it.' Spit. Rub. He was passionate. Proud. 'Blue gum here, but don't be fooled – when it's dressed it's deep pink.'

We tramped from one stack to another for almost an hour. Malcolm and Jarrod lifted great heavy slabs. Insects, exposed to the light, scurried off in fright. Ants spun in circles before bolting. Malcolm brushed away dried cow poo with a bare hand. Cattle ambled past, heads bent to the fodder. His son tidied up in our wake.

'What's that?' I asked, pointing at a curvaceous slab about two inches thick but way too short for our purpose.

'Mango. Lovely timber, mango. Bit like leopard skin when it's done up. Don't see much of it so I grab it when I can.' Spit. Rub. The timber glowed. Alive. Colour shooting off in ripples, waves, stripes and spots of red, yellow, gold.

'Make a great desktop for your office,' Bob said, raising his eyebrows. I succumbed instantly. We talked money for a moment . . . but I was a goner. It was scribbled in the greedy light of my eyes.

With one deal done, Malcolm returned to the main game: ''Bout the only timber I've got that's the right size for your bench is camphor laurel,' he said.

'Uh, uh,' Bob responded, wagging his head in the negative. 'We're only interested in native timbers.'

'Well, it grew here, mate,' Malcolm said flatly. He led the way to a weathered grey stack that looked more like firewood to me than kitchen bench material. Spit. Rub. Then a pale blond timber with a strong wavy grain and a heady perfume emerged. Beautiful but marred by an almighty, lightning-bolt split that ran from one end to the centre.

'Not a problem,' Jarrod said, easily. 'We'll laser cut a piece of wood to fit perfectly. Glue it in. Blackbutt would tone nicely.'

'Blond wood has a lovely lightness,' I said dreamily, running my hand along the rough edges where bark still clung. Bob sighed. 'Guess that's it, then,' he said, cornered by a lack of choice. He had a philosophy for this house that I'd never quite understood until that point. For him, it was an opportunity to illustrate all he was passionate about. Australian timbers, sustainability, practicality – all strengthened by quality craftsmanship and an eye for detail.

We loaded the timber into the back of the ute, tying it down to hurricane codes, delivered it to Jarrod's workshop and hit the Pacific Highway. Bob was quiet, his mouth drawn in a thin line.

'It will be lovely,' I said, thinking he was disappointed.

'Do you want drawers or open shelving?' he asked.

He'd already moved on.

——

Almost inevitably, the building budget exploded. Every day, I saw the white utes speeding up the hill, like a line of beetles in the distance, and swallowed a gut-churning mix of fear and resentment. Told myself the buck stopped fairly and squarely with us. We'd been seduced by the architect's vision, we'd agreed to nearly every creative detail, and we could blame no one but ourselves in the final analysis.

At one stage, when I looked over Bob's shoulder to read a column of figures, I said, 'Should we call a halt? Delay. Rethink the strategy.'

He shook his head: 'When you're in this deep all you can do is see it through.'

In the last financially fraught few weeks of the project, Bob handed me a glass of wine at the end of a particularly frustrating day. The door fittings, usually simple devices, had been a nightmare to install. Taking time. Time was expensive. But he was pragmatic: 'Might as well bite the bullet and finish properly. No shortcuts. What do you think?'

Wine eased the pain, I thought, but it never eliminated the problem. But all I said was: 'Oh well, we're not saving for our old age – we're in it. And there's no point in stressing the long-term ramifications of major decisions. There aren't any.' But it was a line that was wearing thin, becoming ludicrous. Every project had to have limits.

'Stock market's starting to quiver with a bit of life,' Bob said, 'world's struggling out of the doldrums. Benny's Boys and a few others are ready to be sold, too. Prices aren't great but we'll make a profit. We'll be right.' I felt a lurch of regret. Molière, Flaubert, Camus and Sartre, as well as MacDonald and MacDougall. No old age for them. Everything that is born must die, as the Buddhists – unarguably – say, but the process had a much bleaker tone when it was your hand that gave the execution order.

'Might stay in the house when you send them off, if you don't mind.'

'Good idea,' Bob quickly agreed.

26

EACH TIME WE RETURNED TO PITTWATER, my mother seemed less well. Her feet, ankles and wrists were badly swollen, flesh oozed over the rings on her fingers, her watch, the frame of her shoes. The grey outline around her mouth now stretched across the bridge of her nose, like a mask. Even a fool could see that death was stalking her, could pounce at any moment. But her frailty was physical. Her mind was razor-sharp. The quick, sometimes cruel, often sarcastic one-liners still came hard and fast, but I wasn't easily felled by them anymore. Once or twice I even tried for intimacy, only to have her reduce it to safe banality. So I wasn't prepared for the day the lid blew off our relationship once and for all.

We were eating a picnic lunch in the car because the weather was too foul to attempt what had become a painfully slow and agonising climb in and out of the car followed by a stop-start passage to the restaurant. In an unguarded moment, she said, 'I wasn't that bad. As a mother.'

And so, after a lifetime of tiptoeing around the cracks and fissures in our relationship, she'd swung open the door as wide as it would go. Outside, the sky was black. Rain pelted. Lightning zigzagged like the first signs of migraine. Green mountains of surf crashed onto a blood-red beach while a gale forced an avenue of pines and dune grass into submission. All it would take was a severed branch, rogue wave or a lightning strike and we'd both be dead, I thought. So I told her then that I couldn't bear to hug her hello or kiss her goodbye or even pat her on the back when we parted, because I could never forgive her. I told her I found it hard to listen to her version of my childhood; every time she rosied up old memories I wanted to scream.

'So here it is,' I said. In a clipped, angry voice, I told her what her father did to me in the chook shed, the Humpy, on the nights he offered to babysit while everyone else went off yabbying by the light of a full moon. The holidays when he forced me to walk beside him on the beach, my hand in his pocket. How I hated him and feared him. How he distorted my understanding of love and sex forever.

'You must have known,' I said, staring straight ahead, unable to look at her. 'You must have known and you failed to protect me.' I waited for an unseen force to scoop up the small car in which we sat and hurl it into space. Punishment for giving life to a deeply hidden canker that had defined much of my life, if not all of it. Instead, for a few seconds the roaring apocalypse seemed to quieten.

With a careless wave, she flicked aside a revelation that would break most mothers: 'It probably made a better woman of you,' she said dismissively, as though we'd been discussing whether to buy pork or lamb chops for dinner. And, just like that, a fifty-year-old suppurating sore dried up. And we were both still breathing.

She finished her oysters. I ate the last of my meat pie. The gloom lifted. The wind and rain eased. The lightning shifted out to sea, no more than a flashing white light on a black horizon. I gathered the detritus of our *picnic* and stepped outside the car to dispose of the rubbish.

'Just a minute,' she called. Here it comes, I thought. But what? An apology? A disclaimer? Denial? I bent to see and hear her better.

'Yes?' I asked, warily.

She fastidiously wiped her fingers, each one heavy with those awful rings, then handed me the soiled paper napkin. 'It'll save you an extra trip.' I laughed then. My mother has never known the meaning of retreat, and she clearly wasn't about to start learning.

I drove her back to the Village and helped her out of the car. She shuffled off, a stubborn, mulish expression on her face. Her lips drawn in a thin red line. I roared away before she reached the front door, hit the steering wheel with the palm of my hand. After years of silence and secret shame, why today? She'd been no more acerbic than usual when I collected her. She'd behaved no differently at lunch. Our conversation, stilted and mostly one-sided, was a well-worn script that rarely changed.

Was it the grey tinge around her mouth? The swollen ankles and wrists? The wheezy breaths? Death-in-waiting. The signs were loud and clear. Say it now or I might never know the truth? Or was it the assemblies of courageous childhood victims, many damaged beyond repair, who'd publicly stepped forward with their awful stories? Determined to take on and hold to account the most powerful institutions in the land after decades of secrecy. Distanced enough, now, from the pain and anguish to be able to blow the sanctimonious lids off the most sacrosanct establishments. Healing along the way. I had applauded from deep in my comfortable armchair. Feeling my own shame for remaining mute – how can it ever end if none of us speaks out?

All my life I'd wondered: Did my mother know her father was a degenerate of the most heinous kind? And if she knew, why didn't she keep me out of harm's way? It wasn't until much later that I understood I still didn't have a clear answer.

'She takes no hostages, does she?' Bob said when I told him what had happened.

'That's one way of putting it,' I replied.

'How do you feel?' he asked.

'Lighter,' I told him. 'Like I've emptied myself of a poison I've been carrying around forever.'

'Good!' He said nothing else. Held my hand for a long while. Then went off to make a cup of tea.

———

I picked Esther up the following week on our scheduled day. She waited with rabbit-scared eyes in the reception area. Hoping, no doubt, that we'd perform the traditional Duncan feint-and-parry in the face of battle and let the whole hideous topic slide into a dark recess, never to be resurrected. But as soon as we were on our way, she said, 'I never knew. I swear I never knew. If I'd known I would have killed him.'

I said nothing. The silence stretched out.

'He did it to me, too, you know,' she said. 'I didn't know it was wrong.'

A while later, as we pulled into the restaurant: 'I thought I was helping Mum.'

Once we were seated: 'It made me feel special.'

Inside the restaurant, I went through the motions. Ordered food. Drinks. Paid. Took a seat on the other side of the table from her. 'If you knew what he was capable of,' I said carefully, 'then you are guilty, as charged, of failing to protect a child.'

'I never thought he'd do anything to *you*.'

'Why? Because I was a gangly, freckle-faced kid without an ounce of charm? Not a pretty blonde little tease like you? How could you not understand what was going on?' Anger. Swirling. Cyclonic. Blinding.

She was silent. Fiddled with the tab on a can of bourbon and cola. I took it from her, opened it. Poured.

'Even now, more than fifty years later,' I said, 'I cannot see a man – any man – with a child in his care, without wondering if that child is safe. Why do you think I never had children? I was terrified something terrible might happen on my watch and I would never, ever, forgive myself.'

Our food arrived. We plastered on our public faces. Good Duncan soldiers till the end. Smiling. Polite. Consigning our dirty linen to a basket and snapping shut the lid. I poured her more drink. She asked for a straw and I went to the front counter to get her one.

But later, when I crawled out of my anger: *Her, too*, I thought, overwhelmed by sadness and the beginnings of understanding of the forces that had moulded my mother. *What chance did she have?*

Everything between us changed in ways I could never have foreseen. I raised one more question: 'Do you think Nan knew what was going on?' From this end of my life it seemed impossible to believe she'd been blind to the depravities of the man she'd married.

'I always thought she was wonderful. If she knew, then she wasn't. I can't believe she knew. I'm sure she didn't. We were very careful.' The implications of the word *careful* didn't occur to me until much later.

I remind myself to consider the timeframe. Esther was born nearly a century ago, her mother at the end of the 1800s. It was an era when women without the support of men often perished. He might have – must have, if she knew – seemed the lesser of two evils. Life is life. I had my answers. The sky didn't come crashing down on our heads. And my mother and I were bound for eternity by blood and history.

—

The following week we drove along Pittwater Road, past yachts, dinghies, well-tended houses. People carrying plastic bags, wearing lycra shorts and stretch-fabric shirts walking their dogs along the foreshore at a hectic pace. Arms swinging, jerked backwards every so often by a pooch lifting a leg against a polit-ically correct border of Australian natives: coastal rosemary, grevilleas, unfriendly lomandra with its spiky foliage and flowers. I waited for the status quo to resume, and it kicked in right on cue as we rounded the final corner.

'I'm well looked after,' she said. 'The staff is going to pot, though. The head honchos are cutting workers and cutting hours. I'm lucky to get my unit cleaned once a week.'

'So is there anything you'd like me to take up with manage-ment? Any problems?'

'Have you ever heard me complain? Do I *ever* complain? They treat me quite differently to the others. They love me. I don't know why.' It was said with a funny laugh, as though she knew exactly why and the joke was on everyone else.

'How's Stefan these days?' I asked, to change the subject.

'He died.'

I twisted my head to look at her, frowning. 'He *died*? When? Was there a funeral?'

'I was too ill to go to it.'

'But I would have taken you! He was your friend!'

'You weren't around and anyway, I told you, I was ill.'

I pulled into the five-minute drop-off zone outside the restaurant at the Church Point ferry wharf. Unloaded the walker. Opened the door, reaching across her ample chest to release her seatbelt.

'Oooh,' she said flirtatiously, 'I didn't know you cared.'

'I don't.'

'Hah. I know you love me. So did your brother. I did my best.' Her eyes got a wary look. As if afraid she'd opened the door to more questions. A moment later she clutched her chest. Breathed in short puffy gulps.

'Are you alright?' I asked, not convinced she was ill for a second.

'A pain. It will go away.'

'Want me to take you back to the Village?' I asked slyly.

'No! I can do anything.' She placed one foot on the ground, but the other refused to follow, as though it was hooked up to a separate electric current and the switch was off. Not an act – not this time. 'Giddy-up, giddy-up,' she ordered in a sing-song voice, making tongue-clicking sounds every so often.

I reached inside and lifted her foot out. Placed an arm under hers to help her upright. Standing, with her hands on her walker, she regained her confidence. But she shuffled along painfully, as though the very act of putting one foot in front of the other was a task too great.

'Do you want to sit at a table next to the water or inside?' I asked.

'Inside. I wouldn't want to catch a chill.'

The restaurant was filling with bright young women in skimpy clothing, even though a chill southerly had pushed back summer for the day. Long shiny hair. Perfectly even, beauty-parlour tans. Sandals. Feet with toenails painted blue or mulberry. They sat outside on the deck under red umbrellas, looking festive. I asked for the gas heater to be turned on and settled Esther at a table so close to it that I expected to find her skin toasted brown when I returned from parking the car.

On the way back to our table, I grabbed a bourbon and cola from the fridge, my mineral water, a couple of menus. 'Here you go. The fresh prawns are good. The pasta is terrific. Have a look. Tell me what you want and I'll go and order.'

She studied the menu intently. 'Of course, I'm still seeing double.'

'No, you aren't.'

She snapped: 'How would you know?'

'So, prawns, is it?'

'No. I'll have the seafood pizza.'

'The one with or without chilli?'

She picked up the menu: 'The Waterfront Special.'

'Your eyes are better than mine,' I muttered.

After a short while, the southerly picked up. Umbrellas flapped. The young women giggled and hugged themselves. The flamboyant Italian waiter fetched coloured wraps to tuck around their shoulders, making a huge fuss. My mother watched with envy in her eyes.

'Are *you* cold?' she asked me.

'Nope.'

She gave a shiver, the kind she once would have said meant someone had walked over your grave. Unkindly, I let her wait another thirty seconds.

'Would you like a blanket?' She brightened. 'Not sure how you can be cold when you're practically sitting on top of that heater, but . . . I'll get you one.' I went to stand up.

'Why don't you ask the waiter? It's his job.'

'He's busy.' Her face fell into loose folds of disappointment. I felt spiteful, silly, petty, so I dropped back into my seat.

'A blanket, Mauro, please, for my mother,' I called when he whizzed past.

'*Si, si, bella, bella* mama. I get one right now. Black for you. Is your colour, no? Not the red. Is too bright for such beautiful skin.' I could almost hear her purring.

Our food appeared via Mauro. 'Mario, like the singer,' my mother said, trying to hold his attention.

'Mauro, Mauro,' he responded emphatically.

'Yes, Mario, Mario Lanza – but you're much too young to know about him.'

'Mauro!' he said, throwing up his hands. 'But for you, I am Mario. *Bella* mama.'

When lunch was over, I drove her back to the Village and dropped her at reception with relief. Duty done for another week.

I'd once thought her daily 7 am phone calls, which went on well into my forties, were wearing, even outrageous. Our meals together, though, were even more excruciating as we danced around the past, unwilling to give it weight. We had nothing at all to say to each other. I'm not sure we ever did. I searched through memory. We'd once laughed a lot. But everything my mother tried to teach me – her advice for life – was based on fear. *If you kiss a boy, he will think you're easy. If you're late for work, you'll be fired. If you aim low, you will live low. If you get run over by a bus, be sure you're wearing clean underwear.* Almost certainly unfairly, I remembered little else.

On another car picnic, I asked her, 'Did your sisters ever guess anything was . . . strange about the way you were given special privileges?'

'Not that I know of. Dad never took risks.'

'It wasn't your fault, you know. You were a child. He was evil. Skilled paedophiles groom children. You didn't stand a chance.'

She closed her eyes, rested her head on the back of the car seat. 'All so long ago. But you never forget.'

'No.' I cleared the car of rubbish. 'We're heading back to Benbulla tomorrow. Be gone a couple of weeks at least.'

'You needn't worry about me. I'm well looked after.'

'Does it ever haunt you, what happened?' I asked, curious but no longer angry.

'Not really. What he did to *you*, that's hard to accept.'

'If I know anything about you at all, Esther, you will learn to live with it,' I said, unkindly.

''Course I will,' she replied firmly. 'You can't let tragedies bring you down. You've got to get on with life.' And her casual dismissal turned my new, very fragile feelings of compassion and forgiveness to dust. Here she was, bent over, sinking, and still unable to look beyond her own best interests. *Our bond is always going to be like quicksand*, I thought.

I drove her back to the Village in bitter silence. I couldn't wait to return to Benbulla. To be well away from her.

——

As construction continued, we lived almost permanently at the farm. Some days, progress sped along. But then weeks would go by without seeing much change. 'The devil is in the detail,' one architect friend told me when I grumbled. 'God is in the detail,' another said. Whatever deity ruled, it added up to more expense.

Wherever possible we chose frugality over excess, simplifying trickily designed cupboards, opting for melamine in the dressing room instead of timber. 'Could save a few hundred bucks on the interior doors,' Terry said at one stage. 'Use hollow instead of solid ones.' We checked the stock at Bunnings. Too flimsy. Too light. You'd hear a whisper through them. The extra dollars might hurt in the immediate moment, but this detail out of kilter would irritate forever. And this house was meant to be where we played out the endgame. Do it right, do it once.

There were big moments: The day Jarrod and his team installed the massive double-glazed windows and doors. The timber so heavy even the sliding screens took the strength of four men to raise into place. The day the bathroom was completed. We slid open every panel and stood fully clothed in the shower to test the effect. Inside or outside? It gave a wondrous feeling of both. The day Bob's painstakingly designed, two-way fireplace was installed. While it would warm the house in winter, it would also heat water for household use and the underfloor heating. The day the scaffolding came down. We wandered up and down hills to judge the impact of those lean, sharp lines on a rolling landscape. Strong but not bulky, we decided. We'd trusted the right people. The day the builders cleaned the site of debris. It was the clearest indication of all that at any moment the team we had come to know, whose company we'd enjoyed and whose skills and talent we respected, would move on to a new job. Finally, the day Terry stomped over to the shed, battered straw hat on his head, heavy work boots caked with dust, his face weary and relieved, and said, 'It's done, mate. I'm off.'

His rackety white van made its way down the hill. Stopped. 'He's cutting grass for his rabbits,' I explained to Bob. Once, when he'd pulled up for no obvious reason, I'd guessed a flat tyre and driven off to help out. Found him on his knees with a cane knife. 'All good. But thanks for checkin',' he'd said at the time. The van rolled on and we watched it out of sight. He stopped again to close the entrance gates. Meticulous, scrupulous, painstaking. He wasn't nicknamed Millimetre Terry for nothing.

After he'd gone, we stood alone on the Home Hill, hands entwined. Shed. House. Us. The new triumvirate. We'd either make a go of this effort at sustainability, this daring life, or it would be our downfall. But our generation had been one of enormous and far-reaching privilege. There was nobility, I believed, in trying to repay the debt.

We carried our camp chairs from the shed across the dust and dirt to the house. Set them in front of the fireplace in the breeze-way and plonked our tired backsides down. Blue wrens with their harems of Jennies hopped about the bare earth, scavenging for insects. In the distance, a magpie warbled sweet notes. Way beyond, the high piping of bellbirds floated, echoing like pings on crystal. Neither of us spoke for a long time.

'Need to clear the rubbish in front of the solar panels,' Bob said eventually. *A fallen tree, burnt logs, a squillion rocks, large and small – was he kidding?*

'Big job,' I replied. 'Tractor work?'

'Manual labour, mostly. You wear it away.'

'Yeah.' *But, oh god, surely we're too old to be lifting rocks.*

The sun, a blinding orange ball, dipped behind the hills. Shadows fell across the landscape. Purple sky, hills, paddocks.

A kookaburra gave a half-hearted cackle and for a moment the peace was shattered. Then a still quietness resumed, growing deeper as darkness, soft and innocent, crept across the valleys. Nights were respite. Days would become the hard, grubbing reality.

Then the rain, temperamental and flighty in the past, turned flat-out recalcitrant again. One dry week turned into a dry month, followed by a parched spring, summer and autumn. Winter wasn't much better. Bob tried to stay upbeat, but there were sixty steers now and the paddocks were lean.

'Keep 'em alive, that's all you can do,' Foggy told us. 'Gotta take the good with the bad. That's farming. But yeah, it's depressing. Not normal for around here.' Further south, we heard of farmers abandoning paddock management and opening their gates to give stock a free run, hoping they'd scrape enough pickings to survive until the next big wet.

Then, for three days straight, a wicked wind bent trees double. Sent dust skittering under our beautiful new doors. It crept across the bright, glossy floorboards like an incoming tide, piling in corners and crevices. The huge glass windows pulsed and whooped like a wobble board. It was unnerving. Outside, the precious, lean layer of topsoil, raked free of rocks and stones over hot and weary days so it felt as though every body joint had seized forever, swirled high on a gust and was carried off. A luscious, cooling lawn felt like a fool's dream. Depressing didn't begin to describe it.

On the second day of the big wind, Bob shouted across the yard, his voice raspy with dust: 'Get your boots on. A steer's jumped the fence.'

'Can't it wait till the wind drops?' I yelled. But he'd gone off towards the shed to get a bucket of grain. Already a ghostly wraith in a fog of red dirt, one shoulder tilted crookedly.

At the bottom of the hill, Lucca, a half-grown Limousin, cropped innocently, his toffee-coloured coat set off by gyrating yellow, daisy-like flowers that I knew to be fireweed. Killed cattle if they ate it. Along with thistles, stinging nettles, castor oil plants, lantana, Parramatta grass, fleabane, Stinking Roger, crofton weed and too many more to list, they were a rural pestilence.

'Some retirement,' I muttered, slipping out of flip-flops and pulling on the work boots that I'd learned to place handily at the kitchen door. I set off. Dust rampaged up my nose till it hurt to breathe. *Rain would be good*, I thought with a physical longing so strong it was an ache. As far into the future as the weather bureau dared to predict, though, there was nothing but blue skies and temperatures ranging from five to ten degrees above normal, making sense, I thought in small consolation, of our solar panels and rainwater tanks.

I headed down the steep slope of the Home Hill sideways, like a crab. Thirty degrees in early August. I tried to work out the Fahrenheit equivalent so I could judge it against the weather of my childhood. Mentally file the day under *freak* caused by the profligacy of mankind or a previously recorded *aberration* – uncommon but not unknown. I failed, as usual, to make the calculation. It was bloody hot, though – I knew that for a fact. Bordering on a heatwave in what was supposed to be the coldest month of winter, so probably closer to *freak* than *aberration*. Not much consolation there, though.

Bob pointed, indicating we'd creep in from the sides in a pincer movement, but if the steer decided to turn nasty, there was a clear run right up to our front door – and sweet bugger-all we could do to stop him. But Lucca was one of Benny's Boys. They all had sweet, accommodating natures – not like some of the schizo liquorice allsorts we'd bought at the bawling Monday morning Taree cattle sales. We might get lucky.

Lucca raised his head. Saw Bob. And six hundred kilos of prime beef did an immediate bolt in my direction. Swallowing hard, I spread my arms wide, like I'd been taught, and walked slowly and at a slight angle towards him. Lucca skidded to a stop. Bob slipped behind him and opened the gate. Under Lucca's watchful eyes, he walked into the paddock and tipped fattening grain on the ground. A bribe. Slowly, slowly, we closed in. Lucca sussed his options. The grain won. He made his move. Bob grinned.

'It's amazing how fast cattle can go,' I said, almost shouting against the whoosh of the wind, trying to stretch the gate wire so Bob could strain a loop over the fence post. Lucca, unfazed, gave up on the grain and ambled towards the herd like he was on a Sunday stroll. The rolling gait catwalk smooth. Then one of the allsorts, an Angus-Shorthorn cross, spooked and they were all off at a hysterical gallop down the hill into a densely forested gully. *Herd mentality* took on new meaning.

'How'd he get through?' I asked.

'Fencing wire needs tightening.'

And another job was added to a list that already ran off two pages and into three. I pushed harder on the gate. The loop was still an inch short. 'What now?' I asked, frustrated, defeated. Bob winked, took a coil of rope from his shoulder, tied a fancy knot like a hangman's noose, threaded the straight end between gate and post, slipped it through the noose end and pulled. The wire slid over the old mahogany post with room to spare. His face was dirty, hands scabby from scratches, burns and cuts; he looked dead on his feet. But it was another win. He grinned. I returned the smile and slapped his back. We headed up the hill to the house, heads bent into the wind.

We kicked off our boots at the kitchen door. 'Cuppa?' I asked, going inside and filling the kettle. The massive windows continued to wobble against the gale. I hoped like hell they held.

'If it cools down and the wind drops by tomorrow,' Bob said hoarsely, 'we'll light a few fires and clear some rubbishy paddocks.'

'Oh. Terrific.'

27

ON A COLD DAY TOWARDS DUSK at the end of winter, Richard, our neighbour who'd cleared the landslip, turned his truck into the gateway. Bob and Eric had walked twelve steers, blissfully unaware of their fate, into the cattle yard without incident. From the sitting room window, I watched Richard back his truck hard up against the race. Then turned away.

I lost track of time. Cooked dinner. Lamb. Out of respect for our *boys*. Looked up when Bob appeared at the door. 'Can you come down and help?' he asked, sounding stressed. 'We're having a few problems.'

'Yeah, sure.' I turned off the curry. Bob went in search of torches. Outside, the night was now pitch-black. The cold, biting. There'd be a frost dusting the valleys in the morning. 'What sort of problems?' I asked, trying to sound unconcerned.

'First lot went off ok. Sweet as a nut. These bastards won't go near the truck. The more we push and yell, the more stubborn they get.'

'Right.'

Down at the cattle yard, Richard, in shorts and a windcheater, gumboots to his knees, shouted at his dogs: 'Get behind, Bron!

Get behind, Ben!' But they were overexcited, yipping, nipping and stirring up the cattle. One beast got the heebie-jeebies and, like a rabid infection, the others quickly caught a dose of panic. Frustrated, Richard locked his dogs in the truck. Strode back to the pens, urging with shouts and whacks on the rumps from a piece of rubber piping. Bob yelled and pushed a golden rear-end. Then a black one. Careful of the hooves.

I stood uselessly beside the ute, without a clue what to do. Then one beast, two beasts, lumbered unwillingly up the ramp. Richard raced to slide shut the partition between the front and rear gate. Returned to the yard. The gate slid open. The steers backed out. Spooked the animals coming behind. More panic. More bellowing. Begin again.

Richard resorted to a low-voltage, battery-driven cattle prod. The batteries were flat. 'Never had to use the bloody thing,' he said, shaking his head.

'Get up to the house. Get new ones,' Bob told me, sounding desperate. 'And call Eric. We need help.'

By the time I returned to the yard, Eric and his wife, Robyn, were pulling up. Bob changed the batteries but the prod refused to work. Eric jumped in the pen with Richard. Bob joined them. 'Get on, you dozy bastards. Get on,' Eric yelled, but in a way that sounded controlled. Pushing. Shoving. And who knows why – the power of three or tired of revolt or Eric's persuasive voice – within minutes the cattle marched up the ramp like obedient pets. Richard slammed a gate shut behind the first three steers and then closed the rear of the truck, locking in the last three. Easy as pie when it all goes to plan.

'Cuppa before you head off?' I asked.

Richard shuffled his feet and shook his head. 'Nah. Get this lot delivered and head home for tea. Jenny'll be waiting.'

'You got a date with the Rabbitohs?' Eric asked, aware of Richard's devotion to his footy team.

Richard waggled his head, grinning. 'On to me, are ya?'

Eric, Robyn, Bob and I stayed around the cattle yard until he swung onto the road. 'Don't know about you, but I'm ready for a glass of something restorative,' I said with feeling.

'Right on!'

Back in a cosy house, warm from the day's heat trapped by double glazing, with a fire blazing hot and strong, I poured wine for Robyn and me, handed Eric a beer, and sloshed a serious amount of whisky into a glass for Bob. He looked shattered. Then the phone rang. It was Richard's wife. Yes, Richard had arrived safely at the abattoir. But the lock hadn't caught. Three steers were missing. Fallen out of the back. Richard was already out looking for them. Dead or alive, there was no way to tell.

We put down our drinks and headed off.

'Looks like he'll miss the big game,' Bob said, climbing into the ute.

'He'll have told Jenny to record it. Stake my life on it,' Eric said, grinning and heading for his ute.

Out on the road, my easy job was to flag down oncoming traffic. Warn of cattle on the loose. The others set off on foot, searching for one red, one white-faced and one black beast on a black night. *Bloody, bloody hell.* Headlights approached. I stepped forward, waving my arms. The ute slowed, pulled up. The passenger window rolled down, a head leaned across from the driver's side. I explained: 'Lost a couple of cattle. Well, three. They're somewhere on the road. Fell out of the back of the truck. Take it slowly, ok?'

The driver, a young fella with an open face, wearing the kind of wide-brimmed hat young men on the land favour, smiled. 'Oh yeah,' he said in a long drawl, 'happens like that sometimes.' And in a moment, his words took the sting out of the whole shambolic operation. *Shit happens*, I thought. It's not entirely the result of our inexperience. 'Give me a minute to pull over,' he added, even more laconically, 'and I'll give you a hand.'

We heard it at the same time. Crashing through undergrowth up ahead. The Good Samaritan darted off into the darkness. I stood at my post. In a few minutes, the group returned triumphant.

'Two back in the paddock. One to go,' Bob said.

Richard's truck appeared in the distance. 'Mate, mate,' he said, shaking his head in apology. 'Can't find the other one. Least it's not dead on the road.'

'Jenny recording the game?' Eric asked. Richard nodded, sheepishly.

We all searched a while longer, our torchlight flashing eerily over scrubby strips of roadside land. Trouble was, there was no way of knowing where the steer had parted company with the truck. Could be wandering the streets of Wingham by now, looking for a warm bed. We were dead lucky, we all agreed, that the others had fallen out so close to home and we'd found them before they'd caused an accident. To keep searching was probably pointless. Time to go home. See what the morning dealt.

'Let's finish that drink,' I said to Eric and Robyn. The Good Samaritan waved goodbye. Richard said he'd keep looking all the way home.

We'd just sat down when the phone rang again. 'Relfie called Jenny. Thought one of our cows was on the road. Reckon it must be your bloke.'

'We're on our way,' Bob said. There was excitement now. A tangible sense that things might turn out ok. Eric and Robyn took off. We followed. At the gate to Richard's property, Jenny waved us down.

'Steer's up ahead,' she explained. 'Richard, Eric and Robyn, Dan, too – I think you met him – and Dan's father, Bill, they reckon they'll get him into our paddock.'

'Fingers crossed,' I said.

We heard voices, then the steer was so close you could smell him. But Richard's thoroughbred, a normally sweet-tempered, affectionate mare that had done well at country race meetings, spooked. Reared up, snorted, whinnied loudly. The steer threw back his shoulders, raised his head and, a poofteenth away from lock-up, bolted. Bob chased. Robyn passed him at a flat-out sprint. Eric on her heels. Trying to head him off before he hit the bridge and crossed into no-man's-land – or that's how it felt.

No one quite knew why, but the steer crashed through a barbed-wire fence instead, and kept going until he pulled up in the middle of Richard's best breeding herd. Safety in numbers perhaps. Whatever the reason, when luck shines on you you don't question it. We gathered, victorious, at Richard's front gate.

'Now, Richard,' I said. I felt Jenny stiffen beside me, probably thinking ignorant newbies like us didn't understand that the potential for stuff-ups in farming was limitless and I was about to make a complaint. 'When we moved to the country, we were looking for a quiet life . . .' Laughter. Mostly relieved. Every kind of tragedy, the kind that might make headlines on the ABC's rural report, had been averted. We stood around for a while, chatting in the cold night air.

'Wish I'd seen your face at the abs, mate.' Eric said. 'Bet you let loose with a few choice words, eh?'

Richard, a man who takes his time even though his words are few, waggled his head, still feeling the shock: 'Nah. I was speechless. I thought, *gee, what's happened here?* I couldn't believe it.' Another headshake. 'Just couldn't believe it.'

The group stood around in a circle by the side of the road, the way people gather after a church service to meet and greet. They discussed cattle prices, rain, foxes, a dodgy gearbox in the tractor, Richard losing a couple of calves for no reason anyone could fathom. Relfie, who was multi-skilled like most farmers and who'd worked on our house in between showing his stud cattle at agricultural shows, was – like Richard – immune to the cold in shorts, work boots and a windcheater. Jenny was wrapped in a horse blanket she'd grabbed on her way out to help with the round-up. The rest of us, dressed for indoors and heated cars, stamped the ground occasionally, rubbed our hands to get the blood circulating.

'Well,' Bob said after a decent interval, 'we're off home before our feet go numb.'

'Yeah. Right. See ya!' Eric said.

'Thanks for all your help,' Bob added.

'Right. See ya!' Richard said.

We drove off. No one else moved.

'What do you think went wrong with the cattle prod?' I asked on the way home.

'Stuck the dead batteries back in instead of the new ones.'

Three months later, after the bruising on the steers had faded, Richard transported the cattle to market. They were heavier and prices had picked up. 'Did us a favour,' Bob said, slapping him on the back. 'Made us a fortune. Owe you big-time.'

———

Esther sparked up when I told her about the runaway steers. 'Will you have a horse at the farm?' she asked. Before I could reply, she continued: 'We had a cunning draught horse called Old Bob. Got it into my head to ride him one day. Had to climb on his head so I could wriggle down his neck and onto his back. Of course I ended up facing the wrong way. Old Bob promptly bolted for the apple orchard. Knocked me off under a tree. Mum saw the whole thing. Stood there shouting that I'd be the death of her. Her!'

'What happened to him?'

'He died. Old age. Your grandfather –' She saw my face, broke off. Held up her hand in a stop sign. 'Alright, alright. I know. No need to say anything.' She patted the air with her hand, as if to press down unseen turbulence. 'Anyway, it was winter. He was a big horse and no one felt like digging for too long in the hard ground, so they cut off his legs and piled them on top.'

'Yetch. But you've told me that story before.'

She thumbed her nose at me. 'Are you going to breed?' she asked.

'Nope. All steers.'

'Pity. Calves are beautiful little creatures. What a woman wouldn't give for their eyelashes. Cows make good mothers. Well, not all of them. We had a cow once that refused to have anything to do with her calf. Hand-fed it until it was time to be butchered.'

'Your pet calf! Off to the abattoir?'

'No. Your grandfather shot her. Butchered her himself.' The hand signal again. 'I know, I know. Anyway. You'd better get used to sending them to market.' She paused. Thought for a while. Sighed heavily in a way that indicated a bout of emotional black-mail coming up. 'I'll never see the farm, will I?' She sounded sad. Resigned. As if I'd abandoned her forever.

'Of course you will.'

'No. I'm aware I'm fading.'

I laughed inwardly. 'Well, you're not twenty-one anymore, but with a mattress in the back of the ute and a bottle of whisky for company, you can lie down all the way. You'll make it.'

'Is that legal?'

'Of course not!' And we laughed.

She said, 'I've always enjoyed breaking rules. Of course, you were such a goody-two-shoes.'

'I was terrified of you.'

'Were you really?' she asked, her eyes brightening at the thought.

'Yeah. But not anymore.'

'No – now *I'm* terrified of *you*.'

'About time.' And we laughed again. 'See you in a couple of weeks. We're off to Benbulla tomorrow.'

SUSAN DUNCAN

'Do you think you'll go there for good one day?' Esther asked, her voice serious.

I thought of a squillion evasive answers, opted for truth. 'If anyone had told me I'd ever leave Pittwater I would have laughed in their face. Not now.'

Esther nodded, fiddled with her rings. And that's where we left it.

28

OUR FIRST DAY BACK AT THE FARM was wild and windy. The noise was like a crashing surf, rising and falling with each new gust. We worked through the turmoil, building a vegetable garden with raised beds inside a netting tent to keep out marauders, such as rabbits, bats and birds. Late in the afternoon, when soil saved from our road building had been weeded and raked into two wide beds, I sat on the tractor wheel guard, holding two shovels, and we went in search of cow poo to add to the mix.

Cattle have a habit of camping in one – usually shady – spot for days, even weeks, so they were easy pickings, although Bob handled the fresh stuff, which turned my stomach. I sought out respectable, innocuous dried pats. When the tractor bucket was filled, we made our way back. It was almost beer o'clock, knock-off time. While I went off to prepare some nibbles, Bob dug in the manure. At sunset the wind dropped, as if a switch had been flicked and the volume turned down. We watched, entranced, as daylight crescendoed from pale insipidness into a roaring red furnace that set the distant mountains on fire. All of it framed and contained – or so it felt – within the walls of our home. It was an affront when my mobile phone went off. No caller ID. I debated answering it. Bob nudged me into action: 'Might be important. You never know.'

'Hello?' I said.

'Susan?'

'Yep.'

'It's Chris. Esther's doctor. She's very, very ill.'

'Oh shit,' I said before I could stop myself, feeling an unexpected surge of grief.

'She's refusing to go to hospital,' he continued.

'What's the problem?' I asked.

'Her pulse rate is dangerously low. Her heart and kidneys are failing. We need to get her into hospital, quickly.'

Why, I thought? If all her vital organs were failing, what difference would it make? 'Well, Chris, she has a right to choose whether or not she gets treatment, and she's been telling me for months that she's had enough and she's ready to die. It's her choice.'

'It's a very, very painful way to die. An awful way to die. I'd like to call an ambulance and get proper medical attention.'

'No one should be in pain. I'll give her a call and get back to you, ok?' I disconnected and turned to Bob. 'Esther's crook. Really crook this time. Chris reckons she's dying.' I called her number.

'Hello,' Esther said, sounding chirpy.

'How are you?' I asked, feeling my way. 'I just had a call from Chris and he told me you're not too flash.'

'I'm alright. I don't understand what all the fuss is about. I'm not in any pain. I'm quite happy and comfortable. And I'm ready to die if that's what's going on.'

'Chris wants you to go to hospital.'

'What for? There's nothing they can do for me. I told you, I'm quite happy and not in any pain.' I felt a wave of relief. For her or for me? I wasn't sure.

'I'll drive back to Pittwater tonight. We can talk all this through in the morning.' I saw Bob raise his eyebrows, shake his head *no*.

'As you wish,' she said, as though we were talking about taking milk and sugar in a cup of tea. I ended the call.

'Esther's dying. I've got to go.'

His voice was soft and calm. 'It's too late to set off now, and a few hours won't make any difference. Wait till the morning and we'll go together.'

'Chris says she's really, really bad. Her heart and kidneys have packed up.'

'Don't worry, your mother's a tough old bird. We'll leave very early. Trust me, this is a better, safer way.' He reached for my hand. I sank down beside him.

Sometime during the night, I woke. Moonlight flooded the landscape, ghostly and beautiful. How hard, I thought, to think of leaving the physical world forever. It occurred to me that I could not imagine life without the presence of my mother. There would be a hole, dug over sixty years and more, growing deeper with time. Time. It didn't heal all wounds. No matter what the experts said. It merely dried the edges into scabs.

Bob drove along the Pacific Highway in silence. We hit a light drizzle on the outskirts of Sydney. Maybe it would move north, I thought. Maybe the weather forecasters had got it wrong and we'd get a welcome drenching.

We parked the car, walked in the back entrance to assisted living. Up a few tiled steps to her door. I took a deep breath. Knocked.

'Come in if you're good-looking.'

Her legs were tree stumps, her feet footballs. 'You don't look crash hot,' I said. Understatement. Duncan-style.

Bob kissed her cheek. 'Good to see you, Esther,' he said in a sunny tone.

My mother waved us towards the red leather chairs, as if she were hosting a salon for acolytes. 'I feel pretty good,' she said. 'There's no pain, and I've told you I'm ready to go. I won't be alone up there. Your father's waiting for me, and so is John.'

There was another tap at the door. Chris arrived, shook our hands, felt Esther's pulse. 'Ready for hospital yet?' he asked.

'No! I'm perfectly happy where I am, thank you.' She smiled around the room. Incredibly, she seemed nonchalant. Airy-fairy.

Chris asked a few more questions. In the end, he said, 'You need a pacemaker, Esther. Think about it and let me know. But don't take too long.' Pacemaker. The word hung in the air like the promise of a reprieve from death row. My heart sank. Here we go again, I thought, another bloody horror round of hospitals. She'd pushed her luck and beaten the odds once. It was impossible to believe she'd pull off a miracle a second time.

'Nah. I'm not dying or anything. I'll be fine,' she said. I held back a sigh of relief. Puzzled over the words: *I'm not dying or anything.*

I realised later that in her nursing experience she'd never seen death without pain. And there was no pain. In her opinion, death was way, way off.

'Do you need anything?' I asked.

'No, Denise will be in shortly. She'll see to everything. She's like a daughter to me, you know.' Nothing changes, I thought, swallowing a scream, holding back tears. And now it's too late. But anger helped. It wiped out sadness, even compassion. Gave off an energy all of its own.

Outside, I asked Bob, 'Do you think she has any idea what's really going on?' He shrugged, grimaced slightly, as though the workings of my mother's mind were her own affair and trying to suss the subtext was a fool's errand. We barely spoke going home. In the tinny, I said, 'Nothing quite makes sense. I can't believe she's going to take the noble path. She's not built that way. She'll call an ambulance at the eleventh hour. I'd stake my life on it.'

'Probably,' Bob agreed.

The night-duty carer, Larry, a good-hearted, funny, larrikin offshorer – the sort of bloke who always had a lead role in Scotland Island theatrical productions and whose idea of comedy veered towards risqué but stopped well short of filthy – called at around eight o'clock in the evening.

'Your mum wants an ambulance and it's on the way,' he said.

'Ok, I'll come over now. Thanks, Larry.'

'I'm fond of the old girl, you know. She's quite a wit.'

'Yeah.' I put the phone back in the cradle.

'It had to be the pacemaker word,' I said to Bob. 'Soon as Chris said it, I thought, *Oh shit. She'll have a go.* Not sure whether I'm impressed or depressed.'

'Told you she was tough.'

Esther lay on a stretcher in the ambulance. Larry stood outside the rear doors. 'She looked shockin',' he said. 'Said she was in terrible pain.'

'Thanks, Larry. She adores you, you know. Can't remember how many times she's told me the python story.'

He rolled his eyes. 'Meant to be a bit of fun. Liven things up. Your mum understood that. Not many of the others did, though.'

'Yeah. She's a one-off, my mother.' I said something flippant to the paramedic. I can't remember the words. Shades of my mother, never far from the surface. Whatever it was, he took it the wrong way and bit my head off. Not many people, I thought, could or would understand the forces that drove the relationship between us. I didn't understand them myself. 'Thanks again, Larry. See you on the water.' He gave me a hug. Went back to his duties.

'We don't need a siren for this one,' said the paramedic. 'We'll take it nice and slow.'

'Yeah. Good on you.'

In emergency, I presented myself to the triage nurse. 'No paperwork yet. Take a seat and I'll call you,' she said. A few minutes later, people coming and going, she called me over and handed me a clipboard. 'Fill these in, please, and they'll let you through as soon as your mother is stabilised.'

In a corner, the television flickered. Mute. A mother with a young child flipped through a children's book, talking softly about fish and dolphins. The child had overheated red cheeks and glassy eyes, and tried hard to concentrate.

—

'Sorry, Sue,' my mother said in a small, apologetic voice.

'What for?' I asked, not understanding. I stood by her bed.

'I know you're busy and I hate being a nuisance.' The nurses looked at me oddly. I let it go through to the keeper. If she wanted to make out I was the bad guy, well, maybe I was and always had been. There were format questions – age, living arrangements, medical history – all leading up to the ultimate question: do you want your mother to be hooked up to life support if necessary?

Esther leapt in before I could reply: 'I'm ready to go. I've had enough.' The doctor looked relieved. The nurses let out long breaths and smiled. The electronics were unplugged and wheeled away. The beeping, squealing and clock-like ticking ceased. She was comfortable and smiling.

'I used to be a nurse,' she said. I opened my mouth, closed it. Tiny white lies didn't really matter. Not on the final lap.

'We'll make sure you're comfortable and never in any pain,' said the doctor, a dark-haired young man with a South African accent. He had the gentlest touch as he inserted a cannula in my mother's swollen hand. Stroking, soothing, making small jokes. 'Let's get a catheter sorted and we'll find you a bed in one of the wards.'

'She's been here before,' I told him. 'The resident heart specialist saw her last time. That's when she had a triple bypass and a heart valve replacement.'

'Can you remember who it was? We'll get him to take a look her in the morning?'

I gave them his name. Couldn't resist adding: 'He had the bedside manner of a Rottweiler.'

The staff grinned in unison. 'You either hate him or love him. His style doesn't suit everyone, but he's very good at what he does.'

'Yeah.'

I walked off, unable and unwilling to hang around while Esther's clothes were removed, a catheter inserted.

'All done,' called one of the nurses. I returned to Esther's bedside. 'We managed to remove all her rings except one,' the nurse said. 'It may have to be cut off.'

'No!' screeched Esther.

'Well, love, it could interfere badly with your circulation,' she said reasonably

'No,' Esther repeated, quieter this time.

'Let's see how you go, then,' said the nurse, kindly.

'Ok,' I said, 'you're all set. You're in good hands. I'll be back in the morning.' I patted her shoulder. 'The specialist will take a look at you. Tell us what to expect.' I did not, for one millisecond, believe my mother would choose a noble death. She'd heard the word pacemaker. It was her trump card. All we had to do was wait for her to use it. At home, I slid into bed beside Bob. His hand reached for mine. Neither of us said a word.

A few moments before I climbed in the tinny to return to the hospital, my mobile rang. It was the specialist. 'If you want your mother to survive,' he said in his favoured tone that managed to sound accusatory, judgmental and hectoring at the same time, 'she will need a pacemaker.'

'Oh, for god's sake, look at her. She's ninety-two. Barely functioning. What's the point?' It was not one of my finer moments.

'I see,' he said, sounding tired and as though I'd whipped the hubris out of him. I suddenly felt sorry for him. He had an awful job.

'Anyway, it's up to her, isn't it? I'm on my way to the hospital now. We can discuss all this in front of her. As I recall, that's the way you prefer to do it.' I phoned Bob from the dock: 'Could you come with me? I think we might need a referee.' Five minutes later, we cut across the water. It was a blazingly beautiful morning. As always, I thought that no one, given a choice, would give up the promise of an extra day.

———

There were three other patients in Esther's room. The woman on her left was in a deep, drugged sleep or a coma. A man diagonally opposite, who appeared to be at least one hundred and ten years old, didn't appear to be breathing. His eyes were closed. Mouth open. His legs were purple and blue, as though all the blood vessels under his skin were leaking. Directly opposite, an alert but aged man waved hello.

'He served in the war, too,' Esther said, sounding cheery.

'How are you?' I asked, standing back as usual while Bob gave her a kiss. She wheezed in reply, but I was immune to that wheeze. 'You look pretty good.'

'What? For someone who's dying?'

'Have you seen the specialist?'

She gave a limp-wristed little wave. 'Oh, he's been and gone.'

'What did he say?'

'Nothing much.'

I left her with Bob and went searching for him. Found him in the cluttered hallway further along the corridor next to a nurse holding a clipboard. 'North Shore. The San. Manly,' I heard him say. I guessed he was farming out the night's intake to specialist hospitals. I waited politely. He eventually looked my way. 'Esther Duncan,' I said, meeting his eyes. 'We're ready when you are.' He walked off, ignoring me. I returned to Esther's room to wait.

An hour later he swept into the room like royalty. 'Your mother,' he said firmly and for the second time (which made me wonder if he had a set routine for every situation), 'needs a pacemaker. Without it, she will die.'

My mother lay back, quite still except for her eyes, which darted from Bob to me. 'What would you do?' she asked. It struck me how young her voice sounded, even now, a day or two from death, three days at the most.

'It's not my decision, it's yours,' I said, refusing to be drawn in. If I understood anything about my mother, anyway, her mind was already made up. She was just playing the scene for all it was worth.

Esther gazed at the specialist standing at the foot of the bed. She gave off an air of submissiveness, a helpless little woman putting her life in his hands. But then, when she was young, doctors were gods. Early training, as I well know, is impossible to shake off. 'I'm not afraid of dying,' she said, sounding sensible. And then: 'But what do *you* think I should do?' The specialist turned away without answering. Over his shoulder he told us all to think about it, discuss it and let him know what we'd decided, but we didn't have all day. He was getting the schedule sorted for transfers.

I followed and dragged him back into the room. 'My mother needs to know the facts. What's the upside, what's the downside?' I said, familiar with the system this time.

'A pacemaker won't fix anything else that's wrong with her,' he replied, looking at me as though she wasn't there. 'It will keep her alive. That's all.'

'What are the risks?'

'She might die. She might come out of surgery with full-blown dementia. She might suffer a stroke during surgery. She's in the very high risk category because of her age and the fact that her health issues are a long way along. If she'd come even a week ago, there might have been a better prognosis.'

'And the outcome,' I insisted on him repeating it, 'the best possible outcome is . . .'

'She'll be alive, have all her faculties, but nothing else will change.' In other words, the general crumbling would continue and escalate, but the head-on collision with death would be postponed for a month, two months, perhaps longer. Nobody could say.

This time, when he walked away, I let him go. Then I stood at the foot of my mother's bed and looked directly at her. 'Did you hear all that?' She nodded. 'Ok. You have all the information. It's your decision.'

'But what would *you* do?' she asked again.

'It's not a decision I can make and it's not fair to ask me.' But I knew she wanted me to encourage her to struggle on, tell her she was the centre of my life, that I would wilt – even succumb – without her. I couldn't do it. To offer affection, I knew from bitter experience, invited ruin. Exposed a weak point where the knife could plunge. I'd stopped taking the risk so long ago that I couldn't play the loving daughter now. Not even if it meant her life. Whether it was deliberate or not, she brought out the shameful worst in me. The thin, complex wiring of mothers and daughters, or perhaps just this mother and daughter. Surely we were an aberration.

She settled her gaze on Bob then and asked the question once more. 'I know what I would do in your circumstance,' he said, 'but I can't tell you what you should do.'

Her eyes went flat and hard and her lips thinned. 'In *my* circumstance,' she said, enunciating each syllable very clearly, sarcastically, 'tell me what *you* would do.'

Bob, a decent man, gave it to her straight: 'I would say no. You've had a good run, Esther. Nothing is going to improve from now on. It's going to get worse. But it's your choice.'

She turned her face – pale, puffy and disappointed – towards a window filled with blue sky. 'Tell them no,' she whispered, scrunching, like a caterpillar, deeper into her bed.

I let out a breath I didn't realise I'd been holding. 'I'll let them know,' I said. 'For what it's worth, I hope I would have made the same call.'

She nodded. 'I'd like to be buried in the dress your brother bought me. The one with the blue diamond pattern.'

'Buried?'

'Well, whatever. As long as I end up next to Wally. There's still room for me there, isn't there?' And we switched, Duncan-style, into absurdity to cancel out despair.

'Of course there is. Plenty of space. And you'll have the chooks for company. They're great little yabberers. You've always loved chooks. There's a brush turkey mound close by, too. We have chicks nearly every year. Cute little things.' It didn't occur to me until later how bizarre we must have sounded. Life. Death. The two most powerful driving forces in humanity, and there we were, once again discussing whether there would be enough room for my mother's ashes next to her old Rottweiler. Later, I realised it was a clue: the seriousness of her situation hadn't hit her. She'd shut away every grim detail in an airtight compartment while she focused on her deathbed performance.

'I'll find out where we go from here and be back shortly,' I said. I glanced at the old bloke opposite. He gave me the thumbs up. Did the same for my mother.

I heard the scream as I stepped in the corridor: 'Give me the pacemaker! Give me the pacemaker!'

29

ESTHER WAS TRANSFERRED TO ROYAL NORTH SHORE the same afternoon. The following morning she was quickly and slickly fitted with a small electronic device under the skin near her collarbone. It would keep her heart beating steadily, the blood flowing, for as long as she had the strength to keep breathing. For as long as her heart remained steadfast. I wondered at her iron will to survive.

The surgery went well, but Esther's mind seemed to have short-circuited. She talked in riddles. Refused to get up. 'The pain,' she said, clutching her chest, 'the pain.'

The *overnight* procedure stretched into one, then two, then three days. The head nurse, a young bloke, rushed off his feet and hard to pin down, said, 'The pacemaker is working perfectly, her heart is beating strongly. She's just not responding the way she should.' He paused, looked at his feet. 'She can't stay here any longer. There's nothing more to be done.'

I grappled to understand what was really going on: 'She's improving, though?'

'She's stable.'

'So . . . not in any danger?'

'No.'

'Will she be able to go back to her old life in assisted care?'

'We have a very good social worker who'll come and talk to you. She'll explain the options.'

My heart sank. When my first husband was beyond help, the hospital sent a social worker. I immediately understood that Esther had slipped a rung. 'What happens now?'

'We'll move her to another ward.'

I sat in a chair in a corner of my mother's room. 'I wish I could tell you that when you get over this you'll be seventy years old again, but I can't,' I said. I felt incredibly sad. The next step was a nursing home. Hadn't my mother always told my brother and me, *Whatever you do, never put me in a nursing home. Knock me on the head first.* Her image was locked into an early-twentieth-century nightmare of filth, madness and cold, overcrowded cells, half insane asylum, half dumping ground for the near-dead. The kind of ugly, depressing place, I suspect, she and my father found for Uncle Ted after dementia blew his mind to bits and he tried to kill Esther. Choices were limited in Melbourne in the '60s, and they'd done their heroic best before committing him, but I knew my mother was still haunted by the decision. Afraid, perhaps, the same fate awaited her if she dropped her guard.

To raise the bond money, I would have to sell my house. Or ask Bob to step in. But I wouldn't do that. Family takes care of family. Blood dictates. My mother came first. If I believed she had failed me all those years ago, I could think of no valid reason to justify failing her now. I sat there for a while then crossed the room without another word.

'I'm sorry,' I heard her say in a very small voice. So not completely gaga, I thought. Post-anaesthetic confusion, maybe. Not necessarily dementia.

Outside in the corridor, the head nurse told me he'd made an appointment with the social worker for the following morning.

I promptly burst into tears. 'Oh god, sorry. It's just she told us she wanted to die and then she changed her mind, and now a whole new existence needs to be sorted out. Which is fine. But where is the upside here? I mean, really, where-is-the-upside? Forgive me if I sound ungrateful, but my mother is ninety-two. It's not as though she has a bright future waiting for her. Really. Was there a point to all this?' I knew I sounded childish, selfish and even cruel. But to see my vain, witty, tough old mother slip unknowingly into an unlovely, empty-minded, demoralising living death was unthinkable.

The nurse was kind: 'Will you do me a favour? Let me know how your mother's going in a few weeks.' Where do they find all that kindness?

'Yeah, sure,' I said, knowing even as I said it that I would not stick to the bargain.

The following day, Bob accompanied me to the hospital to meet the social worker. While we waited in Esther's room, he went through the rituals. 'You look great, Esther. More lives than a cat.' And he leaned down to kiss her.

'This is a very good hotel, you know,' she said in a whispery, sly, confidential tone. 'They even wash your bottom.'

'You're in a hospital,' I said quickly, nervously, willing her to focus. Return to the feisty woman I knew. 'You'd better not lose your marbles, Esther, because no one will want to know you.' Hoping toughness would jolt her back to reality. She threw me a black look. Closed her eyes, shutting me out.

The social worker was a pretty woman with fair hair, a good figure and a soft voice. My mother warmed to her immediately. 'You're a natural blonde,' she said, à propos of nothing. She added: 'I used to be a blonde once. Blondes are always more fun.'

The social worker, whose name I can't recall, smiled. 'I was blonde a long time ago and now I have three young kids, so the fun part is debatable.'

'I was a nurse like you,' Esther said, sounding sly again.

'I'm not a nurse. I'm the social worker, my job is to work out what's best for you because you can't stay here forever.' There was a look of naked panic in Esther's eyes.

'You've been here nearly a week,' I explained, 'and it's an overnight procedure. The system isn't geared for longer stays. The thing is, Esther, you can't go back to your old home — you're not fit enough. We have to organise a halfway house until I can sort something out.' She lost all interest in the conversation. Switched off. Her eyes seemed to empty of interest, emotion, life. 'Do you understand, Esther?' I asked, my voice louder than it had to be. She turned away from me.

The social worker said, 'There's a shocking shortage of hostel accommodation for someone like your mother, but I'll get on the phone to see what we can find.' Hostel accommodation? I had no idea what that meant. Like Bonegilla? Esther would have a fit.

The next day, the social worker told me my mother had asked to see her to explain that neither Bob nor I had her best interests at heart, that her son, my brother, was the only one who'd loved her. I was furious.

'My brother has been dead for nearly twenty years. When he was alive, he banned her from his house. Even when he was dying he told his wife not to let her in. I have been looking after her ever since. I cannot remember a single word of thanks.' I shook my head. 'One day, I will turn my back and walk away. I will wash my hands of her and her name will never cross my lips again.' I closed my mouth tightly. Took a deep breath. 'Sorry. You don't need to hear any of this.'

The social worker smiled with understanding. 'You have no idea what we see in this ward. Women like your mother cling to their sons and are monstrous to their daughters. It's unjust and irrational, but I've seen it over and over again. In my experience the boys don't do much. It's the daughters who end up with the dirty work. And, by the way, you won't walk away. If you haven't done it by now, you never will.'

'No. Of course I won't. But god, she goes too far. She goes way too far.'

'Would you like a cup of tea,' she asked kindly.

'No, thank you. I'm fine. Over it now. Wanted you to know that I'm trying to find a bed for her in the country, near Taree. We spend most of our time on our farm there, so it makes sense.'

'Sounds like a great idea. Let me know how you go.'

The following day Esther's condition deteriorated for no obvious reason. I could have told them what was going on in that devious, manipulative mind of hers. Hospital was safe. There was always someone around if she felt threatened. She was plotting to stay as long as possible – preferably forever – and she wasn't known as Sarah Bernhardt for nothing. Confused or not, her cunning instinct for self-preservation was as inviolable as ever.

I spent less than fifteen minutes with her. Both of us silent except for a polite word or two with the cleaner who mopped out the bathroom – a happy woman, or so it seemed as she hummed away under her breath. Thanking her lucky stars, perhaps, that she wasn't lying in a hospital bed with a death sentence hanging over her. In the end, everything is a matter of degree and circumstance.

In a new ward, a geriatrician took charge of Esther's wellbeing and called me each night with a report. 'Very, very frail,' she said. A few days later: 'Her heart, her kidneys, are worn out.' Another time: 'Three weeks or three months, I cannot say.' Finally: 'She will need high care for the rest of her life.'

No way, I thought cynically, *she's conning the lot of them*. But as always, doubts niggled. And nobody, not even my mother, lived forever. I decided to trust the experts and plan accordingly.

—

Beds in high-care nursing homes are hard to procure. Essentially, someone has to die before there's a vacancy. I rang around the countryside on a daily basis, aware that snagging a bed boiled down to luck and timing. Or timing and luck. I was amazed to find, though, that in the country very few facilities demanded bonds. Fees were based on income and assets alone. It felt like someone had lifted a concrete hat off my head.

One evening, over a couple of drinks with a neighbour, she told me there'd been a cluster (three) of, er, *check-outs*, from the nursing home where she worked. Happened like that, she said, as though the Grim Reaper ordered in bulk to save a second trip. Called Alma Place, it was named after a nursing Sister who'd lived and worked at Bonegilla during my mother's era. The connection, as flimsy as it was, might comfort her. I chose to see it as an omen. Shades of my mother, again and again.

The following day, I rang at opening time and hurriedly booked a bed, agreeing to pay the daily rate until my mother's arrival. A few days at the most, according to the geriatrician. I told Esther the plans during a visit. A day later she took a turn for the worse. Two weeks later, still in the geriatric ward at Royal North Shore, she announced she'd really prefer the nursing home at the retirement village.

'Ok,' I said, as cunning as her, 'I'll raise the money somehow, but I won't be able to visit very often. We'll be at the farm most of the time.' A day later, I found her coming out of the bathroom on her walker. It was the first time I'd seen her upright in four weeks. She'd always preferred the country, she said. It was a much healthier lifestyle. I should have been inured to the games, her ruthless determination to turn events to her advantage no matter the cost to others. But I wasn't. I didn't feel angry anymore, though. All I felt was tired.

Back at Pittwater I began the process of minimising Esther's life once more. To be sure I wasn't transgressing any unwritten rules of compassion and decency in the pursuit of practicality – and to give myself the chance of saying, *Denise told me to do it this way*, if Esther complained – I asked that good, common-sense woman for her advice.

'Three of everything,' she said flatly. 'Shirts, skirts, nighties, bras. Shoes – one pair only – and one pair of slippers. One dressing gown. No trousers.' The geriatrician had warned that Esther would be catheterised to the end.

I chose her room. Light, spacious, with a view of a garden, a private bathroom – it was lovely, and if by some miracle she became truly mobile, there was a spacious sitting room with tea- and coffee-making facilities right outside her door. With her gift for rearranging facts to suit her desires, she could pretend it was a swank hotel.

I went shopping. How often had I seen my mother hold a new garment up to her face, inhaling the scent of new with greedy pleasure? I put a photo of my brother on the bedside table. Another of her and Stefan smiling cheek to cheek. Another of her loyal friends from Wallacia, where she lived before the retirement village. Warm-hearted people who'd visited her regularly over the years. I bought expensive hand cream and make-up. Her favourite deodorant and a soft hairbrush. Lavender soap – I couldn't find any Yardley's April Violets, her favourite. They were small touches meant to console her for what I'd been warned over and over would be a short time. Her future laid down in packs of threes: three days, three weeks, but not more than three months. I lay the leopard-skin dressing gown on the end of the bed.

Esther was flown (for once, I was thrilled I'd kept paying her private medical insurance) from Sydney to Taree in the very early hours of the morning. So early, the thoughtful staff at Royal North Shore didn't want to call and wake me. But I'd been waiting, staring out the bedroom windows at a rising dawn, anxious to be there when she arrived. I didn't want her to feel frightened, lost or helpless. Pointless worry, as it turned out.

'First time I've ever been in a helicopter,' she told me as I walked through her door. She sounded as excited as a kid. 'Wish I'd been able to see where we were going, but I was well looked after. A lovely young man took care of me. Not handsome but very kind. A woman, too. She was very thoughtful.' And she launched into a detailed account of dealing with the embarrassing demands of an overflowing catheter bag mid-air, when once she'd pretended to have a heart attack to avoid mentioning her haemorrhoids.

I put this new lack of inhibition down to the sedation she'd been given for the trip. But it ramped up as time passed, with a fixation on her rear end: 'A lovely man washed my bottom this morning. He was so thorough he polished every grape, one by one.' And then: 'They all love me, you know. This morning, when Fred [name changed] applied cream to my bottom – it's red raw – he treated me as gently as a baby. Never thought I'd enjoy having a man wash my bottom. But he does it so efficiently.'

The day she ripped out the catheter, I knew she had a future even if I couldn't guess how it might take shape. A day later, I arrived to find her still on the bed, lying at an angle that would cripple lesser women, but she was fully dressed.

'There's a hairdresser on the premises,' I said, wheedling shamelessly, and I watched her eyes light up with pleasure.

'I'd like a Friday appointment. Late morning.'

'She only works on Mondays.' Esther pouted. 'Yes or no?' I asked.

'Yes!'

For a few weeks, I visited every day. Stepping through a weighty, cathedral-like timber door into a thick, gagging fog of floral air-freshener, determined to do my duty, or, more accurately, alleviate my guilt for plucking her out of Sydney against her wishes and being selfishly thrilled I didn't have to sell my house.

'Morning, Teena,' I'd say with a wave to the receptionist before marching on. Past the kitchen and two dining rooms. Then through a doorway and across a vast expanse of an always morbidly vacant sitting room with gold brocade chairs scattered around like a formal drawing room.

I always found her stretched on her side, resting on her elbow, head in her hand. Clean clothes the sole signal of a brand-new day.

'Still breathing, then,' I'd say automatically. And, automatically, she would thumb her nose in my direction. Then she'd run her hands along the smooth, unwrinkled, unblemished skin of her legs, drawing attention to them. 'Not bad legs for an old girl,' she'd say if I forgot to comment.

My own legs were scribbled with broken veins. My feet a mess of crooked toes broken on docks and in boats. 'Oh, you were born with hammer toes,' she said dismissively when I lifted a foot to make a comparison I thought she'd relish. 'Like your father. I wanted the doctor – Vern, do you remember Vern? He took your tonsils out and you haemorrhaged – to break and straighten them when you were a baby, but he said no. We thought we might lose you over those tonsils.'

These are the bonds, I thought, that knotted us forever. These are the bonds that overrode all else. 'I'm tough. Like you.'

'I'm not afraid of dying, you know. Never have been.' I resigned myself to a familiar monologue, but she surprised me. In a piping, childish voice, she said, 'It's just . . . well, I'll never be ready to die.'

'I'm not sure anyone ever is,' I replied after a moment, unsure whether to feel happy or sad for her, even more unsure of my own response in her circumstances.

'You're stuck with me, kid,' she said, smiling, patting the bed to emphasise the point.

I recalled a harried nurse in the emergency ward at Mona Vale Hospital, dealing with a violent, roaring old man determined to cheat death. 'The ones who won't give in have the worst deaths,' she'd said. 'There's nothing peaceful about them, that's for sure.'

Esther, fully dressed, stayed on that bed for a long, long time. Months. Most days she spun around so her feet rested on the pillow. It bamboozled the staff for a while, but I knew it gave her a view of the comings and goings of medication trolleys, laundry deliveries and meals. And the surprising number of visiting family and friends who rolled up regularly, as though they were having a fun day out. In Esther's former home, the crowds appeared on Mother's Day and Christmas. Otherwise, the streets were eerily empty beyond the residents and the staff.

For lunch or dinner, Esther steadfastly refused to join her comrades in wheelchairs, open-mouthed and prone on stretchers, or glued to walkers. 'I'll dine in my room,' I heard her say over and over, as if she was ordering room service in a hotel or on a cruise ship. She snapped at any suggestion by the patient and good-humoured staff that she join activities for the day (sing-alongs, bingo, storytelling), and remained prone on her bed. I didn't blame her, but I didn't think it was good for her either.

'You've always loved singing,' I said, trying to sound jolly.

'I don't know any of the songs.'

'Of course you do – even I know most of them. Learned them when we had the pub. Remember the Saturday night sing-alongs with Old Gil? How she pounded the keyboard with her twisted fingers?'

'Will you come with me?'

I almost choked.

'Hah!' she said, spitting out the word in triumph.

———

It had been, and still was, a complicated time emotionally. But there were subtle shifts in our relationship. Driven more by dependency, probably, than our reconstructed personalities. The fight went out of her. And me. She became kinder, less critical. I found patience. Every so often, she thanked me. Every so often, I thanked her.

'You gave me a great education. It set me up for life. I'll always be grateful,' I said.

'I had to fight your father every step of the way. We made a lot of sacrifices for you two kids, you know.'

'I know.'

They were unexpected turning points.

I found the more I did for her, the more my rage about the past resolved. It also took the edge off guilt, which I realised was often the trigger for flaring up over what boiled down to nothing at all. She was who she was. Me too. If vanity and self-absorption drove her, did it really matter? If believing she was special and loved by one and all gave her a reason to open her eyes each morning, could anyone deny her that? It was time to stop holding up as prima facie evidence of failure what I so effortlessly forgave in myself. Most of all, she was consistently stoic in a situation that would have broken most spirits, and I admired that above all else. She'd made her bed, as she and my grandmother used to say, and she was damn well lying on it. Even if it meant being imprisoned in a facility where rational conversations were rare, where she was confined to a room no matter how well-appointed, where television became her closest soulmate and the staff her substitute family.

'It's TV or the clickers,' she said.

'Clickers?'

'The ones who have had strokes. They click their tongues. Makes sense once you get the hang of it.' I filled the third drawer in her room with chocolates and sweets to tempt the staff into making extra visits and talking to her in plain English.

'I've realised there's a lot for me to do here,' she said earnestly one day. 'There are quite a lot of very ill people, so I'm going to read to them. I can manage that. I've always been a good reader, so they tell me.' I knew it would never happen. *But see*, she seemed to be saying, *I'm going to make myself useful. The pacemaker was worthwhile. It was the right decision.*

'Of course, that's the first-class end,' she said one day, pointing to the far end of the corridor, implying I'd stuck her in the bargain basement. A comment like that would have made me furious once. But how many people lay under blocks of marble in cemeteries, exhausted to death by their bitterness?

'That's the dementia wing, Esther. Be happy you're nowhere near it.'

'I'm not complaining. Have you ever heard me complain? I'm well looked after.'

'Yes, you are. You're a very lucky woman.'

'Haven't I always said that?'

'You've always been a model mother.'

'Don't go too far, kid.'

On another visit, she said, 'They put me in dead people's nighties every night.'

'I have no idea what you're talking about,' I said, alarmed that it signalled an irretrievable mental shift.

'I don't mind. It's rather funny.'

'What makes you think that's happening?'

'Well, they're not my nighties. I assume they're passed on to me because their former owners don't need them anymore.'

'But you've got plenty of nighties.'

'No. They've all disappeared.' She made a *poof* motion with her hands.

'I'll check it out,' I said, not sure what to think. The front desk called the laundry, laundry sent me to a lost clothes cupboard. I rummaged around. Found two shirts, a pair of trousers. No nighties. Name tags were missing, explained laundry.

'Ah.' I told Esther I'd buy some new stuff anyway. 'You're a bit short in the clothes department. None of us expected you to live this long.'

'Hah! There's plenty of life in the old girl yet.'

By now, she was ninety-three years old and I was sixty-three. Both of us firmly aware of the impact of time and the inescapable end result of living. The point, I thought, of her long survival, was the time it gave me – not her – to reach détente. Admittedly wobbly, but a state of mind nevertheless.

30

ESTHER SEEMED WELL ENOUGH ONE DAY to attempt taking her out. I wasn't sure of protocol, so I lined up behind a nurse at the front counter to check the routine.

'I need some sticky tape,' said the nurse.

'What's it for?' Teena asked.

'Mr Smith's blow-up doll has sprung a leak.'

'You need something stronger than I've got,' Teena said, unfazed. 'Speak to maintenance.'

'Blow-up doll?' I spluttered, butting in, incredulous.

'There's nothing wrong with it; whatever brings comfort in this life,' said the nurse firmly, daring me to disagree with her.

'Yes, no,' I mumbled, embarrassed.

'Mr Smith's a lovely old man,' Teena said.

Just then, a sparrow of a woman strode up purposefully in a neat pink tracksuit. I stood aside. 'You're a wonderful employee, Teena,' she said, writing out a cheque in perfect lettering. 'The best worker I've ever had. I think you deserve a raise.' She tore off the cheque carefully, placed it on the counter. Teena smiled kindly but didn't move. Odd, I thought. The woman turned, took a few steps, then spun back, her face riddled with rage. 'You're fired!' she spat out. 'You're no good. You're a lazy girl, Teena. You're fired.' She snatched back the cheque, stomped off furiously.

'Hell. What was that all about?' I asked, shocked.

'Mrs Jones used to run her own business. She thinks she's still in charge.'

'Doesn't it bother you? The abuse?'

Teena – young, beautiful, impeccably groomed and dressed, clever and competent – shrugged. 'She's not too bad. You get used to it. It's not her fault, really. It's just age and illness.'

'Yes. I see. Ha-ha. I bet you've got a thousand stories to tell.' I gave another stupid sort of laugh, feeling way out of my depth. 'I was wondering, would it be ok to take Esther out?'

'Of course! The staff love it when people are taken out.'

'Right. Good. Thank you.' And I marched off. Head reeling. Blow-up dolls? I held back a roar, swallowed it whole. Bob always said the last thing in a man to die . . . well, why spell it out?

'Esther!' I boomed from her doorway. 'You've always wanted to see the farm. Today's the day. Get up off that bed and put on your shoes – we're heading out.'

'Give me a minute, kid.'

It took almost an hour, but she struggled along the hallway on her walker, puffing and panting, stopping every few feet, closing her eyes, opening them, giving herself a shake, plodding on.

'You're doing well,' I said, when once I'd been impatient, convinced it was an act. Well, once it *was* an act. 'We're nearly to the front door. Turn left just ahead. I'll go and get the car and bring it to the entrance.' I took off at a fast walk.

In the dining room, people with baby-fluff white hair, vacuous faces and bibs were being spoonfed by staff. Others, still able to lift a fork slowly to their mouths, ate sparingly. Cutlery clicking on china echoed loudly. I quickly looked away. *I'd never leave my room either*, I thought.

—

'Bum first,' I told Esther, holding the car door with one hand, removing her walker with the other.

'I know, I know.' And *snap* – we fell back into a well-worn routine like a couple of old vaudeville players. 'How far to the farm?' she asked.

I leaned across and buckled her into her seat. 'About half an hour.'

'You don't want to waste time with me.'

'Nope, but I'm prepared to do it anyway.'

'Just as well.'

'I'll buy fresh prawns for lunch.'

'The food is very good where I am. But they don't serve oysters or lobsters. They should address that problem.'

'Ok, ok, I've got the message. You'd prefer oysters, but lobster would be even better.'

'Prawns will do very well,' she said primly. She looked out the window: 'This is a big town, isn't it? And such pretty houses. I thought you were dumping me in a cold, old hollow when they brought me here.'

Two shocking facts hit me at the same time: My mother's world had reduced to a single room, and it could have been in Timbuktu for all she knew. And she thought I was capable of doing truly dreadful things to her. I scrolled back through history, searching for the basis for her distrust. I may not have been a perfect daughter – or even a barely adequate daughter – but, as far as I could tell, I had always responded to genuine need.

'Why would you think I'd dump you somewhere awful? Or even more important, have I ever dumped you anywhere awful?'

She ignored the question. 'Look at all these beautiful trees. Aren't trees beautiful?' And in my new state of being, I let her comments slide off when once I would have held them hard up

339

against my chest. Used them as an excuse to skive off doing my duty for a while.

'Here we are,' I said a while later. I turned into our gate, began the climb up the Bottom Hill in first gear. Waved to Bob as we passed the shed. Perhaps *beckoned desperately* is nearer the truth. Opened the car door. Spot, a ball of brown and white fur, bounded into the car, scrabbling across my legs, landing in Esther's lap. Licking her face, her hands. Tail wagging madly.

'Oh, she's beautiful,' Esther said, laughing.

'Out, Spot,' I said. 'C'mon, out, out damned Spot.' I grabbed the dog, chucked her through the door.

'Did she scratch you? Are you bleeding?' I went around to the other side of the car to help Esther.

She sat without moving, just looking. 'This isn't what I expected,' she said in a critical tone I recognised from the old days.

'Well, you don't have to live here – we do,' I replied, bristling.

'It's different. I'll give you that,' she said, trying to nullify any hint of disapproval. 'I wouldn't call this a farmhouse, though.' She paused, making no attempt to move. 'How many bedrooms are there?'

'Just one,' I lied, because I knew immediately where she was headed.

'The shed would do me.' I caught the glint in her eye.

'It's yours anytime you like,' I said, calling her bluff.

'No, I'm well looked after where I am. They really love me, you know.'

'Would you like a whisky when we get inside?'

'Well, perhaps just a small one.' I left Bob to sort her out. Went to put on the kettle.

Later, still curious, I asked her again: 'Have I ever dumped you anywhere awful? Ever?'

'Not yet.'

—

After the success of our first outing, Esther came to the farm for prawns on a fresh bread roll, or eggs from our new brood of chooks boiled and served with toast cut into soldiers – a new favourite – at least once and often twice a week. She sat in one of the red leather chairs we'd brought from her unit and breathed in the hills and valleys, as though they were life-giving.

Once, I said, 'It's a view that reminds me of Donvale.'

She shook her head: 'This is much more beautiful.' And we said nothing more about her childhood or mine.

If the weather was too wild and wet to tackle our dirt track with confidence, I took her to a funky little restaurant and old wares shop on the edge of the great Manning River in Taree. There, the shopkeepers treated her like a fragile treasure and made the kind of fuss she loved. She always had a story for anyone game enough to listen. The little toe-tapper dancing for pennies on the pavement will never die in her.

On one occasion, I discovered she'd whispered that she was on the verge of her hundredth birthday.

'You're ninety-four,' I said, insisting on the truth, as always.

She shot back: 'Well, today I feel at least a hundred. Even older.' And we all cracked up.

'You never admit defeat,' I said, driving her back to the nursing home.

'Defeat never gets you anywhere,' she retorted.

As a joke, during the drought, I told her to make herself useful. 'Get on your knees and pray for rain,' I said.

Now, whenever water falls from the sky, she takes the credit. 'I have a direct line to God, you know,' she said.

'That's handy. I'll keep it in mind.'

'Don't get too greedy, kid. I don't want to wear out my welcome.'

But by the tail end of winter, 2015, her mind was wandering more and more. She left sentences unfinished. Broke off mid-thought as if she'd become knotted in a tight tangle. I knew something was seriously out of kilter the day – running late – I rushed to pick her up straight from mowing a paddock. I was stinky, dusty and my clothes were filthy.

In her room, Esther smiled sweetly. 'You look quite lovely today,' she said.

'No, I don't, and you know it.' But her eyes shone with hurt.

The official diagnosis was Stage One dementia. The happy stage, I was told. And although my mother had already softened, it changed her personality to such an extent I had no idea how to handle her. I felt wrong-footed by kindness, lost my moral compass for a minute or two and floundered – uncertain whether to laugh, cry or applaud. Sometimes I felt I could have been talking to a stranger. But there were just enough days when she reverted to form and I'd breathe a sigh of relief.

One day she looked at me with dull eyes and said, 'My mind is going wonky, isn't it?'

'Yes,' I replied, as though it was no big deal.

'Didn't think you'd noticed.'

'I've always kept a close eye on you.'

She nodded in acknowledgement but had nothing to say for a while. 'It feels like there are big black holes,' she said.

'Any pain?'

'No. But I don't think I've got long to go.'

'You'll be right.'

'You never could tell a decent lie.'

—

One morning, when we'd returned to Pittwater, Bob opened the courtyard gate and Spot dashed past him, ran off to the boatshed. It was very early on a Sunday when no one was about. Somehow she got her pretty little head stuck in an empty crisp bag, fell in the water and drowned. Bob was gutted. I couldn't leave the bedroom for three days. It took me a week to find the will to get out of my pyjamas.

'No more dogs,' I said to Bob vehemently. 'No more dogs. Ever.'

When I told Esther about the tragedy on a visit to her room, she shot me a gimlet-eyed look and, in a voice sharp with blame, said, 'You let her die, did you? That beautiful little dog.' I stood up and walked out. 'I was only joking,' she called after me.

It will always be like this, I thought. *Expect nothing more.*

A few days later, on the drive to the farm, she suddenly sounded quite lucid and asked, 'Are you going to write about my sins?'

'They were not your sins, Esther,' I replied. 'Never think that for a moment. You didn't stand a chance against your father.'

'He was a bad man, wasn't he?'

'The worst.'

'And yet everybody loved him. I'll never understand it.'

'The only thing you have to understand is that none of it was your doing.' And because I know she believes in God and heaven and hell, I added, 'You carry no sin. None at all. Remember that.'

'So you don't blame me?'

'No. Never again.' A small sob escaped on the back of a deep, shuddery sigh.

'I know I haven't got long to go,' she said, and I couldn't catch a whiff of manipulation. 'Your father and John are waiting for me. God knows, they've waited a long time. Mum, too.'

'Don't worry about your father. He'll be in the other place.'

'Maybe. But God is all-forgiving, isn't he?' She sounded hopeful when I'd expected her to feel angry or at least bitter, and I understood at that moment that she'd loved him deeply. The men who followed were simply transactions. A means to an end.

'It's your birthday in a couple of months. We're planning a party for you. Ninety-five. Not a bad innings, eh? You'd better hang around for that.'

She made a fluttering motion with her hand. Non-committal.

—

When it became clear my mother would live to celebrate another Christmas, Bob and I began discussing options. To take her to Pittwater was out of the question – she would never physically cope. Should we swap our traditional family, waifs and strays celebration for a quiet one at the farm? Or should we decide in favour of the pleasure of the majority? Either way, there would be losers.

While we agonised over the dilemma, I decorated her room, making sure to put a wreath on her door. Without a wreath, she once instructed me after I'd failed to hang one, you couldn't call it Christmas.

'You don't have to bother,' she murmured as I strung baubles along walls, placed poinsettias and small fake fir trees where she couldn't knock them over.

'But you love Christmas,' I said firmly.

'I'm well looked after here. Everyone spoils me, you know.'

On another visit, she said, 'The staff needed the decorations for the rest of the building. I gave them away.' That's when I knew she'd sensed we were going to abandon her. Powerless, she struck out in the only way left to her. For once, instead of throwing up my hands in angry resignation, I found some red-and-gold floral fabric in a shop. Eric's wife, Robyn, a skilled seamstress who'd made dust covers for our furniture, sewed a vibrantly gay quilt.

'Don't give that away,' I ordered, 'we can use it again next year.'

'I won't be around next year,' she responded.

'We're having an early Christmas dinner for you at the farm,' I told her, trying to make amends. Adding, as a blatant bribe, 'Would you like me to find a new outfit for you to wear?'

She remained hunched and small. 'No. What's the point? Nothing matters anymore.'

'You love red. How about a red dress?'

Her eyes lost their dullness. 'Well, not too bright. Perhaps something green to go with it.' And the battle was over.

'Of course.' I smiled inwardly. We invited neighbours to lunch on a Sunday afternoon. I couldn't find a red dress so I bought her a pair of green trousers and a bright red, flowing shirt.

'How do I look?' she asked when I picked her up.

'Fabulous.'

'Will you be wearing what you've got on? Or will you change?'

'Haven't decided yet.'

'You might want to find something more festive.'

'Yeah. Maybe.' She made her way down the corridor of the nursing home, supported by her walker, stopping every few steps to rest. A look of such agony and distress on her face that I wondered if the effort might kill her. She didn't even come alive at the party, and an hour and a half later, her face pinched with exhaustion, I drove her back to the room.

'Do you realise,' she said accusingly on the way, 'you didn't invite a single soul I knew?'

I let it slide through to the keeper. Said not a word. Wondered if she would ever understand that being ungrateful made it easier to leave her.

'Just so you know,' I said, 'if you die before me, I will not have a twinge of guilt. I have always done the best I can for you.'

Her face went slack with shock, as though I'd whipped the scaffolding from under her and left her hanging. Then a few days before we quit our high, quiet hill for our high, rough hill, I went to take her to lunch to say farewell, to tell her we'd return in a couple of weeks. I found her lying on her side, curled into snail tightness.

'Sit down,' she said, pointing at a chair.

'Why?'

'Because I think I'm dying.'

'Think? Or know?'

'You'll be sorry when I'm gone.'

'Are we going out or not?'

'No. I want to know where I'm going to be buried.'

I gave in. Sat down. This was such familiar ground, I didn't even have to think. 'With Wally. Where else?'

'There's not enough room now you've put Spot next to him.'

'There's heaps of space. You'll be beyond worrying by then anyway.'

She rolled on her back, unwinding until her legs extended like two swollen stumps. I helped her struggle upright, shoved a pillow behind her head. 'Give me a minute and I'll be back,' I said.

'Where are you going?'

'To the front desk to top up your hairdressing account,' I lied.

'Don't be long.'

I went looking for my white-haired neighbour to get at the truth. Margaret barely reached my shoulders but kept large mad men under control using laughter as a tool and, as a kindness, kept me updated on my mother's condition.

'Esther reckons she's dying,' I said when I located her in the dementia wing, doling out medication.

'Rubbish, her pulse is strong as an ox,' she said. I swallowed in relief, for once happy it was a quintessential Esther con, and waited while Margaret finished pill duty. I followed her back to Esther's room. At the doorway, she whispered, 'Stay out here and listen.'

'What's this I hear about you dying?' Margaret said in a no-nonsense voice.

'Oh, I'm alright.'

'I know that. So I might as well tell you, you're not good enough for up there, and not bad enough for down there. So forget all this dying business until you've racked up a few more credits to get through heaven's gate.'

'All I want to know is where I'll be buried,' Esther said, her voice turning small and childlike, seeking sympathy.

'Where do you want to be buried?' Margaret asked, her voice still firm.

'On that big hill at the farm. I'd have a wonderful view and I'd be able to haunt Susan forever.'

'You won't be haunting anyone for a long time yet,' Margaret said. 'Now pull yourself together and go out with your daughter. The drive will do you good.'

Outside Esther's bedroom, Margaret gave me a firm talking to. 'Your mother's got you wrapped around her little finger. It's time you stopped letting her get away with it.'

'Yeah. Thanks, Margaret.' But I knew it was way, way too late for either of us to change.

When I told Bob about her desire to haunt me, instead of laughing, as I thought he would, he said, 'There's no way her ashes are going anywhere near the farm.'

'Ah, what does it matter?'

'Trust me. No way.'

'We could put her way over in the back paddock, couldn't we?'

'Still too close.'

—

I never thought I would be capable of leaving my mother to eat institutional food in a nursing home on a day when everyone was supposed to be wrapped in the joy, angst, fury, rivalry, boredom – whatever – of their families. But I did.

We ate Christmas dinner on the lawn on a perfect day. 'Where's Esther?' one guest after another asked. 'Too hard to get her here,' I explained.

'Oh, that's sad. Not the same without her. Who's going to snaffle the table decorations this year?' But I'd be lying if I said I didn't feel relieved – freed – by her absence.

Early in the evening, a fierce storm blew up out of nowhere with gale-force winds and torrential rain. Our last hangers-on scurried to the far end of the verandah where Bob and I sleep in summer. We dropped the awnings, filled our glasses and hunkered down to sit out the deluge, too replete to make the effort to shout above the bedlam, mesmerised by the sight of towering spotted gums rocking back and forth, as though at any moment they might come loose from the earth and crash down. Then Boatshed Michael called to say someone's tinny was about to sink and everyone took off at a gallop.

There was a brief moment when I stood alone in the hallway and picked up the phone to call my mother. I put it down. No matter what either of us said, it wouldn't sound right.

———

On our return to Benbulla, Esther came to lunch at the farm.

'How was your Christmas?' I asked.

'Best I ever had. By a mile.'

'Good to hear. I was afraid you might miss us.'

She smiled smugly. 'Oh, I know you think about me all the time.'

'So what did you do? Lunch in the dining room? A few crackers and party hats?'

'I woke up on my own, ate lunch on my own and went to bed on my own. It was the most peaceful Christmas I've ever had.'

'I'll try to do better next year,' I said.

'I'm not being sarcastic. I mean it. I didn't have to worry about a thing.'

I had no idea if it was a knife being thrust in my gut or a gesture of extraordinary graciousness. It was ever thus.

———

I still wake occasionally in the dead of night and wonder if my mother was complicit in what happened to me as a child. Surely the signals, signs, operandi had to be as familiar to her as getting dressed each morning to go to school. Then I remembered Cousin Jayne's anecdote: 'Your mother coped [with the distress, shame, trauma of being unmarried and pregnant] by making up a mad story about rushing home to help June recover from an abortion. When June heard, she wanted to rip out Esther's hair.' By the time I was born, plucking one or two words out of a conversation and reinventing the facts around them, or taking refuge in phantasmagorical denial, was a skill she'd mastered. Without it she'd probably have been felled by grief and disappointment decades ago.

At some point, I can't remember exactly when, I realised Cousin Jayne had a right to know about the material in this book. Felix was also her grandfather. She has children and a grandchild who are his descendants. But I also had a deeper, underlying motive. She'd lived within arm's reach from her birth to her marriage. Had he done to her what he'd done to my mother and me?

I phoned to tell her Bob and I were driving to Melbourne, and on the way we'd like to meet for lunch in Wangaratta. I had a couple of *things* I wanted to talk to her about. On the due date, I rang to confirm a time and place.

'I have no idea what this is about, but I've just had a check-up and all this secrecy has sent my blood pressure sky-high,' she said. 'You'd better tell me what's going on now so I can let go of a thousand nightmare scenarios that are currently rocketing through my head, not least of which is that your cancer is back and you're dying.'

So in the end I blurted out the reason for our visit over the phone.

'Oh, for heaven's sake, don't believe a word your mother says,' she said without taking a moment to think.

'It wasn't just her,' I said. 'It was me, too.'

'Oh god, oh no, oh god, that's different. That's entirely different.' She paused. I heard her breathing heavily. 'You know, I always thought Auntie Jean and Susie were the goody-two-shoes in the family and never understood why. I'm glad I was the bad egg now.'

Half an hour later, we sat across from each other in the restaurant. I couldn't look her in the eye. Even now, when we have both lived the greater part of our lives and are comfortable in our skins, I wondered if this new knowledge would come between us and skew her attitude towards me forever. A fear, I suspect, that lies firmly at the core of the long silences of abused children. Would revealing our damaged history result in standing forever isolated with the word *victim* tattooed invisibly on our foreheads? Deeply different from every other child through no fault of our own?

'What about you?' I asked, once again failing to meet her eyes.

'He never put a foot wrong. Not once. God, all those years and none of us saw what was happening.' She shook her head in disbelief.

'I didn't let him win, though,' I said after a long while. 'He didn't destroy me.'

'If Frank had known what he'd done, he would have killed him.' *My father, too.*

She stabbed her pizza. And we left the dreadfulness there once and for all.

'We've planted some fruit trees at the farm. If you've got time, we'd like a few tips on pruning,' I said.

'It's all about choosing strong buds,' she said, stabbing another piece of pizza with her fork.

'You'll have to show me.'

She let go of her cutlery and reached across the table to grab my hand. Nodded.

EPILOGUE

OFTEN, ON A SWELTERING EVENING when only birdsong breaks the silence like a single riff being repeated over and over, I think back to the cool damp day we climbed the Great Hill and found the inspiration – and backbone – to make the mental and physical shift from the known world to the unknown. Back then, as one rainbow after another made harlequin streaks across the sky, my imagination ran amok with dreams of gardens heavy with perfect tomatoes, cucumber, beans, peas, broccoli and every other kind of vegetable. Fruit trees bending under the weight of oranges, apples, lemons, plums, figs, peaches, apricots, quinces and pears. Walnut, almond and pecan trees. Perhaps an olive tree. And a flower garden meant only for cut flowers for our house. I dreamed of winter nights with open fires, slow-cooking beef emblazoned with a startling array of herbs and spices plucked from the yard, and in autumn, when there was a glut of fruit and vegetables, days spent tending huge simmering saucepans until jars of preserves were lined up like soldiers on the pantry shelves. Nothing ever wasted. The heart and soul of farming, I have learned, is profoundly domestic. And even though I was standing on a bleak summit redolent with cow dung, I remember the eerie sense that there was a whiff of baking quinces in the air. (A few years later, that is not as weird as it sounds. My permaculture neighbours down the hill, Annette and Les, are passionate bottlers and preservers of their organic produce, so it is quite possible sweet scents of simmering jams wafted to the tip of the high hill as we stood there with our dreams running amok.)

At the time, I'd dismissed it all as romantic sentimentality. I was well aware of the backbreaking slog required to establish a successful garden. I had seen at close range, when I covered stories as a journalist, the heartbreak of droughts, plagues, floods or disease. Understood we'd always battle bats, birds, possums and rabbits. But I reckoned without the backbreaking work of a good man, who never wavered in his commitment to bring a dream to life, and romantic sentimentality has become a deeply satisfying reality. With Eric's help, Bob built a netted enclosure, now known as 'Wimbledon', to thwart greedy wildlife marauding our fruit trees. I felt for him when a gale ripped through five hundred square metres of netting before he had time to tie it down securely, and for a string of wind-whipped days, all we could do was watch it flapping wildly.

'Still blowin' so hard I've got white caps in my teacup,' Eric said, looking into a mug I'd handed him when they began repairs, his hands numb with cold. Bob was twenty feet off the ground on a ladder braced against a tractor bucket. I couldn't bear to watch, but I held back from pointing out the danger. Most fears are plain to the risk-taker and best left unspoken.

Living off-grid has delivered far more joy and comfort than we ever imagined and gone way beyond our expectations. In winter, double-glazed windows provide effortless warmth. On even partially sunny days, the inside temperature averages twenty-three degrees – T-shirt stuff. Soars to twenty-seven sometimes in full sun, so even when it is frigidly cold (around eight to ten degrees outside) I throw open windows for a while for relief. When the sky is overcast the indoor temperature lingers around eighteen and a light sweater is enough to hold the cold at bay. The underfloor heating, installed to run off a fire we believed would burn day and night right through winter, will never be used. Not even if a freak blizzard veers so far off-course that it lands on the doorstep.

I quickly learned closing doors and windows at three in the afternoon locks in the heat and our long, slim main room stays toasty until well after bedtime. Mind you, bedtime in the country is closer to nine than eleven. In the very early days of living off the power of batteries, we reckoned solar energy would entail using one major appliance at a time. But I can run the washing machine, vacuum and dishwasher without hesitation. Power to both our fridges has never failed and the backup generator lies unused under the house. Although, it is wise to check the level of power after a few overcast days in a row and plan accordingly. We also use solar power to run the pump from the dam when my mother's link to the Almighty wobbles for a while and the rain forgets to fall. I am amazed over and over, by the mental freedom that is attached to living sustainably, and I have never used a dish-washer so profligately in my life.

We picked our first lemons and limes in the summer of 2014, our first golden peaches in the late spring of 2015. And mid-summer 2016, we bit into the sweet, winy flesh of a white peach that made our senses reel. Next year, we're hoping the plum, fig, tropical apple, pear, avocado and mango trees will also bear small crops.

Bob has planted young grapevines that will take time to mature, but we've eaten corn, tomatoes, cucumbers, onions, spinach, potatoes, rocket, sweet and burning chillies, snow peas, broad beans, bush beans, lettuce, rhubarb and learned new recipes to cope with a glut of radishes. Pickled a strong crop of beetroot, spiced with cinnamon, cloves and orange peel. Herbs grow like, well, weeds. Even pernickety French tarragon thrives. But I would be lying if I failed to admit that, every season, there are many hard lessons amongst the successes. Most answers, we've learned, lie in the soil, so we collect cow manure for composting and, under the house, worms as thin as threads toil day and night, improving the biodiversity of our good and fruitful earth.

When it became clear we would be spending more and more time at Benbulla, Bob built a henhouse, and now ten chooks roam free in Wimbledon, roosting safe from foxes at night. There are no words to describe the pleasure of handing a passionate cook a clutch of eggs still warm from the henhouse.

At least once a week from spring through to autumn, I pick armfuls of vibrant red, purple, pink, mauve, yellow and orange roses. Their rich perfume beats back the ripe smell of cattle when they've camped near the house on very hot days.

We now have two dogs. Scruff is a punk-haired, mulish Jack Russell with a chocolate box face. Feisty and independent, she's harder to pin down than a firefly. Red Girl, a roan cattle dog, is all muscle and sinew beautifully knitted together. She sprints like a racehorse, stalks like a lion and has a sweet, loving nature. One day, we're sure, she will overcome her fear of the steers.

In the evenings when we come inside, knackered but happy after weeding, mowing, digging or moving our now almost seventy-strong herd from one paddock to another, we throw our boots onto a rack Eric built from scraps of metal, grab a cold beer and discuss how we might do it better next time. We never stop learning, which at our age is a rare gift and saves us time and again from falling into the trap of heckling – safe from criticism – from the fence. No shades of my mother there, at least.

During the past two years, the seasons have been kind. On a morning walk, dew soaks our trousers as high as our knees, the cattle are fat and sleek. We now generate enough farm income to qualify as bona fide farmers. A milestone. But the greatest endorsement came from a bloke called Hank. Eric wrote down the gist:

'I always reckoned the country through Blackflat Lane was so piss poor that a mouse would have to pack a cut lunch to walk through there. But that place [Benbulla] looks so f★★★★★' good. The best it's ever f★★★★★' looked. I was checkin' out the bullocks in the front paddock and they looked pretty f★★★★★' good, too.'

P.S. 'Hank says f★★★★★' a lot. I might have missed a couple in the transcription.'

—

At this stage of Esther's life, her world is closing in rapidly. She believes the medical alarm button in her nursing home to be a bird call. She hears a loudspeaker regularly announcing she's the most popular patient in the home and everyone loves her. She tells me over and over how lucky she is. And more and more often she thanks me for taking care of her. It is oddly disturbing to see my mother needy and humble to the point of obsequiousness.

A few weeks after our conversation about the 'sins' of her father, my mother slid down another rung on the dementia ladder. Each day, compassionate and tender staff settle her in a mobile chair called a *fall out* chair (it's impossible to fall out of it) and wheel her along the corridor to a large sitting room where erratic and unpredictable patients are kept under constant watch. On a visit one day, she called me closer to her side.

'I have something to tell you,' she said in a small voice tinged with shame.

'Oh? Yes . . .' I said, wondering where she was going.

She struggled forward, her voice dropped conspiratorially: 'I fell in love.' She looked sheepish. 'I've had a baby.'

'No, Esther, you're confused.'

Suddenly feisty: 'No, I'm not.'

'You're ninety-five years old. Your child-bearing years are long gone.' Her eyes widened, she struggled to make the links in her mind.

'That's what I thought. But I've had a baby. Truly. It's just . . . I can't find him and I'm worried he's starving.' She looked at her hands, played with a gaudy ring in the shape of a large ladybird – costume jewellery, a gift from a friend of mine who'd visited from New York and remembered my mother's love of glitz. 'The shame I've brought on the family,' she said, 'it's terrible.'

Her eyes, foggy with confusion, filled with tears. Her hands shook violently, the ring shooting shards of light like a sparkler. Despair riddled her face.

'Let's eat these oysters,' I said, trying to soothe her. 'Sydney rocks, your favourite. From the fish co-op in Taree. So fresh you could smack their faces.' She opened her mouth like a chick and, one by one, I fed them to her on a fork. A dozen, as usual. I repeated: 'There is no baby, Esther. There's nothing to worry about. Everything is fine.'

I pressed my fingers against my lips, the same fingers against her chalky white cheek in a facsimile of a kiss. Only death, I thought, releases us from a corrupted childhood. Until then, it's an endless struggle to put the terribleness aside just to function.

When I stood to leave, she grabbed my hand and held it tightly. 'Don't go,' she said, 'please don't go. Not yet.' I pretended I didn't hear. She let go her grip.

'I'll see you on Tuesday. Today is Friday, Monday is hair-dressing day, and then it's Tuesday.' I arranged her chair in front of the television with the others patients, who were hanging on by the thinnest threads. 'Don't forget. Tuesday,' and again I raised my fingers to my lips and then pressed those fingers against her cheek.

Alone in the car, I rested my head on the steering wheel and wept for the awful fragilities that lie hidden in all of us.

Secrets lose their strength and dissolve into the atmosphere the moment you shine a light on them. Tackling demons, even at this late stage of my life, has uncluttered the path ahead. My only regret is that fifty years ago I lacked the courage to confront my grandfather and tell my mother what was going on. In the best of all possible outcomes, it might have ruined him and helped to heal her. But, then again, perhaps not. We now know many brave, frightened children spoke out, only to be told: This stays in the family forever. Or: It must be your fault. Or: What did you do to make this happen? Or even more tragic: You're lying.

The other day I emptied my handbag and found a scrap of paper where I'd copied a few lines I must have read somewhere: *Release from the wounds of childhood is a task never completed, not even on the point of death.*

It is enough for me now that the process has begun.

AUTHOR'S NOTE

In 2015, Benbulla won the Australian Institute of Architects' Country Division for Residential Architecture and was short-listed in a group of ten for the top New South Wales residential award. It was described as a house that 'encourages you to breathe quietly, slow down and just appreciate the delicate balance offered between landscape and shelter'. Michael Baker's slim and striking bricks, which anchor a light design elegantly but forcefully, are a triumph that helped Terry Cross to win best use of bricks in the Master Builders Association Excellence in Business Awards Newcastle. He also picked up top awards for best use of glass and sustainability, which is a tribute to Jarrod at Bago Wood-works and Bob, who worked tirelessly to set up energy and water systems to make Benbulla both sustainable and a wonderfully comfortable house in which to live. Every so often, though, we still go camping and the magic never fades.

ACKNOWLEDGEMENTS

For many reasons, this has been the most difficult book I have ever attempted. Without the patience and understanding of, first, Fiona Henderson and then Nikki Christer, who gave wise advice and much encouragement, I would have abandoned the project altogether. Thanks to Brandon VanOver for his sensitive editing and many kind words. Thanks, too, to all the wonderful people who chugged up the slightly winding track from the gateway to make our House on the Hill such a wondrous place to live and learn, and who generously let me include their stories.

ABOUT THE AUTHOR

Susan Duncan enjoyed a 25-year career spanning radio, newspaper and magazine journalism, including editing two of Australia's top-selling women's magazines, *The Australian Women's Weekly* and *New Idea*.

Susan has published two bestselling memoirs, *Salvation Creek* and its sequel, *The House at Salvation Creek*, and two novels, *The Briny Café* and *Gone Fishing*.

Esther Jean Duncan 1921–2016